YORKIST PRETENDERS TO THE TUDOR THRONE

To Barbara, Niamh, Ciara and my five wonderful grandchildren

YORKIST
PRETENDERS
TO THE TUDOR
THRONE

WHO WERE LAMBERT SIMNEL
~ and PERKIN WARBECK? ~

KIERAN MOLLOY

PEN & SWORD
HISTORY

AN IMPRINT OF PEN & SWORD BOOKS LTD.
YORKSHIRE – PHILADELPHIA

First published in Great Britain in 2024 by
PEN AND SWORD HISTORY
An imprint of
Pen & Sword Books Ltd
Yorkshire – Philadelphia

ISBN 978 1 03610 521 1

Typeset in Times New Roman 10.5/13.5 by
SJmagic DESIGN SERVICES, India.
Printed and bound in the UK by CPI Group (UK) Ltd.

Pen & Sword Books Limited incorporates the imprints of Atlas, Archaeology,
Aviation, Discovery, Family History, Fiction, History, Maritime, Military,
Military Classics, Politics, Select, Transport, True Crime, Air World,
Frontline Publishing, Leo Cooper, Remember When, Seaforth Publishing,
The Praetorian Press, Wharncliffe Local History, Wharncliffe Transport,
Wharncliffe True Crime and White Owl.

For a complete list of Pen & Sword titles please contact
PEN & SWORD BOOKS LIMITED
George House, Units 12 & 13, Beevor Street, Off Pontefract Road,
Barnsley, South Yorkshire, S71 1HN, England
E-mail: enquiries@pen-and-sword.co.uk
Website: www.pen-and-sword.co.uk

or

PEN AND SWORD BOOKS
1950 Lawrence Rd, Havertown, PA 19083, USA
E-mail: uspen-and-sword@casematepublishers.com
Website: www.penandswordbooks.com

Contents

Acknowledgements

I would like to thank Gail Peacock, fellow Ricardian and member of the Somerset Branch of the Richard III Society, for her helpful critical comments and suggestions. Any errors that remain are entirely the responsibility of the author.

I would like to offer my thanks to the staff of Pen & sword, particularly Charlotte Michel and John Wright for guiding me through the minefield that is copyright and Laura Hirst and Tony Wilson for help with the latter stages of the production process.

Image Credits

Introduction

The Wars of the Roses – three decades of civil war between the houses of Lancaster and York – did not end on a battlefield near Leicester. The fighting had not yet stopped, and the political unrest had more than a decade yet to run. The new king, Henry VII, was an unknown quantity, having spent the previous fourteen years (exactly half of his lifetime) in exile in Brittany. His victory at Bosworth relied on an *ad hoc* amalgam of die-hard Lancastrians – men who had been in the shadows since the Battle of Tewkesbury (1471) and the death of Henry VI days later – and disaffected Yorkists, more loyal to the southern Woodville faction than Richard III's northern affinity. After more than three decades of unrest between England's nobility – punctuated by set-piece battles, changing loyalties and tit-for-tat executions – a return to peace and tranquillity were by no means guaranteed under the new Tudor monarch.

In the decade after Henry VII's victory at Bosworth in 1485, two serious claimants to his throne emerged to challenge his tenuous hold on the crown. In 1487, 'Lambert Simnel' was crowned king in Dublin, although in whose name is far from certain. He may have been the imposter whom Henry VII claimed him to be, although he might also have been either Edward V (the eldest son of Edward IV and one of the 'Princes in the Tower'), Edward, Earl of Warwick (son of the Duke of Clarence, brother to Edward IV and Richard III) or – though rarely suggested – Richard, Duke of York (the younger of the two Princes in the Tower). After the Battle of Stoke Field in 1487, a boy later named as Lambert Simnel was captured and put to work in King Henry's kitchens, commensurate with him being an innocent dupe of surviving Yorkists. Henry, though, admitted he wanted one of the leading Yorkists, John de la Pole, the Earl of Lincoln, captured alive 'so that by means of that man the entire source of the conspiracy could be revealed'. Unfortunately for Henry, de la Pole died in battle. The overwhelming balance of historical comment has been that Simnel was an imposter, although challenges to this orthodoxy have been made. Indeed, the identity of Lambert Simnel is a greater mystery than that of the second claimant, Perkin Warbeck.

In 1491, this second 'pretender' – from the French verb *pretendre*, to claim – emerged in Cork, on the south coast of Ireland, acclaimed by his supporters to be Richard, Duke of York, the younger son of Edward IV. Henry VII spent most of a decade trying to secure his capture, whilst at the same time claiming he was another imposter by the name of Perkin Warbeck, a boatman's son from Tournai in Flanders. After 'Warbeck's' failed invasion of 1497, he was captured by Henry but, unlike Simnel, was treated with some courtesy until he was eventually executed in 1499 after two failed escape attempts. Like Simnel, the balance of opinion has Warbeck as another imposter, largely based on his post-capture confession. Others have argued that this confession, quite probably made under duress, is meaningless and that the feasibility of teaching a non-native to learn both the English language and the background to Edward IV's court stretches the plausibility that Warbeck was an imposter beyond the limits of credibility. For these commentators, this pretender truly was Richard, Duke of York.

What has largely been the accepted narrative concerning Simnel is that of Polydore Vergil, whose history was written at the behest of Henry VII. Generally taken as fact, this work has formed the basis for subsequent authors, from Francis Bacon in 1622 to Nathen Amin's 2020 work, *Henry VII and the Tudor Pretenders*. There are, of course, exceptions to this broad view, as noted below; but, nonetheless, ask the general public what (if anything!) they know about Lambert Simnel and you will get the response that he was a fake (an imposter, in old money), reinforced by the rather comic nature of his name. Similar comments can be made about the name Perkin Warbeck, which, when added to that of Simnel, forms a double act of pantomime proportions. However, this interpretation of their names has, over the years, unconsciously served to reinforce their impostor status in the histories of these two anti-Tudor rebellions. As A.F. Pollard's nineteenth-century *Oxford Dictionary of National Biography* (*ODNB*) entry for Simnel states, 'no serious historian has doubted Lambert was an imposter'. Who, it might credibly be asked, would back a Lambert or a Perkin to be king of England?

This book is not a conventional history book; it is part detective story and part courtroom drama, with a dose of speculation layered on top. It is not an account of the years 1486–99 in a conventional sense, but is limited to only those aspects which relate to the identity of the two pretenders, the relationship between them and the aftermaths of their failures. Was either the Battle of Stoke Field or the execution of Warbeck the end of their stories?

In the case of Simnel (Part I), I am indebted to the work of the late Dr John Ashdown-Hill (*The Dublin King*, 2015), who, so far as I'm aware, is the only contemporary historian to have given serious credibility to Simnel actually being the Earl of Warwick. Whilst I agree with much of the argument made by Ashdown-Hill, I have tried to develop the theme with alternative perspectives and additional comments. This is the more complex history to unravel, as several options are possible for Simnel's identity.

With regard to Warbeck, the information is presented in the form of a dialogue which allows readers to form their own judgement, since the options here are binary: Warbeck was either the real Duke of York, second son of Edward IV, or an imposter from Flanders. For this section of the work (Part II), the author is indebted to four books which provide all the background information, each with a different perspective on Warbeck. Ian Arthurson (*The Perkin Warbeck Conspiracy 1491–1499*, 1994) has no doubt that Warbeck was an imposter, and his book is primarily concerned not with the latter's identity but with the European power politics of the late fifteenth century; Warbeck was simply a pawn to be played in this game. Similarly, the recent book by Nathen Amin (*Henry VII and the Tudor Pretenders*, 2020) covers both Simnel and Warbeck, and, as may be expected of a founder member of the Henry Tudor Trust, also views the pretenders as imposters. At the other extreme, Diana Kleyn (*Richard of England*, 1990) argues firmly that Warbeck was the true second son of Edward IV, widely believed even to this day to have been one of the murdered Princes in the Tower. By far the most exhaustive treatise on all aspects of the Warbeck affair is Anne Wroe's *The Perfect Prince* (2003). Heavy on detail and primary sources, the author is even-handed in her treatment but never comes down on one side or the other. For my own part, I have heavily referenced the statements made by the various participants and am grateful to Wroe's book for making this relatively straightforward. Thus, although delivered in a dramatic (literally) setting, it is also meant to be historically accurate, and original sources (not just the opinions of contemporary historians) can be examined by readers, wherever possible online.

During the production process of this book, the ground-breaking work of *The Missing Princes Project* (*TMPP*) was published, culminating in both a book – Philippa Langley's *The Princes in the Tower: Solving History's Greatest Cold Case* (2023) – and a TV documentary, which shattered many widely accepted, if largely unproven, narratives concerning Richard III. In providing evidence for the survival of the two sons of Edward IV, the belief that Simnel and Warbeck must be imposters simply *because they were dead* no longer holds true. The implications of the *TMPP* for this work are two-fold. In the case of Simnel (Part I), *TMPP* results largely support what is presented herein, though I have tried to highlight where another opinion is still possible. In Part II, since the trial of Perkin Warbeck is presented as a drama, with information known only up to 1499, then the only casualty is the reader's possible foreknowledge that much of the case against Warbeck is not as watertight as previously supposed. I have not adjusted this, as hopefully, it will still provide a new and easily accessible way of looking at the traditional opposing standpoints. I have retained in Scene 3 of Part II discussions of who might have killed the two princes, simply as a counterpoint to the road travelled for so many years by modern-day Ricardians; it may now be easier, by retaining this time-old debate, to see the opposing stances with a more open mind. I have taken the liberty of incorporating a little of the new information contained in Langley's book, where appropriate and with due reference, to improve the arguments presented and clarify what would otherwise be errors on this author's part.

PART I

Lambert Simnel

ENGLAND, 1486

'Uneasy lies the head that wears the crown': words put into the mouth of Henry IV by the Bard of Stratford, but words that must have been at the forefront of Henry VII's mind a year after he usurped the crown of England at the Battle of Bosworth on 22 August 1485.[1]

Before Bosworth, Henry Tudor's claim to the throne was gossamer thin. On the paternal side, his father, Edmund Tudor, was the son of the probable marriage between Catherine of Valois, dowager queen and wife of the late King Henry V, and a courtier, Owen Tudor. Since this marriage had been made in secret (and not made public until after Catherine's death) and was against the law preventing dowager queens from re-marriage without the consent of the new monarch, Edmund Tudor was technically illegitimate. On his maternal side, Margaret Beaufort was descended from the illegitimate liaison of John of Gaunt and his then mistress, Katherine Swynford. Although this couple eventually married and their children were legitimized by Richard II, Henry IV barred their right to succeed to the throne.[2] Henry Tudor's support at Bosworth was far from all-pervasive, lacking the kind of widespread acclaim that had propelled Henry Bolingbroke's usurpation of Richard II's kingship nearly a century earlier. Instead, it came from a mixture of remnant Lancastrians who saw Tudor as their only hope of re-establishing their house to the primacy it had once enjoyed during the reigns of Henrys IV, V and VI; but equally, it came from Yorkists disaffected by the accession of Richard III at the expense of the elder son of Edward IV, nominally Edward V.[3, 4] Tudor's army at Bosworth was built around troops given to him by Charles VIII, King of France, to where he had fled after exile in Brittany for some fourteen years,[5] bolstered by Welsh support gained after landing at Milford Haven and from his march to the English Midlands. Tudor himself was no battle-hardened warrior, and Bosworth would have been his first full-scale encounter; his ultimate victory, against numerical odds, was largely due to the military skill of John de Vere, Earl of Oxford, the inertia of some of Richard's army (primarily the Duke of Northumberland in Richard's rearguard) and the duplicity of the Stanley brothers.[6] While Thomas Stanley sat impassively on the sidelines, waiting to commit only when the outcome of the clash was certain, it was the late entry into the fray of his brother, William, on Tudor's side that turned the tide of battle at the point when Richard was, literally, within striking distance of his opponent. What England would make of this unknown Welshman, a foreigner to most after his years in exile, who had won a battle but not hearts and minds, was far from certain.

Henry VII's first year on the throne was thus engulfed in the uncertainty generated by his meteoric rise to the monarchy. Ricardian loyalists were still at large, primarily Sir Humphrey Stafford and his brother, Thomas, and Francis Lovell, the three of whom had initially taken refuge after Bosworth at the Benedictine abbey of St John the Baptist in Colchester but were now at large and fermenting rebellion. The Staffords, minor members of the family once headed by Henry Stafford, Duke of Buckingham – who had rebelled against Richard III in autumn 1483 – had led a short-lived and abortive rebellion in their native Worcestershire around Easter 1486 which ended with Sir Humphrey's execution.[7] Francis, Viscount Lovell, whose name is writ large over the Simnel affair, was another matter. Lovell, whose father died when he was only 8, became a ward of Edward IV but was subsequently passed to the guardianship of Richard Neville (Earl of Warwick, better known as 'The Kingmaker'), where he met Richard (then Duke of Gloucester, later Richard III), becoming a lifelong friend and die-hard supporter of the future king.[8] At the age of about 10, Lovell had married Warwick's niece, Anne Fitzhugh, whose father supported Warwick and Clarence against Edward IV in the brief period leading to the readeption of Henry VI. Lovell, still under-age in 1471, suffered from this association, and although he was pardoned, he was placed in the guardianship of Elizabeth of York and her husband, the Duke of Suffolk, after Warwick lost his life at the Battle of Barnet. It was during this period that his path crossed that of John de la Pole, son of the duke and duchess. From April 1486, Lovell was in the north of England, attempting to coordinate Ricardian resistance to the new monarch, something the king stubbed out before it could gain traction, but which culminated in an abortive assassination attempt during Henry's visit to York.[9] During the latter part of 1486, Lovell moved unimpeded across the country, a measure of the level of covert support still available to the House of York, finally emerging at the end of the year as an integral part of the Simnel rebellion.

In addition to overtly hostile Yorkists, a number chose the politically expedient course of accepting the new regime despite their past. Most significantly among this number were the de la Pole family of East Anglia. John de la Pole the elder, Duke of Suffolk, was from an essentially Lancastrian family but had married Elizabeth,[10] sister to the two Yorkist kings, and served both rulers faithfully. He was, however, a pragmatist and accepted the new king with equanimity. His son, another John de la Pole, had been created Earl of Lincoln by Edward IV in March 1467, played a prominent role in Richard III's coronation and had supported this king during both the Buckingham rebellion of 1483 and at Bosworth in 1485. The de la Poles were treated leniently by Henry VII, allowing them to keep their lands and titles in an act of reconciliation towards one of the country's leading families. The younger John, like his father, had toed the party line with regard to the new monarch up until early

1487, when he aligned himself with the Simnel plot. He was, like his mother, an implacable Yorkist at heart.[11] Lovell, whom we have noted had at one time been under the guardianship of Lincoln's mother, Elizabeth, and Lincoln were to become brothers in arms on behalf of the first Yorkist pretender.

Perhaps more worryingly for the new king was not these tangible threats to his kingship but the intangible ones presented by the sons of Edward IV. Despite every effort, Henry had failed to establish with any certainty the fate of these two boys after the summer of 1483, when they had been declared illegitimate by their uncle, Richard, the Duke of Gloucester. Their illegitimacy was based on the testimony of Robert Stillington, Bishop of Bath and Wells, who had come forward with the revelation of a secret marriage between Edward IV and Eleanor Butler in May 1464, which was still valid at the time the king entered into a second secret marriage with Elizabeth Woodville.[12] Henry's problem was straightforward: he had reversed *Titulus Regius*, the Act of Parliament which had validated Richard III's right to the throne based on the bastardy of Edward IV's children,[3, 4] as a necessary prerequisite to his marriage to Edward's eldest daughter, another Elizabeth of York. This was the cornerstone of Henry's attempts to shore up his claim to the throne by, in effect, uniting the houses of Lancaster and York and offering an end to the so-called Wars of the Roses.[13] However, this also legitimized *all* the children of Edward IV, who, if they were alive, included his eldest son, Edward V. Nothing had been seen or heard of these two boys for over two years, and despite common rumour that they were no longer alive, there was no hard evidence at the time that either or both boys were dead. A living prince would make Henry's position as king untenable, and it was under this cloud of suspicion and uncertainty that the Lambert Simnel affair had its genesis.

BACKGROUND TO THE REBELLION

Before attempting to explore the question 'Who was Lambert Simnel?', it is necessary to give a short synopsis of the events and timeframe of the rebellion, and a brief consideration of the available sources of contemporary, or near-contemporary, evidence that relates to it.

The Simnel rebellion was a relatively short series of events, particularly when compared to that around Perkin Warbeck. Sometime in early to mid-1486, rumours were heard that the Earl of Warwick, presumed to have escaped from the Tower of London, where he had been held since soon after Bosworth, was at large and in Ireland. At some point – it is not recorded with certainty when, but towards the end of 1486/early 1487 seems likely[14] – messengers and an unnamed herald[15] were sent to Ireland to investigate, and these messengers appeared to be convinced that whoever it was they questioned – and it is not stated who this was – was genuine. In February 1487, we get the first official evidence for a plot, involving a priest from Oxford and an unnamed boy trained to impersonate the Earl of Warwick. Henry countered this by parading his Earl of Warwick for all to see at St Paul's Cathedral in London. At this point, John de la Pole, the Earl of Lincoln, fled Henry's court for Flanders. It was also in the wake of the plot's revelation that the dowager queen, Elizabeth Woodville, retired to Bermondsey Abbey to see out her days.

During the spring of 1487, an invasion force gathered in Flanders under the leadership of Francis Lovell, a committed Yorkist and close friend of Richard III, and the Earl of Lincoln, with support in the form of German mercenaries supplied by Margaret, Duchess of Burgundy, sister of the last two Plantagenet kings. This force landed in Ireland in early May 1487, and a young boy was crowned King of England in Dublin on 27 May; neither the name nor regnal number of this king is known with any certainty.

The Yorkist army, enlarged by support from Anglo-Irish nobles and native Irish troops, crossed to England in June, landing in Cumbria, but their march south ended with defeat at the Battle of Stoke Field, near Newark, on 16 June. A young boy, later named as Lambert Simnel, was captured and the Earl of Lincoln killed, while Francis Lovell seems to have escaped, although his ultimate fate is not known with any certainty.[16] The boy Simnel was spared and put to work in the king's kitchens. Fuller accounts of these events are given elsewhere for the interested reader.[17–19]

There are four chroniclers who wrote about the Simnel rebellion and they fall into two camps, each with their limitations. The two most closely related to events temporally are Adrian (sometimes Adrien) de But and Jean de Molinet. De But (1437–88) was a monk-chronicler at Les Dunes Abbey in Flanders who wrote extensively on the history of Belgium under the Dukes of Burgundy. He spent some of his youth in Mechelen, the seat of Margaret, Duchess of Burgundy. While his information from England must have been second-hand, what he wrote of events in 1486–87 must have been almost contemporaneous, given the date of his death.[20] Molinet (1435–1513) was a French poet-chronicler who succeeded the better-known Georges Chastellain in 1475 as official chronicler to Charles the Bold of Burgundy, then to his daughter, Mary, and finally her husband, Emperor Maximilian. His account was written about 1500.[21] Both De But and Molinet were foreigners and were not present when the events happened, and Molinet in particular is known to have had confused views of the reign of Richard III.[22] Both could possibly be deemed to be hostile to the new English king, although their chronicles mostly relate to facts as they knew them and not opinions.

The two chroniclers based in England were Bernard André (sometimes cited as Andreas) and Polydore Vergil. André (1450–1522) was a blind French Augustinian friar who was tutor to Prince Arthur, son of Henry VII. He wrote a history of that king's reign up to 1497, probably between 1500 and 1502;[23] he could be considered as Henry VII's first official biographer.[24] Vergil, who did not arrive in England until 1502, was encouraged to write his *Anglica Historica* by Henry VII, the first version of which, covering events up to 1513, was completed about that time. However, revised versions appeared in 1534, 1546 and 1555,[25] with significant changes relevant to the Simnel rebellion. For example, later editions included the rumours that the sons of Edward IV were alive after 1483.[26] Vergil's account is, nonetheless, the one most commonly used as the basis for subsequent accounts of the Lambert Simnel affair.[27] Both André and Vergil's closeness to Henry VII must have had an influence on the partiality of their histories, and Vergil's in particular lacks consistency over its various editions. Not surprisingly, both believed Simnel to be an imposter – what other position could they take? – but still of relevance is *who* they believed he was impersonating.

None of these four historians are therefore without potential bias, although it would be wrong to dismiss what they say out of hand unless there is genuine proof that they are in error, or highly likely to be. To selectively choose some aspects to fit a desired narrative whilst ignoring others which may be contradictory would be wrong. In what follows, all perspectives are given due consideration.

THE SONS OF EDWARD IV

There are three realistic possibilities for the identity of 'Lambert Simnel'. He was either one of the two sons of Edward IV – namely Edward, nominally Edward V before his claim was nullified by the Stillington revelation of illegitimacy, or Richard of Shrewsbury, Duke of York – or Edward, Earl of Warwick, son of George, Duke of Clarence, the late brother to Edward IV and Richard III. In mid-1486, Henry VII had no knowledge of the fates of Edward's two sons. Despite rumours, they had been murdered at the behest of their uncle, Richard III, that was all these were: rumours. The whereabouts of the Earl of Warwick was more tangible, as he had been removed from Sheriff Hutton Castle (along with other children of the House of York)[28] immediately post-Bosworth and was firmly secured in the Tower of London. Any of these three could, in principle, have been the focus of the ensuing rebellion, but equally, the boy later known as Lambert Simnel could have taken on any of them as a false persona.

Of the two brothers, the stronger case can be made for the elder, Edward, although any such evidence is circumstantial. While none of the four chroniclers ever claim the pretender to be Edward V, Edward is by far and away the most common name associated with the pretender crowned in Dublin (hereafter referred to as the Dublin Pretender). Unfortunately, in only one instance contemporaneous with events is the name associated with a regnal number, and then it is VI, not V. This sole citation linking name and number comes in a letter from the Dublin Pretender, written at Masham, to the city of York in June 1487.[29] Unfortunately, only a copy of the original exists and the body of the letter does not contain either name or regnal number to identify the king. However, added to the copy by the scribe is a comment stating the letter is a 'Copie of a letter … in the name of the king calling hymself King Edward vjth'(vj = VI, sixth). Firstly, it should be noted that the widely read twentieth-century citation of this letter by Raine incorrectly transcribes this margin addition as 'King Edward vth'.[30] Secondly, we do not know when this addition was made, nor can we rule out the fact that the truth may have been altered to support a desired narrative; a master forger would not have been required to change 'v' to 'vj'. In other words, while at face value the evidence supports Edward VI, i.e. Edward, Earl of Warwick, it does not entirely exclude the possibility it was for Edward V.

In addition to this letter from the king is another written by the Earl of Kildare in the name of the king, starting 'Edward, by the Grace of God, King of England, France and Ireland …', dated and sealed 13 August 1487. A letter issued after the Battle of Stoke Field must itself raise questions, but quite possibly reflects the lack of administrative ability of the earl to process something ordained before the Dublin Pretender's invasion of England.[31] The letter has an attached seal impression, though this is damaged, with only a small fragment remaining;[32] sadly, this includes neither name nor regnal number. The letter is, however, dated as 'on the thirteenth day of August in the fist [*sic*] year of our reign'. Since regnal years date from the year of accession to the throne, not the date of coronation, this must refer to Edward VI; Edward V would be in his fifth regnal year after his accession in 1483, despite never having undergone a coronation.[33]

The other obvious milieu for an official record of the identity of the Dublin Pretender is coinage, which unfortunately leads us into a numismatic minefield. The issue is complicated by the existence of coins existing with the name 'EDWARDVS' or 'RICARD' relating to the two last Yorkist kings. Furthermore, it was the practice not to include regnal numbers in addition to the name, or year date. At the end of a complex analysis of coinage style and value,[34] the most that can be concluded is that, in all likelihood, some coins were issued in Ireland (but not England) in the name of the Dublin Pretender, but this takes us no closer to knowing the identity of that individual.

With regard to Edward V, none of the four chroniclers mentioned earlier suggest that the rebellion was in his name. What scant evidence exists for the fate of Edward IV's sons, other than the rumour of their murder, is consistent with the elder having died of natural causes. Mancini[35] tells us that Edward was being seen daily by his physician, Dr Argentine, and that 'he [Edward] reckoned his death was imminent', and goes on to say 'now there was suspicion he was taken by death … and by what manner of death so far I have not at all ascertained'; no comment of any sort was made about the ill health or fate of his brother, Richard.

An entry in the Oath Book of Colchester for September 1483[36] also seems to suggest Edward V was dead. As ever, though, it's not as simple as this. The wording of the entry clearly states Edward IV is dead, recording, '*Edwardi quarti nuper Regis angliie, iam defuncti*', which translates unambiguously as 'Edward IV, late king of England, now deceased', before adding, '*Regis Edwardi* [blank, erasure] *qui nuper filii dominii Edwardi quarti*', i.e., 'King Edward V [blank, erasure] "late" son of Edward IV'. Thus, it lacks the qualifying addition '*iam defunctii*' ('now deceased'), which clarifies the translation of '*nuper*' which, in addition to 'late', can also mean 'formerly', 'lately' or 'not long ago'. This evidence, therefore, *could* be interpreted as Edward V having died, but it is certainly contentious.

Mancini's ignorance of Edward's fate, cited earlier, is instructive and merits alternative analysis. Surely the natural instinct of any parent or guardian in charge of a seriously ill child is to keep a medic constantly at their bedside until all hope is lost and their fate sealed. Argentine's dismissal while not knowing the boy's fate suggests his medical condition was not terminal. Moreover, if Edward was dying naturally, it seems remiss of a supposedly usurping and malicious Richard III not to have simply allowed nature to take its course, with the option then of murdering his brother and claiming another natural death before displaying the two bodies and then burying them with due reverence. In addition, there is no mention of a requiem mass for Edward V, something a pious man like Richard would have deemed a necessity. Neither of these two points accords with a natural death for Richard's eldest nephew. To this can be added the behaviour of the boys' mother, Elizabeth Woodville. While defenders of Richard III have cited Elizabeth's action to leave sanctuary and at least accept (however grudgingly) her brother-in-law as king as evidence she believed the boys were alive, a second aspect of her behaviour has gone unremarked: she never commissioned the building of a chantry chapel for prayers to be said for the repose of their souls and a speedy passage through purgatory. During the years of Richard's reign this may be seen as inevitable and thus inconclusive evidence, but, after 1485, she had time and money to instigate such building work. Doesn't this also suggest she thought her boys were still alive?

The idea that Edward V had died, either naturally or otherwise, thus remains speculative and cannot be accepted as fact to rule him out of being the Edward of Dublin Pretender fame. In fact, there is one snippet of information, found in Vergil, that *does* support the crowning of Edward V in Dublin. Vergil[37] writes, 'and although both the Germans [i.e. Martin Schwartz] and the Irish in the force announced they had come to restore the boy Edward, recently crowned in Ireland', the key phrase here being '*ad resitiuendum*', to restore, which can only apply to Edward V, who had been replaced as king by Richard III after the Stillington revelation.

While there is clear evidence for the focus of the rebellion to relate to an Edward, with what there is tending towards Edward VI, the evidence for the involvement of Edward IV's second son, Richard, Duke of York, is almost non-existent. Of the chroniclers, only Bernard André makes this assertion,[38] referring to the crowning of Edward IV's *second* son in Dublin.

Vergil, describing the confession of the pretender's tutor, a priest named Simons, only states, 'he [Simons] changed the boy's name and called him Edward';[39] the name change being from Lambert to Edward (Earl of Warwick). Francis Bacon, whose work is closely based on Vergil, does specify the son initially mentioned as being Richard, but as this narrative is some 100 years after the event, it has little in the weight of either originality or authenticity.[40] There is no official documentation which in any way implies that the Dublin Pretender was Richard, and no further consideration of this possibility will be made.

THE EARL OF WARWICK

The Earl of Warwick, real or as imposter, presents a far more complex issue. Standard history books will relate the life of Edward, Earl of Warwick, as follows: Edward was born on 25 February 1475, the second child of George, Duke of Clarence, brother of Edward IV, and his wife, Isabel Neville, eldest daughter of Richard Neville, known now to history as 'Warwick the Kingmaker'. A daughter, Margaret, had been born earlier, on 14 February 1473 at Farleigh Hungerford Castle in Somerset, an event which ultimately had some bearing on the life of her younger brother. In October 1476, Edward's mother, Isabel, gave birth to a second son, Richard, though both were dead within a fortnight of each other, by 1 January 1477. Around mid-1477, for a number of reasons peripheral to the current narrative, the Duke of Clarence was imprisoned on grounds of treason, being held in the Tower of London for some six months before his trial and execution.[41, 42] The supposed manner of his death – drowning in a barrel of Malmsey wine – is arguably the best-remembered moment in the duke's life story.

Now an orphan, Edward, who inherited the title Earl of Warwick from his grandfather upon Clarence's death, was placed in the care of successive households. The first of these was probably the royal household, as Edward IV was his godfather and had most likely attended his christening. In 1480, he was made ward of Thomas Grey, Marquis of Dorset, eldest son of the queen, Elizabeth Woodville, by virtue of her first marriage. After the death of Edward IV, the exile in Brittany of Thomas Grey and the accession to the throne of Richard III, Edward went to live with Elizabeth of York (Edward IV's daughter, later wife to Henry VII), and probably her sisters and some cousins, at Sheriff Hutton Castle north of York under the watchful eye of John de la Pole, where he remained until the aftermath of Bosworth. He was then brought to London at the behest of Henry VII, initially placed in the household of Margaret Beaufort, the new king's mother, before eventually being secured in the Tower of London.

When the Simnel plot officially emerged in February 1487, Henry must have felt a sense of both relief and confusion, along with the threat posed by a possible challenge to his crown. Relief, because the threat he must have feared most – from a surviving son of Edward IV – appeared not to be the case; confusion, because Henry had the Earl of Warwick safely under lock and key. Or so he thought.

George, Duke of Clarence, was convinced his wife and infant son had been poisoned, probably at the behest of Elizabeth Woodville. There had been bad blood between the two from the time when Clarence and 'The Kingmaker' had executed her father, Richard Woodville, Earl Rivers, and her brother, Sir John Woodville, after the Battle of Edgecote in July 1469, during the brief period when both Clarence and Warwick were supporting the readeption of Henry VI. According to the *Crowland Chronicle*, in the aftermath of his wife's death, Clarence was 'not without reluctance to eat or drink in the king's abode'.[43] What is surprising is that Clarence's first instinct after the believed poisoning of his wife was not to seek out the perpetrator(s), but to disappear for about three months. While we have no certain knowledge of his whereabouts during those months, the Act of Attainder, issued at the time of his treason trial[42] and given below, must give a significant clue:

'And also, the same Duke purposyng to accomplisse his said false and untrue entent, and to inquiete and trouble the Kynge, oure said

Sovereigne Lorde, his Liege People and this his Royaulme, nowe of late willed and desired the Abbot of Tweybury [Tewkesbury], Mayster John Tapton, Clerk, and Roger Harewell Esquier, to cause a straunge childe to have be brought into his Castell of Warwyk, and there to have putte and kept in likenesse of his Sonne and Heire, and that they shulde have conveyed and sent his said Sonne and Heire into Ireland, or into Flaundres, oute of thise Lande, whereby he myght have gotten hym assistaunce and favoure agaynst oure said Sovereigne Lorde; and for the execution of the same, sent oon John Taylour, his Servaunte, to have had delyveraunce of his said Sonne and Heire, for to have conveyed hym; the whiche Mayster John Tapton and Roger Harewell denyed the delyveraunce of the said Childe, and soo by Goddes grace his said false and untrue entent was lette undoon.'

The Abbot of Tewksbury was John Strensham, one of Edward's godfathers.

There was clearly a two-fold plot at hand, involving relocating the surviving son, Edward, to either Ireland or Flanders for safety, and replacing him in Warwick Castle with a lookalike. We cannot be certain whether or not this plan came to fruition. Tapton and Harewell denied carrying out their part of the plan – but naturally they would have said that when faced with possible execution – and this has generally been enough for historians to believe the whole plan came to nought.

However, Taylor (sometimes Taylour or Taillour) does not seem to have made a similar denial – possibly he was in Ireland or Flanders and could not be questioned – and the same Taylor went on to be pardoned after Stoke on 2 January 1489.[44] He later entered into the early stages of the Warbeck conspiracy under the (erroneous) belief he was doing so on behalf of Clarence's son, so as late as 1491, and with the Earl of Warwick officially in the Tower of London, he believed the real earl was at large.[45] In addition, Clarence's absence for three months would certainly suggest that success should not be dismissed out of hand and is at least consistent with him having accompanied Taylor and his eldest son abroad.

There are two questions that need to be addressed in trying to resolve this issue: is there any written evidence that the scheme succeeded, and could it feasibly have been carried out?

Firstly, both Ireland and Flanders would have been plausible options for a safe location for his son. In Flanders, there was Margaret of Burgundy, Clarence's sister, to whom he was generally believed to have been close. Although Flanders and Margaret figure in the later stages of the rebellion,

Ireland is the more likely choice between the two possibilities. Clarence was born in Dublin in October 1449 at a time when his father, Richard, Duke of York, was Lieutenant of Ireland, and Clarence himself had become a close friend over many years of Gerald Fitzgerald, 8th Earl of Kildare and Ireland's leading noble. Fitzgerald, born around 1456, was younger but of broadly similar age to Clarence, and his mother, Jane Fitzgerald, was the daughter of one of Clarence's godparents, James Fitzgerald, 6th Earl of Desmond. Gerald had been made Lord Deputy of Ireland under Clarence, but he lost the post for a short period after Clarence's subsequent execution. There must have been a bond of trust between Clarence and Gerald Fitzgerald, which would have made the latter the ideal protector for Clarence's son.

Written evidence from Ireland that the Earl of Warwick had been raised there is supported by comments from the two overseas chronicles. Molinet[46] wrote:

> 'One scion taken from royally born stock, however, had come on splendidly among the fertile and aristocratic shrubs in Ireland, who, when he was full grown, in the flower of manhood, and, raised up in force, wished to repair and return to resplendent honour the glorious arch and triumphant house of York, of which he is issue. This most noble scion is Edward, son of the Duke of Clarence.'

While de But is uninformative as to where the earl came from, he also is clear that the rebellion was in favour of Warwick: '*Mensibus novembri et decembri superhabundabant nix, ventus, pluvia, gelu,..., rumorque factus est de rege Angliae deponendo et filio ducis Clarentiae introducendo tanquam vero herede*' which translates broadly as 'In November and December there were many problems with wind, rain and frost ... The rumour spread about the deposing of the King of England and introducing the son of the Duke of Clarence, the true heir.'[47]

The Annuls of Ulster, however, cloud the issue:

> 'A great fleet of Saxons came to Ireland this year (1487) to meet the son [*sic*, grandson] of the Duke of York, who was exiled at this time with the Earl of Kildare ... And there lived not of the race of the blood royal that time but that son of the Duke and he was proclaimed king on the Sunday (whitsunday, June 3) of the Holy Ghost in the town of Ath-cliath [Dublin] that time [1487].'[48]

While the grandson of the Duke of York is consistent with the Earl of Warwick, it could equally relate to Edward, first son of Edward IV. Furthermore, the same source earlier states:

'The king of the Saxons, namely, king Richard [III], was slain in battle and 1500 were slain in that battle and the son of the Welshman, he by whom the battle was given, was made king. And there lived not of the race of the blood royal that time but one young man, who came, on being exiled the year after, to Ireland.'

In other words, the Dublin Pretender did not arrive in Ireland until *after* the Battle of Bosworth, which would only be consistent with Edward V. This dichotomy, 'either/or' or 'both', is a common thread in the Simnel narrative.

It is one thing to present evidence suggestive of the Earl of Warwick being raised from the age of about 2 in Ireland, but the corollary of this is that the pretence has to have been successfully affected and maintained in England for a decade. In other words, was it feasible? The simple answer, over the majority of the decade in question, is 'yes'. The substitute Warwick first passed to his uncle, the king, who probably had not seen him since he had been christened; he is hardly likely to have noticed a swap had been made more than two years later, even if he had been completely attentive at the baptismal ceremony. Thomas Grey, his next guardian, had probably never seen Warwick before he received him into his household, and Richard, as Duke of Gloucester, would only have met him, if at all, during those periods when he was being raised and presented as the real Earl of Warwick. No coaching along the way was needed: the replacement was raised as an earl from such an early age it would have been unnecessary, and he would probably, in time, have come to consider himself the real earl. By the time Henry VII took charge of him, the process had become a self-validating sequence of events: the more hands the surrogate Warwick passed through, each believing he was the real Warwick, the more of a truism this became. It would have been unthinkable for Henry to believe anything other than that he had the real Earl of Warwick under his control in 1486.

More problematic is the switch within Warwick Castle, assuming the denial of Tapton and Harewell was false and purely self-serving. There is no indication of precisely when this might have taken place, but to some extent, it must have coincided with Clarence's absence for the three-month period shortly after the death of his wife and second son. Did nobody in the castle notice a new 2-year-old boy had suddenly appeared as the duke's son? The explanation of how this might have been possible lies in the strange tale of Ankarette Twynyho.

Ankarette Twynyho married into a middle-ranking Somerset family from Keyford (sometimes Cayford, now subsumed into part of Frome, Somerset), though her maiden name was either Burdon or Hawkeston(e).[49] There are numerous wills recorded in the Somerset county archives for members of the wider Twynyho family to suggest in general they were not poor and that Ankarette's married home in Keyford, a small manor house named 'The Nunnery', was substantial; however, only one of their number reached national importance. John Twynyho (*ca.* 1440–85) was a wealthy wool merchant, one-time MP for Bristol and Attorney General to the future Edward V.[50] Ankarette married John Twynyho's elder brother, William, in 1441,[51] who was dead before the events of 1476 transpired;[52] they produced at least four children: William, John, Elizabeth and Edith.[53] Ankarette's association with the Duke of Clarence – or more realistically, his wife, Isabel – would have come through Clarence's ownership of Farleigh Hungerford Castle, some 6 miles from Frome, the birthplace of his daughter, Margaret, later to become Margaret Pole, Countess of Salisbury, and a victim of Henry VIII's vindictiveness.[54] There is no record of when Ankarette joined the Clarence household, but it is highly likely her brother-in-law, John, facilitated the matter, plausibly to allow Ankarette to support herself after her husband's death.[52] William was a member of the Clarence household when he died.[53] John Twynyho must have been known to the Duke of Clarence, from whom he once received a gift of a silver cup.[53] Ankarette moved with the Duke to Warwick Castle, where she no doubt played some part in helping raise Edward, the royal couple's first son, during his first two years.

When Clarence returned from his three-month absence, he accused Ankarette of poisoning his wife at Warwick on 10 October,[56] though the accusation is somewhat confused. Isabel's second son, Richard, was born in Tewkesbury on 6 October, so it is highly unlikely Isabel could have travelled to Warwick four days later; 12 November is the more acceptable date associated with this move.[57] Therefore, Ankarette could not have administered poison on 10 October to someone who was in Tewkesbury on that day. The confusion is compounded by the assumption (without proof) that Ankarette would have been in Tewkesbury with her mistress during labour, but it is equally reasonable to consider she really was in Warwick taking care of son number one. In other words, the charge of Ankarette poisoning Isabel Neville on 10 October in Warwick was a trumped-up one.

On 12 April, after his reappearance from somewhere unknown, Clarence ordered the arrest of Ankarette, who was now back in Somerset. It is superficial to simply accept she had left the Clarence household as a result of the Duchess's demise because there is also a second consideration: given that Isabel was dead and Clarence absent from Warwick, who was looking after the 2-year old Earl of Warwick if he was still there? Ankarette's absence gives further weight to the idea that Clarence *and* his son were no longer in Warwick Castle. Subsequent to Clarence's orders, Ankarette was taken by a force of some twenty-six men, and by 14 April she was back in Warwick. A day later, she was tried and executed within three hours. The whole process was something of a kangaroo court. Some jurors are alleged to have asked her forgiveness for their verdict, which they said was made in fear of their lives.[56]

What is remarkable about this case is the speed with which it was carried out and the dubious nature of the charges. Clarence may well have wanted vengeance on somebody for, as he saw it, his wife's murder, but surely he would have wanted to know who was behind it all, the full story. In reality, it seems he wanted less, rather than more, known about the accusation of poisoning. Did he really believe that this aging servant had carried out the murder of her employer and source of livelihood because of some personal grievance? Was there any credible link that would have made her act on behalf of the Woodvilles, the faction, in Clarence's eyes, behind the poisoning? It has been suggested that her son, John Twynyho – who was later (by March 1483) working with (not for) Anthony, Earl Rivers, and Richard Grey – provides such a link, but this John Twynyho is more likely to have been her brother-in-law of the same name, a higher-ranking individual and in 1476 a Clarence adherent.[58] Moreover, such a rationale is tenuous, given the long service the Tywynhos had given to Clarence: Ankarette's husband, William, was a member of the household (1470–72),[53] while their sons, John and William, were ordered to pay bonds to Edward IV in April 1470 as a result of their support for Clarence during the period of Henry VI's readeption.[59] It is surprising, therefore, that history has accepted without question that the motive for Clarence's execution of Ankarette was Isabel's poisoning, rather than considering this unlikely act was a screen for something else.

Bringing the trial back to Warwick certainly enabled Clarence to pack the jury to achieve the desired outcome, but was this the sole reason? An alternative explanation is that this was a warning to anyone at Warwick Castle who may have been suspicious, as Ankarette might have been, of the arrival of a surrogate elder son. The message was clear: stay quiet or else you know what fate will befall you.

Two other aspects of the Twynyho case can tentatively be added in support of this hypothesis. Firstly, why did Clarence accuse Ankarette of poisoning his wife and child in early October, when their deaths occurred in late December? Not only does this seem medically implausible, given the time over which it requires for the poison to be effective, but if he truly believed his wife had been poisoned by Ankarette, why not accuse her of carrying out the poisoning in, say, mid-December, when both she and Isabel were known to be in the same location? The reason for this can only ever be speculative; indeed, the dating has been dismissed as a clerical mistake (albeit made repeatedly),[56] citing the date as 10 October when it should have been 10 *December* (but why accept all other aspects of the written word yet ignore this inconvenient example?). Addressing the issue rather than dismissing it, perhaps Clarence wanted to uncouple the timing of the poisoning (his stated reason for Ankarette's execution) and the disappearance of his son (the actual reason behind her execution). Secondly, Ankarette's daughter, Edith, and her husband, Thomas Delalyne, who were both in Warwick at the time of the trial, having followed Ankarette from Keyford along with their servants, were ordered to leave and go to Stratford-upon-Avon.[56] Clarence seems to have been concerned that they too might have known whatever Edith's mother did.

Support for an at-large Earl of Warwick is evident from the summer of 1486, the time of the failed Stafford rebellions. De But notes this in his chronicle,[60] and a rumour was in circulation that the earl had been 'set free in the isle of Guernsey' about this time.[61] This phrase is somewhat clumsy, but implies that the earl had been set free from the Tower of London and was seen in Guernsey,[62] a rumour generally discredited because it seems evident in hindsight that the earl in the Tower of London had *not* been freed. However, if the phrase is considered in reverse – i.e., that it is the true Earl of Warwick who was seen in Guernsey – then the implication is that it is the need for liberation from the Tower that is wrong, that the falsehood is not in the sighting but in the explanation for it. In other words, the real earl *was* seen in Guernsey because an Earl of Warwick, other than the one in the Tower, was making his way from Ireland to Flanders. This is supported by an entry in the records of the Feast of St Romboult in Mechelen (named Malines by the French) for 1 July 1486 of 'a gift of eight flagons of wine to the son of Clarence of England',[63] which now brings Margaret of Burgundy into the equation as Mechelen was her home city. This evidence has also been dismissed, like the Guernsey rumour, this time as a clerical error (again!) since the Earl of Warwick was assumed to be in the Tower of London at this time; but if the real Earl of Warwick was on his way from Ireland to Flanders via the Channel Islands, then both rumours take on the aura of truth.[64]

A final cryptic comment relating to the Earl of Warwick can be found in a letter from Thomas Betanson, a priest of St Sephulcre-without-Newgate Church in London, to Sir Robert Plumpton dated 29 November 1486,[65] where he notes, among personal news and the general whereabouts of the great and the good, that 'Also here is but little speech of the erle of Warwyk now, but after christmas, they say there wylbe more speech of'. Ignoring the unlikely possibility that the priest Betanson was somehow involved in, or aware of, a clandestine plot to free the earl then in the Tower, then we must take it that another incarnation of the Earl of Warwick was being implied. The rumours seem to have been widespread enough within the capital to have come to Betanson's ears, plausibly hailing from ships entering the city from abroad.

Having established that the boy crowned in Dublin was an Edward, and that this may have been either Edward V or the Earl of Warwick (as Edward VI), is there anything about the known age and appearance of the pretender to suggest which might be the more likely? In fact, the only written information we have, that 'oone Lambert Symnell, a child of x [ten] yere of age … to be proclaimed … as Kyng of this Realme', is given in the 1487 post-Stoke Act of Attainder, referring back to the Dublin coronation of May of that year.[66] Of course, from Henry's perspective, this statement had to correlate with the age of the boy in his possession some months later (after Stoke), and may or may not have any bearing on the age of the boy actually crowned in Dublin. Several authors have tried their best to link their favoured candidate for who Simnel was (or was impersonating) to this single fragment of information of dubious value. Ashdown Hill, who favoured the 12-year-old Earl of Warwick, has argued that Warwick may have been small in stature like his father, Clarence, and hence looked more like 10 years old, but this ignores the fact that an offspring may follow the mother's genes as probably as the father's. Smith, backing Edward V, has ignored the Act of Attainder and favoured the Dublin Pretender being older, based on a speculative interpretation of a slur that Margaret of Burgundy had given birth (metaphorically, not literally) to two princes (Simnel and Warbeck) aged 180 months, i.e. 15 years old,[67] a view reiterated by Bacon but who based his history on Vergil, who had erroneously stated the Earl of Warwick was 15 in 1487 when he was only 12.[68] In short, there is no reliable age for the Dublin Pretender in 1487. This polarized argument has not been helped by futile attempts on both sides to read into the adjectives which describe the Dublin Pretender, either 'boy' or 'lad', a quantitative measure of his age.

The only additional information which can bear on this matter is the account of the coronation ceremony, which does not seem to be disputed, that the crowned king was small in stature and 'for that the throng of the people was such that he could not be seen, the child was borne in, and upon Great Darsey of Plantan's [Great Darcy of Platten's] neck, that every man might see him'.[69, 70] This would seemingly rule out Edward V, who was approaching 17 at the time, would surely not have been described as a child and would have been too tall – and probably too embarrassed – to have subjected himself to such a display, but would just be plausible for a 12-year-old Earl of Warwick. Of course, in the euphoria of the moment, a teenager might be unable to resist the wishes of the crowd to be seen more clearly, or perhaps it was another, younger key participant in the ceremony (Warwick) who was being shown to the crowd. Either/or, or both?

The weight of evidence thus far is that the Dublin Pretender was the Earl of Warwick, but there is sufficient ambiguity that Edward V cannot be permanently excluded. Furthermore, the question 'was he real or an imposter?' remains. It is now time to consider the official account of Lambert Simnel.

THE LAMBERT SIMNEL VERSION

The 1486–87 rebellion has been almost universally accepted down the centuries as a far-fetched attempt by the House of York to regain the throne by force of arms, in support of the Earl of Warwick, a man under lock and key at the time of the rising. If Henry's army was defeated, so the logic goes, the real earl would be freed from the Tower of London to become king. A less common variation on this theme is that it would have been John de la Pole, Earl of Lincoln, who would be crowned. The hold this version of events has had on history lies largely in the fact that it is the one that Henry VII wanted us to have, and, through Polydore Vergil and subsequent authors who have based their work on his, it has become accepted as fact. As A.F. Pollard's early *ODNB* entry for Simnel states, 'no serious historian has doubted Lambert was an imposter'.[71] As is often noted, history is written by the victors, so Henry VII's version of the Simnel (and indeed, Warbeck) rebellion is the one that has gained common acceptance. It is partially based on the assumption that the sons of Edward IV were dead, another 'fact' that has no substance but was one which was necessitated to validate Henry's right to rule and has subsequently determined the portraiture of Richard III as the ultimate villain. In this light, the Simnel story needs careful scrutiny.

News of a plot brewing in Ireland, seemingly in favour of the Earl of Warwick appears to have emerged sometime in mid-1486, causing Henry to send messengers there to find out more. Although Nicholas St Lawrence, Lord Howth, claimed credit for this act of loyal disclosure, a Statute Roll of the Irish Parliament of 1496 attributes it to a Thomas Butler.[70, 72] The Butlers were a rare Lancastrian-leaning family in an otherwise pro-York country. It is clear from what happened at the royal council, held at Sheen from 2 February 1487, that Henry was fully aware of the emerging rebellion, if not its details. He issued pardons for any Yorkists who remained loyal to him and ordered that the Earl of Warwick be brought from the Tower and paraded at St Paul's Cathedral for all to see, to discredit any notion the Earl of Warwick was in Ireland.[73] It is also after this council meeting that there was a dramatic change in circumstances for the dowager queen, Elizabeth Woodville, the significance of which is discussed in the next section. Greater detail of the rebellion only came to light about a fortnight later, on 17 February, at the Convocation of Canterbury, held in Westminster, when the Archbishop of Canterbury, John Morton, related the confession of a priest, William Symonds:

'A certain Sir William Symonds was produced, a priest, of the age of twenty-eight years, as he declared, in the presence of the said lords and prelates and clergy who were there, as well as the mayor, aldermen, and sheriffs of the city of London. He publicly admitted and confessed that he took and carried off to Ireland the son of a certain [blank], organ maker of the University of Oxford, the which son was there reputed to be the Earl of Warwick, and that afterwards he was with Lord Lovell in Fuvnefotts [Furness, Cumbria]. These, and other things were admitted by him in the same place. The said most reverend father in Christ [meaning John Morton, Archbishop of Canterbury] asked the aforesaid mayor and sheriffs, that the above mentioned Will. Symonds brought unto the Tower of London, to be kept there for him, since the same most reverend father was holding another of the company of the said William, and had [space for] but one person in his manor of Lambeth.'[74]

On 19 February, in accord with the king's orders, the 'official' Earl of Warwick was taken from the Tower of London and paraded at St Paul's.

The essence of this confession and the ensuing account of Lambert Simnel will be dissected piece by piece: his name and where he came from, the name (or names) of the priest, what his other admissions might have been and the fates of the various conspirators, named and unnamed.

In fact, the name Lambert Simnel, missing from the priest's confession, only came to light in the Act of Attainder issued in November 1487, some five months after the Battle of Stoke Field. The priest in his confession does not name his protegé, and the boy captured in the immediate aftermath of the battle was named 'John' in a herald's report: 'And ther was taken the lade that his rebelles called King Edwarde, whoos name was in dede John, by a valyent and gentil esquire of the kings howse, called Robert Bellingham.'[75] The name 'Lambert' has only become accepted because of Vergil's history, to the point where the name in the original herald's account was changed from John to Lambert in a 1774 version.[76]

The surname Simnel is far less unusual than currently thought. There is no support for the notion the name Simnel is foreign, as sometimes suggested.[77, 78] It is, however, the diminutive form of Simon, which had variants in the fifteenth century of Simons, Symons, Symunds, Symonds, Simondes, Symondes and Symondys;[79] other variants – Symenel, Symnell, Siminell – seem to have largely died out by the mid-fifteenth century.[80] A note added to the margin of a manuscript copy of the *Book of Howth* calls Simnel 'Simon's son',[81] but the likelihood that Lambert was the biological son of his priest mentor is too remote to merit further discussion. Lambert's father is not named in the confession, which does not help, but the Act of Attainder names him as 'Thomas Symnell, late of Oxford Joynoure'.[66] Henry VII, on the other hand, in a letter to the Pope, described his captive only as a 'spurious lad',[82] while in a papal Bull of January 1488, Pope Innocent VIII stated he was 'a boy of illegitimate birth'.[83] The ambiguity in the story continues with the varying assertions of Thomas Simnel's trade, which spans baker, shoemaker (André)[84] and organ maker (Priest's Convocation confession), as well as the joiner, mentioned in the Attainder.[66] Validation that such a man called Thomas Simnel (or its variant) existed is in Bennett's *ODNB* for Lambert Simnel, where he states that 'Thomas Simnel worked in Oxford in the late 1470s and held a tenement on the conduit towards St Thomas's Chapel from Osney Abbey in 1479'.[78] Specifically, there is a 1478 citation of a Thomas Symnell, a carpenter living in Oxford and a neighbour of a William Wootton, a more prosperous citizen of the city. Wootton was, in 1488, commissioned to hire a team of workmen to build a pair of organs for Magdalen College, and Thomas Symnell may have been part of this team, which may be the origin of some of the confusion concerning the precise description of Thomas Symnell's work.[80] Moreover, Thomas must surely have had a son called Lambert, or, as Marie Barnfield has pointed out, the falsehood of the Simnel biography would be easily proved.

Two points are worth noting about this record of a Symnell family from Oxford. Firstly, while it may be correct it does not mean it is related to the Dublin Pretender. In creating a false history for the man in whose name rebellion was being waged, Henry could hardly present a narrative which was easily disproved. Assuming the priest William Symonds was genuinely living in Oxford, he would have been well placed to construct a story based on individuals known to him. Secondly, if the joiner Thomas Symnell was alive and working in Oxford in 1488, why was he not questioned in the aftermath of the Battle of Stoke Field about his son's involvement in the conspiracy? This has led to the unproven assumption he was dead,[78] but, as we shall see later, could equally be one of many opportunities to get to the truth that was deliberately ignored.

This potpourri of family names and professions cannot inspire confidence in a coherent narrative and has led to a variety of alternative suggestions for the origin of the name 'Lambert Simnel'. The similarity of the Pretender's surname and that of the priest-tutor smacks of suggestion by association rather than authenticity, a means to an end rather than a statement of truth. Other suggestions (but not proof) of the origin of the boy's name, all of which support the idea that it was a fabrication, link it with John Lambert (father of Edward IV's notorious mistress, more commonly referred to as Jane Shore), Roger Machado, possibly the herald sent by Henry VII to Dublin at the outset of the conspiracy, who owned a house in Simnel Street, Southampton,[85] or just the Simnel cake served during Lent.

This ambiguity in the official narrative continues with what we are told about the priest Symonds. The confession has him – William Symonds – in the Tower of London in early 1487, never to be heard of again, while Vergil asserts the 'false boy-king was indeed captured, with his mentor Richard' after the Battle of Stoke Field;[86] the *Book of Howth* also has the priest captured with the 'feigned king' and 'commanded to perpetual prison'.[87] This circle has been squared by assuming there must have been two priests, both named Symonds (William and Richard), possibly brothers, though the coincidence must raise eyebrows. In fact, rather than *two* priests, the available evidence, or rather the lack of it, suggests that there were *no* priests of that name that fit the bill. Thus, while Vergil has the priest William studying at Oxford,[88] the records of Oxford alumni do not unequivocally support this; the only credible entry in Emden's *Register* for a suitable candidate is a William Symonds, who was not admitted to the university until 1503.[89] This entry could only relate to Simnel's mentor if he enrolled after the failed rebellion (and Vergil was only partially correct in his version) and he had received benevolent treatment from King Henry, which, of course, is also possible. However, there is no mention of a priest named Symonds (or it's variant) in any of the Patent Rolls for the years 1476–1509,[90] nor is there an entry in a biographical list of registered clergy between 1300 and 1542.[91]

The next aspect of the official account to explore is whether or not a humble priest (not a high-ranking clergyman) could have tutored a young boy to impersonate one of the three possible contenders for the identity of the Dublin Pretender.

Given that the plot could not have had its genesis until late 1485 at the earliest (i.e., after stock had been taken of the cataclysmic events at Bosworth), and that the boy must have been in Dublin by autumn 1486, the period of tutelage can only have been a maximum of six to nine months. Allowing for identification of a suitable candidate at the outset and travel time to Ireland at a later date, the shorter end of this range appears more likely. It seems highly improbable that the priest Symonds would have had the necessary court knowledge to train a 10-year-old artisan's son to act as a prince, but the location of the origin of the plot – Oxford – does allow for other possibilities. Oxford had several connections with the House of York which may have been brought to bear on the job.[92] Both Francis Lovell's household at Minster Lovell and the de la Pole residences at Ewelme and Wallingford are only 13 miles from Oxford, while Abbington, home of Abbot John Sante, an Oxford theologian, is closer still at 8 miles. Sante was implicated in the Stafford rising of Easter 1486[93] and sent funds to Flanders to support Simnel in 1487;[94] he was later attainted in Parliament for his part in supporting John de la Pole and the 1487 rebellion.[95] However, the individual who attracted most attention from the monarch was Robert Stillington, Bishop of Bath and Wells, whom we have met before with regard to the bastardization of Edward IV's offspring (including the now queen, Elizabeth of York). Stillington was briefly imprisoned by Edward IV at the time of the Clarence treason trial, the suspicion being that Clarence had learnt of Edward's illegal second marriage from the bishop, but this is only conjecture as the bishop was subsequently released. It does, however, suggest a closeness between Stillington and Clarence which would justify Henry's interest in what he might know about events in Ireland.

On 7 March 1487, at the point where news of the brewing rebellion emerged at the Canterbury Convocation, Stillington, then residing at the University of Oxford, was summoned

> 'ffore certen grete and urgent caases touchynge owre personne and the quietenesse off thys owre [Henry's] realme, sent fore the bysshoppe of bathe, … as we be enformyd that he there contynueth, usyng certan practyses prohybyte by the lawes off holy church, and othere damnabyll conjurecies and conspiraes, as it ys probabylly shewyd, as wele agenst us as to the subversione off the universall wole and tranquillyte off thys owre realme.'

Stillington was protected for some time by the university, which was compromised by obligations to both parties, but eventually the university relinquished[96] and Stillington was taken to Windsor for questioning,[97] where he seems to have remained until 1489; he died in 1491.[98] Henry clearly had no trust in Stillington's loyalty.

Is it reasonable that any of the men mentioned could have tutored Symond's boy to the level of prince incarnate? Lovell was in sanctuary in Colchester for some months post-Bosworth, and after that seems to have operated solely in the north of England, so is an unlikely candidate. Abbot Sante was involved in a plot to release the Earl of Warwick from the Tower of London in late 1489, which means that he did not know of the other, possibly authentic, earl in Ireland in 1486, but it does not preclude him having played a part in tutoring an imposter. It is still questionable whether or not he had enough court knowledge to do an effective job as tutor. Stillington is the most plausible candidate, particularly as he resided in Oxford and was well known to Clarence and other members of the York dynasty, but if he was involved he seems to have held his nerve and given nothing away. In summary, the period available for coaching an imposter was short and Symonds himself would not have had the knowledge to do the job, but there were others in the Oxford area who *may* have made it possible.

What is a more difficult aspect to unravel concerns the messengers and unnamed herald sent by Henry to investigate matters in late 1486, who returned convinced that the person they interrogated was who he claimed he was. The questions raised are: who were they expecting to find (or being impersonated) and what questions were answered that convinced them of the Pretender's authenticity? Unlike Warbeck, the level to which the Pretender was scrutinized was extremely short; Warbeck was in the public eye for nearly a decade. Thus, the level of preparation needed by an imposter would be somewhat less, and a boy of around 10 would not be expected to be on top of every detail. Such a boy would also be intimidated by any inquisition, no matter how mild-mannered, so some leeway might have been given in accepting the answers. Despite these margins for error, it is difficult to see how an imposter could have won over these emissaries so convincingly. While from his answers he might not have seemed an obvious fraud, according to André the lad 'very readily answered all the herald's questions ... he was finally accepted to be Edward's son by many who were prudent men'.[99] He was, apparently, more convincing than simply plausible. Leaving aside for a moment that André reports the messengers believed the boy was Edward's son (whom André later thought was Richard, Duke of York, almost certainly in error), is it possible that the Pretender was the real Earl of Warwick? If Clarence had secreted his son in Ireland from the age of not much more than 2 with a guardian, Gerald Fitzgerald, who was a native Irish speaker (though he could also speak English),[100] then the person questioned would have had a strong Irish accent, a dialect which was not native English (indeed, similar comments could be made had he been raised in Flanders from the age of 2), and no knowledge of the English court. Furthermore, aside from possibly remembering he was brought to Ireland as an infant, what else could he know about things outside of Ireland? There are two possible explanations for why the herald and messengers were convinced of the authenticity of the person they questioned. Most obviously, the Irish accent and some knowledge of the flight from Warwick could have convinced them they were talking to the real Earl of Warwick, hidden in Ireland for a decade. If, however, the boy spoke with an English accent *and* he convinced them he was who he claimed to be (ruling out an imposter), then we are left with the conclusion they were questioning Edward V, meaning André's claim the person was Edward's son is less of an error than has been accepted. At age 16, he would have had more confidence in answering questions and would naturally have known not only about his life in England but also that of the Earl of Warwick held by Henry in the Tower. This seems an odd conclusion to come to, given all the arguments in favour of the Earl of Warwick over Edward V presented earlier, so is it an indication that there was more than one Yorkist noble at the centre of the Dublin rebellion? The either/or, or both conundrum continues.

If the message came back to Henry that Edward V was alive and in Ireland, he could hardly admit as much. Framing the rebellion in favour of the Earl of Warwick, whom he believed was in the Tower, would have been a logical way forward. It would also explain his urgent need to question Stillington, who, as well as knowing Clarence, had far more to do with Richard III and thus possibly knowledge of the fate of Edward IV's sons.

MISSED OPPORTUNITIES

The level of inconsistency in the Simnel biography is hard to comprehend, as Henry had numerous opportunities to sort this out. William Symonds's confession at the Canterbury Convocation lacks any credible detail and a second conspirator held (supposedly) by John Morton, apparently more senior than Symonds, is never named, nor are 'other things ... admitted by him'[74] expanded upon. The herald, upon his return from Dublin, unconvincingly did not name the individual he spoke to (unless it was a name Henry could not repeat). Great Darcy of Platten, who carried the boy king on his shoulders at the Dublin coronation gave an oath of allegiance to Henry at Maynooth in July 1487, so why was he not pumped for information?[101] Henry himself was still uncertain in July 1487 in whose favour the rebellion had been instigated, because, according to Vergil, he apparently ordered 'that John Earl of Lincoln should not be killed [at Stoke Field] so that he might learn from him more concerning the conspiracy'.[102]

As for the elephant in the room, Lambert Simnel himself, André writes that 'when questioned [after capture] about his family and the status of his parents, he confessed they were thoroughly mean individuals every one, with lowly occupations. In fact, they are not worthy to be included in this history.'[103] This seems something of a cop-out excuse, Henry appearing more concerned with keeping the Simnel story as vague as possible rather than revealing its details. The level of suspicion around Henry's motives is exacerbated by the apparent fate of many of those concerned. The priest, William Symonds, was, we are told, imprisoned, never to be heard from again (unless he was the Symonds cited among the Oxford alumni),[89] although there was no recorded trial or sentencing. The second priest captured at Stoke, Richard Symonds, was spared his life but 'was remanded to perpetual darkness and chains', disappearing without trace from the pages of history.[104] The unnamed conspirator of Convocation fame is never mentioned again, and Thomas Simnel, Lambert's erstwhile father, was never questioned and has thus (without evidence) been assumed already dead in 1487. In a ploy reminiscent of the 1485 attempt to destroy all copies of the *Titulus Regius*, Henry enacted a special Act at the Drogheda parliament of 1494 to destroy all materials relating to a parliament held by the Earl of Kildare (presumably in 1487) which acknowledged the Dublin Pretender as king, and, at the same time, made the keeping of any associated documents a treasonable offence.[70] A cover-up?

The contrast with the Warbeck affair is striking. Whatever the truth or otherwise of Henry's account of Warbeck's family history, over almost a decade it was open, consistent and detailed; Warbeck himself signed a confession of some sort and Henry wanted the details of his pretence known. By the late 1490s, Henry's pretender-management skills appear more finely honed than in 1486/87. Only in one respect do Henry's actions with regard to Warbeck's identity dovetail with his attitude to Simnel: Henry refused offers from both Spain and France to deliver Warbeck's parents to him to settle the question of their (supposed) son's identity, and he never allowed the one person who could definitively answer the question of Warbeck's imposture – Queen Elizabeth, his wife and Warbeck's possible sister – to see him.

Why might Henry have needed a Simnel, somebody to personify a false Warwick? In 1486, Henry was probably not relishing the thought of a Yorkist invasion, but he must have been more confident in his ability to defeat his opponents than he had been when he himself invaded in 1485. He was now based on home soil, had a larger force and, so long as he could stem the flow of remaining Yorkists to the Pretender's banner, would have felt able to win the forthcoming battle. What he lacked is what we now term an exit strategy. How could he prove to his subjects that the defeated pretender was never a credible threat to his reign? If the rebellion turned out to be in the name of Edward V, he could hardly display his dead body as proof of victory – it would have confirmed him as a usurper, a regicide and the murderer of his brother-in-law. Likewise, a display of the body of a 12-year-old claiming to be someone he had been adamant was under lock and key since 1485 would invite accusations of the spilling of infants' blood, the very crime of which he had accused Richard III. What Henry needed was a story and a victim he could parade to the crowds as being a nonentity, proof that there was no living member of the House of York who could challenge him.

If Henry's Simnel story began in early 1487, when did the boy himself come into Henry's possession? He may have been on the Tudor sidelines at the Battle of Stoke Field, waiting to be hailed as the false king. Alternatively, a suitably aged boy could have been captured from the Yorkist ranks in the death throes of the combat. We will never know. Simnel seems to have been well treated by Henry (although a letter between the Mayors of Waterford and Dublin states he was initially kept in the Tower),[105] apparently because of his age and innocence, and he was 'made a falconer by the king after he had turned spit for a while in the royal kitchens and performed other base tasks'.[86]

Related to this is one final event worth noting concerning the life and identity of Lambert Simnel. In July 1488, the recalcitrant Irish lords, including Fitzgerald and Darcy of Platten, finally took an oath of allegiance to Henry, following which a group of Irish lords were invited to England to feast, though the date at which this meeting took place is debated. A date of 1489 has largely been accepted,[106] though a convincing case has more recently been made for it being as late as 1494.[107] Whatever the case, it is not known whether either Fitzgerald or Darcy were there. At the banquet, according to the *Book of Howth*,[108] Lambert Simnel served the wine. Unfortunately for Henry, just one of the Irish lords recognized him as the Dublin Pretender, although this was undoubtedly Henry's intention. Tellingly, the 'one' was Lord Howth himself, no Yorkist supporter and the one guest we know had *not* attended Simnel's coronation in Dublin. Moreover, as the one Irish lord who made the intended identification *and* the author of the account, it could simply have been a means of self-aggrandisement. Convincing as this may seem for those believing Simnel had nothing to do with events in Dublin, it needs treating with caution. The remaining lords may not have recognized the boy pouring the wine simply because he was a servant of no consequence, to whom no attention was paid. Moreover, if the banquet is correctly re-dated as 1494, the appearance of the boy serving the wine would have altered dramatically from 1487.

THE SUPPORTERS

What can an analysis of those linked to the Dublin Pretender tell us, if anything, about his identity? Two of his backers – Gerald Fitzgerald and Margaret of

Burgundy – were, to one degree or another, outsiders, whilst three others – Francis Lovell, John de la Pole and possibly Elizabeth Woodville – were home-grown.

The link between Gerald Fitzgerald and the Earl of Warwick via his father, George, Duke of Clarence, has already been discussed. However, support for the Dublin Pretender was widespread among the Anglo-Irish nobility and clergy,[109] which were largely pro-Yorkist, the notable exceptions being Lord Howth and more generally the Butlers, Earls of Ormond. A John Butler, Mayor of Waterford, refused to back the Dublin Pretender,[110] and Waterford remained staunchly pro-Tudor during the Warbeck rebellion. While it is impossible to read into this whom the Yorkist Irish nobility might have supported, it is notable that Fitzgerald himself gave no significant support to Perkin Warbeck, who claimed to be Edward IV's youngest son. This suggests, however weakly, a stronger connection to the family of Clarence, with whom he was acquainted, than that of Edward IV, though it could simply be a case of 'once bitten, twice shy'.

A similar comment can be made about Lovell. Raised from an early age alongside Richard, Duke of Gloucester, in Richard Neville's household,[111] he was a Yorkist, but even more so a Ricardian. To support a son of Edward IV in 1486 would be to invalidate Richard III's earlier claim to the throne by implying the sons of Edward IV were not illegitimate. Warwick's hurdle to the throne was only a legal attainder, something that could be (and often was) overturned. Illegitimacy was enduring. Henry VII's repealing of *Titulus Regius* and reversing the bastardy of Edward IV's children would have caused a potential rift in the Yorkist camp. For Elizabeth Woodville, irrespective of the validity or otherwise of her marriage to Edward IV, the reversal would have opened new possibilities for her sons, assuming they were alive. For Lovell, support for a surviving son of Edward IV would have compromised his belief in the validity of Richard III's claim to the throne, in effect making him a usurper. Lovell would have found it easier to support the Earl of Lincoln than a son of Edward IV. Where Lincoln might sit in all this is debatable, though his subsequent actions suggest his loyalties to Edward's sons were stronger than his own personal ambition. The early stages of the Simnel rebellion, of which Lovell was an integral part, seem unlikely to have been on behalf of Edward V (at least to Lovell's knowledge), though it is plausible that Lovell could have been persuaded otherwise if stronger support for Edward IV's son emerged at a later point. Pragmatically, selling a re-emergent Edward V to the English nobility and populace would have been an easier prospect than persuading them that a second Earl of Warwick existed, and this post-Bosworth realpolitik may have caused Lovell to rethink his priorities.

Margaret of Burgundy, sister of the Yorkist brothers Edward, George and Richard, was unstintingly a supporter of her dynasty throughout both the Simnel and Warbeck rebellions. It is generally assumed, because of their respective ages, that Margaret was closer to George and Richard than her eldest brother, but this in itself would not have been any impediment to her preference for Edward's, rather than George's, son; she would have supported any legitimate threat to the Tudors. Margaret's support for both Simnel and Warbeck does, however, help in one respect. In medieval times, a king was chosen and appointed by God as his representative on Earth. It was a sacred role, one that would not be debased by elevating a commoner to it. It would have been unthinkable to Margaret, whatever her hatred of the Tudors, to have supported anyone of non-royal blood for king. Any suggestion she may have supported an imposter only to later insert a bone fide claimant is simply wrong. Why would this course of action have merit when John de la Pole, Earl of Lincoln, unattainted and free from the stigma of illegitimacy, was already available?

De la Pole himself was, and still is, something of a conundrum in this affair. As the eldest son of Richard III's sister, Elizabeth, Duchess of Suffolk, he possessed the only legitimate claim to be the rightful heir to Richard III and thus was the only completely valid Yorkist challenger to Henry VII. Supporters of Simnel-as-Warwick have excused this point by suggesting the possibility that, on the eve of Bosworth, Richard reversed the attainder and made Warwick his heir, though there is no evidence for this. After the deaths of his only son, Edward of Middleham, and his wife, Anne, Richard was in the process of arranging a second marriage (probably to the Infanta Joana of Portugal); he was still relatively young and would have retained hope for a direct heir of his own. On the eve of Bosworth, with no direct heir produced, it would have been prudent of him to make succession arrangements, and John de la Pole seems to have been his choice.[112] In an age of opportunity, it seems implausible that, in 1487, Lincoln would defer his legal claim to the throne in favour of someone like Warwick, who was legally debarred. There is only one claimant to whom Lincoln *might* defer as the leading Yorkist claimant, and that is a son of Edward IV, i.e., Edward V.

It is worth pausing at this point to review the timeline of Lincoln's involvement in the rebellion. News that a rebellion was brewing reached Henry's ears in the summer of 1486, with some level of detail – although we are never told what exactly – brought back later that year by his messengers/ herald, who were convinced that the person they questioned was no imposter. If they had news of a surviving son of Edward IV, then the king must have been worried indeed; if it was a rebellion in favour of the Earl of Warwick, he must have been utterly perplexed as he had (or at least, thought he had) this noble under lock and key. In consequence, in February, Henry called a Great Council at Sheen (Richmond), which ran from the 2nd of that month (Candlemass) to 3 March.[113] At this council, two things were discussed which have bearing on the focus of the rebellion: the transfer of Elizabeth Woodville's lands to her daughter (more of which later) and the decision to display the earl held in the Tower to the public.[114] In addition, pardons were offered to any Yorkists who remained loyal to Henry, Acts of Treason were issued against other irreconcilables (Sir John Beaumont, Sir Henry Bodrugan)[115] and a commission was established to negotiate with the Scots against possible invasion,[116] all of which shows how seriously Henry viewed the growing threat. Thus, remarkably, it was left to the southern convocation of clergy – the Canterbury Convocation – to break details of the emerging plot. On 17 February, at the Convocation (which ran from 13–27 February),[117] a priest named William Symonds gave the confession we have discussed earlier. Why it took John Morton, Archbishop of Canterbury, to bring forth the confession is a mystery: why was this not done at Sheen (where Morton was present) when Henry could take the credit for blowing the rebellion apart? Why did Henry not parade the captured priest at Sheen? Why did he feel the need to pass the matter to the Convocation of Canterbury to bring both the priest and the details of the plot to public attention? Is it credible that the priest was conveniently captured between 2 and 17 February? Does this mean Henry was unaware a conspirator had been captured and had a confession to make? We are told (in the confession) that Simonds was with Lovell in Furness Falls, and if true, this must have been immediately before Christmas 1486 as Lovell departed in the new year from the north for Flanders.[118] This only allows a two-month window of opportunity for persons at the heart of the rebellion, particularly the priest, to be identified, found, captured and brought to London and questioned. This was possible, of course, by the king and his network of spies, but surely not by the Archbishop of Canterbury. We therefore have to view with some suspicion this apparent disconnect between Henry's superficial presentation of the Dublin rebellion at Sheen and the details (at least in comparison with what Henry divulged) which Morton presented at the Convocation days later. Is there an indication here that Morton knew more about the plot than the king and chose to keep this knowledge to himself, something that makes no sense unless it concerned Edward V? Or did Morton take it upon himself to fabricate a story at the Convocation that vindicated Henry's earlier assertions concerning the Earl of Warwick, made at Sheen, something he kept from Henry? Morton's Lancastrian sympathies and unswerving loyalty to the first Tudor were hallmarks of his life and career; it would not have been past him to act in such a way to protect his king. Henry's post-Stoke presentation of Simnel to the banquet of Irish lords (discussed above) suggests he was still in need of confirmation as to the identity of his captive.

The banquet and the motive behind Henry's exhibition of 'Simnel' requires one last comment. If 'Simnel' was a plant by Henry to bring public closure to the rebellion, then parading him before the Irish lords who had crowned him was a foolhardy venture, no matter the time gap between the two events. This reflects back on the earlier comments about the disconnect between Henry and Morton's revelations about the emerging rebellion in February 1487. Was Morton acting independently of his king in fabricating the Simnel story as a cover for what was really going on? Is this why Henry continued to need reassurance concerning the identity of the boy now working in his kitchens, and why he saw no risk in looking for that confirmation at the banquet with the Irish lords?

Two days later (19 February), the public display of the Earl of Warwick at St Paul's Cathedral took place.[119] De la Pole is recorded as having spoken to this earl either at Sheen[120] or at St Paul's,[121] after which he fled to Flanders; one report says this happened after the end of the Council (i.e., after 3 March), while the Act of Attainder more specifically gives a date of 19 March. If all this is true, we have to question what it was that Lincoln learned from his discussion with Warwick, wherever it took place, that made him flee the country. The Earl of Warwick whom Lincoln met would have been the same Warwick he would have known throughout his life, particularly when they both were in residence at Sheriff Hutton in 1485. What could this Warwick have said to him in February 1487 that he did not know already and that would have made de la Pole an active participant on his behalf? It's hard to have any answer to this other than 'nothing'.

We can draw two conclusions from this sequence of events. Firstly, whatever Henry knew about the rebellion, he was best served by linking it to the Earl of Warwick rather than one of Edward's sons, so he could demonstrably show it to be false by the parade of his Warwick. In an age with no media, this was Henry's way of winning what we would now call the media war. Secondly, de la Pole's flight, given its timing, must have had something to do with the emerging rebellion, in favour of somebody whom he could support but who could not, rationally, be Warwick. Did the Council have a frank discussion which involved the possible existence of a son of Edward IV and it was this that caused de la Pole to flee? All of which brings us finally to the involvement of the dowager queen, Elizabeth Woodville.

Following the Sheen Council, Elizabeth Woodville was consigned to Bermondsey Abbey (an all-male Benedictine house) until her death in

June 1492. During this five-year period, there is little to suggest she ever regularly left the abbey or received many visitors. It was, to all intents and purposes, an incarceration. She is recorded as having attended her daughter's second confinement at Westminster in October 1489.[122] She died in penury, despite an annuity of 400 marks per year given to her by the king, although the date at which this commenced seems to be a year later (May 1488) and thus something of a hindsight.[123] While 400 marks is a significant sum, it is only just over half of the 700 marks per annum given to her by King Richard when she left the sanctuary of Westminster in 1484.[124] Henry's treatment of his mother-in-law after 1487, including her low-key burial, suggests that all was not well between them. Elizabeth did not seem to want a funeral befitting her status ('without pompes entreing or costlie expensis donne thereabought ... where I have no wordely goodes', according to her will),[125] but the fact that she died penniless gave her little choice. However, this would not have stopped Henry himself arranging something more elaborate if he had so wished. Furthermore, the indifferent and casual nature with which the post-burial ceremonies were performed is noteworthy.[126, 127]

Several explanations have been offered for Henry's treatment of his mother-in-law. Firstly, it has been suggested that this contemplative retirement was something she had been planning and she voluntarily passed her lands to her daughter (for which, read Henry himself). This, however, is inconsistent with the fact that such a move would not require a formal letter to the Exchequer following 'thadvise of the lords and other nobles of our counsaill', which reads as:

> 'have seased into our hands all honours, castelles, manoirs, lordships, knights fees, aduousons, and alle othr lands and tenements, with their apportenaunces and all maner fefermes and annuitees by vs late assigned vnto Queene Elizabeth, late wif to the full noble prince of famous memorye Edward the Fourth, and all and every of the saide honoures, castells, manoirs, lordships, knights fees, aduousons and all other lands tenements with their appertenaunces, fermes, and annuities haue assigned vnto our derrest wif the queene.'[128]

'Seased' is hardly a term which suggests a generous transfer. Moreover, there is no indication of Elizabeth's lifelong piety: she seems rarely to have gone on pilgrimages and (unlike, for example, Cecily Neville or Eleanor Butler) she joined a religious community of men.[129]

Two other suggestions relate to a falling out between the two parties. Henry is said to have been aggrieved by her 'foly and inconsistencie' in taking herself and her children from sanctuary and submitting them all to Richard III's rule, something that might have been true in August 1485 but seems an unrealistic explanation eighteen months later. An alternative suggestion is that it was Elizabeth who lost patience with Henry over his tardiness in having her daughter officially crowned queen.[130] This may well have been the case, but given that her grandson, Arthur, had been born a few months earlier (September 1486), surely this would have overridden any antipathy towards the king.

It is hard not to link the treatment of Elizabeth Woodville with anything other than the Simnel plot. Indeed, Thomas Grey, her son from her first marriage, was imprisoned about this time and not released until after the Battle of Stoke Field,[131] which also implies a Grey/Woodville link to the Simnel plot. The question is, who was Elizabeth Woodville backing? It is inconceivable that she backed any son of Clarence, as the hostility between the two was well-known, dating back to the execution of her father and brother after the Battle of Edgecote (1469) and the possible revelations by Clarence at his trial relating to her husband's pre-contract (i.e., prior marriage) to Eleanor Butler.[132] In supporting any pretender to Henry's crown, she would have to accept the calamitous consequences this would have on her daughter's position as queen. There is only one person who, as king, would make such a move worthwhile: her son, Edward V.

One of the themes of this narrative has been to offer an alternative to the more common 'either/or' debate concerning the identity of 'Lambert Simnel': that is, two opposing camps, backing him as *either* Edward, Earl of Warwick, *or* Edward V, while supporting the assertion of both sides that Simnel – portrayed as an imposter by Henry VII – was a fiction. It is easy for the Edward V camp to dismiss their opponents: there is no conceivable reason why either Elizabeth Woodville or John de la Pole would have backed Clarence's son, though they clearly supported a pretender who was not an imposter. However, the case for Edward V *alone* also has serious questions to answer, albeit of a more logistical and circumstantial nature. Why was it necessary for the coronation of 'Edward' to take place in Dublin when Mechelen offered a better alternative? What better way was there of bringing on-side the remnants of Yorkist support who had sided with Henry Tudor against Richard III than to have an unambiguous coronation in favour of Edward IV's eldest son, openly endorsed by his aunt, Margaret of Burgundy? The sentiments of William Stanley, albeit expressed with regard to Perkin Warbeck, are still apposite here: 'he would never take up arms against the young man, if he knew for certain that he was indeed the son of Edward' (see Part II for details). Why was the coronation so ambiguous in nature – at half a millennium remove, we still don't know with certainty who was crowned? Hardly the way to rally the troops. While it could be argued that a Dublin coronation was preferable as it was, at least in principle, within the realm, any coronation outside of Westminster would have required a subsequent capital-centred ceremony. Secondly, why was the rebellion centred on Ireland in the first place, not Burgundy? Ireland has no precedent as a base for a successful invasion of England, while Edward IV (accompanied by his younger brother, Richard, Duke of Gloucester) had done so from Burgundy in 1471. Furthermore, while Ireland was predominantly pro-Yorkist, it was not exclusively so; Burgundy, under Edward IV's sister, Margaret, had no divided loyalties. Why did the Earl of Kildare in particular back the rebellion when his affinity as a Yorkist was more to the dynasty as a whole than the family of Edward IV?; he would hardly have known either Elizabeth Woodville or her two sons by the late king, and his support for 'Warbeck' was, at best, luke-warm. Why was the army of Martin Schwart sent from Burgundy to Ireland at all when it provided the best trained and equipped component of the invasion force?

There seems no logical answer to these questions without invoking something both independent of Edward V but still of consequence taking place in Dublin. Were the Woodvilles simply using the Earl of Warwick as a front, to see how a rebellion would fare without revealing their true hand?

Taking all the evidence presented in this section as a whole, there seem to be two plots emerging: one in Ireland, backed by supporters of the Earl of Warwick, and a second, based on the mainland, backing Edward V. Other writers on the Simnel rebellion have weighted their arguments, sometimes with logistical acrobatics, in favour of one or the other, but a more reasonable rationale, taking into account all the evidence, is that there was not one but two strands to the rebellion. Ireland (and Burgundy) provided the armed manpower to affect the challenge to Henry in support of the Earl of Warwick, the real one sent to Ireland at an early age by his father. At the same time, those who had knowledge that the sons of Edward IV were alive kept their powder dry by allowing the Dublin movement to proceed, awaiting the outcome. If Elizabeth Woodville had kept the knowledge of her sons' safety from 1484–87, it would have been perfectly understandable had she not revealed her secret until the outcome of the ensuing battle (Stoke) was certain. De la Pole was kin, so he may have finally (in February 1487) been made aware his cousins were alive, whereas Lovell, no blood relative and a staunch Ricardian, may not have been (at least not in autumn 1486).

We can have no idea of the extent to which these two strands of the rebellion ran in parallel or whether they intersected in Burgundy. Did Margaret know of both plans? Possibly, but she certainly expressed surprise when Perkin Warbeck turned up at her court in 1491, implying she was, at least to some extent, in the dark over the fate of her two nephews. Conversely, as we shall see, the Warbeck plot in favour of Edward's second son, Richard, began shortly after the Battle of Stoke Field, and Margaret was again involved.

During the publication process of this book, the stunning revelation by Philippa Langley's *The Missing Princes Project* of documented evidence (dated 16 December 1487, but concerning events of June 1487) that Maximilian I, Holy Roman Emperor, paid for arms on behalf of Margaret 'to serve her nephew – son of King Edward, late her brother ... who was expelled from his kingdom', came to light.[134] This not only shows her support was primarily, if not necessarily exclusively, in favour of Edward V; but more significantly, also proves that one – and probably both – sons of Edward IV survived the reign of Richard III. However, it does raise the issue, acknowledged in the book, that support for Edward V – dated June 1487 – is *after* the main invasion force (under Martin Schwartz) had sailed for Ireland (15 May), and that a two-pronged attack on Henry VII was envisioned. Is this an indication that support for both Warwick *and* Edward V was in play?

In the end, whether Margaret favoured one pretender over the other is an academic point that doesn't affect the overall conclusion: there were two Yorkist horses in this race to the throne.

STOKE FIELD AND ITS AFTERMATH

The Battle of Stoke Field (near Newark) is the forgotten battle of the Wars of the Roses, whilst the Battle of Bosworth and the dynastic change it brought about is seen as its defining event. It did not suit the Tudors to dwell too long on a battle which challenged their legitimacy to the throne, whereas Bosworth was framed in terms of liberation from a tyrannical Richard III. In fact, Stoke was by far the bloodier affair of the two, hanging in the balance until royal reserves arrived to decisive effect; estimates of casualties, though notoriously unreliable, put Stoke at around 7,000, compared to somewhat over 1,000 at Bosworth. The Earl of Lincoln, John de la Pole, was slain, much to Henry's displeasure, as he wanted Lincoln alive 'in order to learn from him more concerning the conspiracy'.[100] Martin Schwartz, the German mercenary leading Margaret of Burgundy's contingent, also perished. For a time, Francis Lovell was also believed dead,[82] but his body was never recovered and it seems he escaped.[16] Indeed, in June 1488, a year after the battle, Lovell and others were offered sanctuary in Scotland for at least a year.[135]

34

The fate of the Earl of Warwick is straightforward for anyone convinced the Dublin Pretender was an imposter – he was simply the boy taken and later named Lambert Simnel, despite being initially named 'John' by his captor, Robert Bellingham.[75] If it is believed that a real Earl of Warwick existed, that he was possibly the boy crowned in Dublin and was the centre of the rebellion, the position is less clear.

Firstly, it is improbable that this Earl of Warwick was the captured pretender, as his pronounced Irish accent would have been a give away that he was not a boy from Oxford. The second alternative is that this Warwick was disposed of on the quiet, although he is unlikely to have been killed in battle as he was too young to fight. This would have served Henry's purpose, and with the presentation of Simnel in lieu of the real Warwick the whole affair could be brought to a close. For sure, nothing is heard of Warwick after Stoke, other than of a person so-named being in the Tower. The third possibility is he escaped, and in this regard, we must again return to the fate of Francis Lovell. The question is less *how* he (Lovell) escaped while all around him were slain, but *why*? For a man dedicated to the Yorkist cause, and someone upon whom Richard III's chivalric bent must have rubbed off, it seems counter-intuitive that he ran in the face of the enemy. This raises the possibility that he did not flee alone, but took somebody, perhaps the young Earl of Warwick – perhaps someone else – with him.

Of course, this is pure speculation, but there are two hints it may be the case. Firstly, Adrian de But's account has Warwick being taken from the field and overseas to Guînes in France when the battle was all but lost. This citation is not as clear-cut as it would appear, as it states that the earl was delivered to France by the Earl of Suffolk, by which he must mean de la Pole's 15-year-old younger brother, Edmund.[136] There is no evidence this younger de la Pole was at Stoke, but it is possible. It's also possible that Edmund was Warwick's courier *after* Lovell, a man on the run, had passed him over. Less credible is de But's assertion that Warwick was first captured by Henry before being taken to France by Suffolk, which would require him to have been subsequently freed from the Tower, something for which there is no credible evidence. Alternatively, it may be that de But assumed that it was Warwick who was taken from the battlefield simply because he had named him as the pretender from the beginning. There may be something in this confused account of Warwick's escape, but it is far from convincing. More telling is the behaviour of John Taylor, a central participant in the Warwick-to-Ireland narrative, who later entered into the early stages of the Warbeck conspiracy under the belief he was doing so on behalf of Clarence's son.[45] Did he have some knowledge of the young earl's survival of the Battle of Stoke Field? Or perhaps he had no idea of Warwick's fate and retained hopes he was still alive. Whatever the case, we never hear of the Earl of Warwick again, except as the person Henry believed was his prisoner in the Tower.

We must also consider the second Yorkist horse in the race, Edward V. He may have been in the background at Stoke and thus it was this Edward whom Lovell escorted from the field of battle, although this would be contrary to the earlier suggestion that Lovell was not in on this strand of the Yorkist plan, until perhaps the last minute. It may be that de But's account was fixated on Warwick and missed the possibility it was Edward V who escaped to Guînes. In any event, a cautious Elizabeth Woodville would have wanted her son kept well away from any fighting until the outcome was known, and it is at this point the name John Clement enters the story.

A John Clement enrolled at the University of Louvain, some 15 miles from Margaret of Burgundy's principal residence of Mechelen (Malines), on 13 February 1488, some seven months after Stoke Field,[137] from which we can guess he was in his mid–late teens as the minimum age of entry was about 16; that is, he was born *ca* 1470. What makes this entry intriguing is it is recorded as being *non juravit*, i.e., not sworn. This was the case for only thirteen student registrations between August 1485 and February 1569 and is usually explained as relating to either privileged college servants or absentees; the Clement entry is the only one without such qualification. A further entry in the same register, also for a John Clement, dated January 1551,[138] is accompanied by the note '*Dominus Joannes Clemens, medecine doctor, anglus, nobilis (non juravit ex rationabili quadam et occulta causa), sed tamen promisit se servaturm juramenta consueta*', which translates as 'The Lord John Clement, doctor of medicine, English, of noble birth (has not sworn the oath for a reasonable hidden cause), but has nevertheless promised to keep the customary oaths'. This registration at Louvain was probably as a professor rather than a student. The qualifying comments on these entries are more than unusual; they are unique among the 49,246 entries in the register between 1485 and 1569.[139]

The identity of this second John Clement is that of a man who became President of the Royal College of Physicians in 1544, when again, uniquely, there is no official document bearing his signature. To quote the author of the Register, 'Making a solemn commitment under the faith of the oath obviously amounts to performing a legal act for which one must have the required capacity.'[139, 140] In addition to this second John Clement being described as 'Lord', he and his wife, Margaret, were buried near the high altar in St Rumboult's Church in Mechelen, near that of Margaret of Burgundy; the years of their deaths were 1572 and 1570, respectively.

In both Clement cases, the inference is that a signature would have had legal consequences for either the university or the College of Physicians because the real name of the individual was being withheld, and that individual (certainly, at least, in the case of the second John Clement) had royal connections.

The two John Clements must be different people, otherwise a single individual would have lived to an age of around 100 (*ca* 1470–1570); not impossible, but highly unlikely. The second John Clement, of whom we know much more, was married to Margaret neé Giggs, a foster daughter of Sir Thomas More, and they both appear in Holbein's portrait of the More family *ca* 1527.[141] Further comments will be made of this John Clement in Part II. Suffice it to say that with respect to the fate of Edward V, the John Clement who enrolled at Louvain some months after the Battle of Stoke Field, and who did not want his real identity to be revealed, was of the correct age to fit the bill. Unfortunately, there is no further evidence yet available to embellish this line of speculation.

There is, however, an alternative for the fate of Edward V after Stoke Field that does have more substance. In the remote north Devon village of Coldridge there is a stained-glass window depicting the boy king, one of only three that exist. The full-length image shows Edward wearing a crown and holding a spectre, though possibly more significant is a second, fragmented head-and-shoulders glass image of a man with a scar across his face, plausibly a wound inflicted in battle. This latter image resembles one on the adjacent tomb of a John Evans, who was at some point (exact date unknown) appointed Deer Parker of the Coldridge estate which was part of lands owned by Thomas Grey, Marquis of Dorset, and Edward V's half-brother; this tomb effigy also has a scar cross the chin. The tomb of Evans has the inscription JOHN EVAS below which appears some inverted graffiti which appears to say "King". The inscription EVAS has been interpreted as Edward V in sanctuary (AS being a truncated form of the Latin ASA, in sanctuary).[142] Other rationales for the iconography at Coldridge have, however, been put forward.[143] It should also be noted that name originally given to the boy captured at the end of the battle of Stoke Field – John – applies equally well to both Evans and Clement.

The evidence available, *in toto*, suggests two fundamental variations to the accepted Simnel story. Firstly, there is every reason to believe that the real Earl of Warwick was alive, living probably in Ireland, in 1486, not, as Henry believed, in the Tower of London. Secondly, the support for the 1486 rebellion by both Elizabeth Woodville and John de la Pole, neither of whom would be natural Warwick supporters, can only be rationalized by including a son of Edward IV – Edward V – at the centre of the rebellion. It was not a case or either/or, but both.

To conclude, the inconsistencies in the accepted narrative, the vagaries of Simnel's background, the implausibility of training a 10-year-old boy to impersonate a prince in a few months and, above all, the missed opportunities to reveal the truth all point one way: A.F. Pollard's early *ODNB* entry for Simnel[71] is surely in need of revision. No serious analysis of the Simnel affair could doubt Henry VII's version was fiction.

CONTINUUM

In 1488, as well as offering a safe haven for Lovell, we get the first link between James IV of Scotland and Margaret of Burgundy, when a mission of around forty people, under the leadership of Richard Harliston, went from Margaret to James IV.[144] Harliston fought on the Yorkist side at both Bosworth and Stoke.[145] Furthermore, letters between Ireland, Scotland and Burgundy were rife in 1488.[146] It is also about this time (a more specific date is not known) that Perkin Warbeck left Flanders for Portugal, and it seems that Henry's spies were on his trail.

Nor were the seeds of continued Yorkist rebellion confined to overseas powers seeking to exploit Henry's vulnerability for their own ends. Sir Robert Chamberlain and Richard White were accused of conspiring on behalf of Charles VIII to bring about the 'dethe and destruccion' of Henry VII on 17 January 1491 and 24 August 1490, respectively,[147] i.e., *before* Perkin Warbeck's landing in Cork and his first appearance on the world stage. The two men, along with eighteen others (two of whom were Chamberlain's sons), had been apprehended by Henry's men, led by Sir Edward Pickering, at great expense: over £140.[148] The arrests were made in Hartlepool, an unlikely departure point for France, but in keeping with a flight to Flanders and the court of Margaret of Burgundy.[149] While there is no written evidence to substantiate a link between these arrests and the emerging new pretender, in a proclamation by 'Warbeck' from Scotland in 1496 he states: 'Henry Tudor has caused to be murdered many nobles of our realm, whom he feared, and whose loyalty he doubted. These include … Sir Robert Chamberlain.'[150]

Chamberlain, the senior partner of the two principals arrested, was a long-time Yorkist, having fought at Towton, Barnet and Tewkesbury and been with Edward IV in his brief exile in Flanders in 1471. Probably because of this previous Yorkist loyalty, he had been beheaded by the time the Act of Attainder against him had reached Parliament. White, described by the lesser title 'Gentleman', was released in 1491 for no obvious reason, but his freedom was relatively short-lived: he was one of the men who landed at Deal in 1495 as part of Warbeck's first attempted invasion and was subsequently executed.[151]

Henry himself never openly linked the Chamberlain/White arrests with anything happening in Flanders; as has been noted, the charges brought were conspiring with Charles VIII to assassinate Henry. How plausible is this? On 17 October 1487 (shortly after the Battle of Stoke Field), Chamberlain was ordered (under pain of a 500-mark fine) to 'abide within the town of Chartesey [Chertsey] co. Surrey and not to proceed beyond a mile thence save by command of his highness',[152] probably because of some perceived involvement with the Lambert Simnel rebellion, though he was not cited in the Act of Attainder after Stoke so was probably not an overtly active participant. Thereafter, up to November 1490, Henry repeatedly held a variety of his subjects as sureties to ensure Chamberlain's loyalty and, when demanded, his appearance before the king.[153] In this light, acting as the agent of a foreign monarch to commit regicide on home soil seems an unlikely charge given the lack of liberty Henry afforded him, which begs the question: was this cover for the real motivation for Chamberlain's action in favour of a second of Edward IV's sons, motivation that Henry wanted to keep hidden?

The Simnel and Warbeck rebellions have been treated by history as two quite different stories, separated by at least four years (Stoke in 1487 to 'Warbeck' landing in Cork in 1491) and up to twelve years (Stoke to Warbeck's execution in 1499), linked only by their (to modern ears anyway) comical names and common masquerades. This clouds what, in reality, was a decade of Yorkist rebellion, the Simnel and Warbeck affairs seamlessly linking support for one son of Edward IV, Edward, with the other, Richard; a continuum, not two unrelated conspiracies.

This story continues in Part II.

PART II

The Trial of Perkin Warbeck

Readers will appreciate that constructing a trial for the identity of the man history knows as Perkin Warbeck requires some flexibility with reality. Crowned heads of Europe – Henry VII, Charles VIII of France, Maximilian I of the Holy Roman Empire, James IV of Scotland, Isabella/Ferdinand of Spain, João II of Portugal – could not be expected to be questioned in a witness box, so in their place are people who were active in their respective courts, who speak on their behalf using documented evidence. Since the aim of this work is to be as even-handed as the available information makes possible, direct questions requiring unknown opinions cannot be used as the answers would betray any bias the author may have. For example, Margaret of Burgundy could have been asked, under oath, if Warbeck was who he said he was, and the answer could only be what this author thought. By using surrogates in place of monarchs, evasive answers and answers with plausible deniability can be introduced. Only information available up to the execution of Warbeck in 1499 has been used in the dialogue of Scene 2 (the trial itself), although Scene 3 includes a wider, contemporary debate about the pretenders to Henry VII and who they might have been if not imposters.

Of the characters in the drama, again some dramatic licence is required. John de Vere, Earl of Oxford, presided over the trial of Edward, Earl of Warwick, but less exalted men may have acted in the trial of Perkin Warbeck (Sir Tom Selby/Sygly, Knight Marshall and Sir John Turberville/Troubilfield, Marshal of the Marshalsea),[1] if indeed any such trial took place. Selby/Turbeville did officiate at the arraignment of those implicated in Warbeck's escape from the Tower in 1499, including John Atwood, who was executed at the same time as Warbeck, and the same source tells us that Warbeck was also present at the same time.[1] That lesser men than de Vere would have officiated in the case of Warbeck would be expected, given Henry VII's claim he was merely a boatman's son. I have, however, taken to using de Vere, the better known historically, as Warbeck's judge, even if its accuracy is unlikely. For the legal teams I have chosen, for dramatic purposes, characters who were not directly involved but each was a staunch supporter of one side or the other: John Morton, Archbishop of Canterbury, for Henry VII, and William Worsley, Dean of St Paul's, for Warbeck. Neither choice is factually correct, indeed Warbeck would have not been defended at all in his trial, if one ever took place, on 16 November 1499.

The witness representing the court of the Portuguese King João II, Rui de Sousa, died in May 1498 and thus before the execution of Warbeck. I have taken the liberty of extending his life by a year. Edward Brampton (Duarte Brandão) is central to the story, but in a trial would have been asked direct questions concerning both the fate of the 'princes' and Warbeck's identity, about which we don't know the truth.* In order to avoid speculative answers or answers (possibly lies on his part) which would introduce author bias, I decided to use Richard Harliston to answer questions on his behalf, as far as facts allow. Harliston and Brampton both served Edward IV and Richard III, and Harliston was Governor of Jersey when Brampton was Governor of Guernsey. However, this also introduces its own problem, as Harliston was a supporter of Warbeck and after the failed invasion of 1495 he returned to Flanders and died there. Having been pardoned once by Henry VII in 1486, he would have been unwise to return to England for any trial of the man he supported in arms in 1495, but this fact has been trumped by literary necessity, as is the fact that the date of his death is unknown other than sometime after 1495.

The trial proceedings have also been adapted for the benefit of the reader. Rather than cross-examine each witness in turn about the whole sequence of events from 1483–99 in so far as each could know them, as would be the current norm, I have chosen to work through the life of Perkin Warbeck, asking questions of the appropriate witnesses as the arguments demand and develop. This affords the easiest way to compare the differing interpretations of Warbeck's life. The testimonies begin with assessing the disappearance of the sons of Edward IV and continue with Warbeck's confession (setting out his parentage) and his life up to the trial.

I have also chosen to place the trial in a contemporary setting, as this has allowed me to introduce elements of events after 1499 which the reader may find interesting. The most obvious setting would be a courtroom, but this would cause some inflexibility, not least of which is the author's limited knowledge of the protocols of courtroom procedures. By setting the trial in the framework of a school sixth-form (years 12 and 13, ages 16–18) I have allowed myself some leeway in the way the trial is conducted while preserving features which will be easily recognized by the general public. It has also meant I can introduce an element of humour, which might make a relatively dry topic more accessible. The format is, though, deliberately flexible and could easily be adapted to another setting: I had originally contemplated it being an 'am-dram'

---

* This comment is now outdated with the recently reported (November 2023) findings of *The Missing Princes Project* (Langley *et al*), which provided documentary evidence, albeit contentious, that Richard, second son of Edward IV, was alive and in Burgundy in 1491. A comment on how this information, which appeared during the production of this work, has been incorporated into the present work can be found in the Introduction.

group holding a lockdown debate over Zoom/Teams in recognition of the time I first put pen to paper (so to speak).

The final scene represents some views on the part of the author alone concerning the identities of Perkin Warbeck and Lambert Simnel. These are speculative, may be of interest and can be read almost as an appendix to the trial itself. For those who wish to put the trial to an unprejudiced verdict, stop at the end of Scene 2 – or at least take a break at that point!

I also hope that the work can be treated as a book as well as a drama, with the readers immersing themselves in a contest that oscillates between the two sides. It should read like an argument between friends who simply want to out-debate each other. Furthermore, this is not a work of linguistic elegance – it is meant to involve the kind of informal talk that the setting affords without being held hostage to accurate grammar or syntax.

DRAMATIS PERSONAE

Judge	John de Vere, 12th Earl of Oxford, fought for Henry VII at Bosworth and Stoke. High Constable of England.
Prosecutor	John Morton, Archbishop of Canterbury, joined Henry Tudor in exile in Brittany and long-time supporter of Henry VII.
Defence	William Worsley, Dean of St Paul's, studied canon and civil law at Cambridge and was also awarded a doctorate in civil law.
Witnesses	Alexander Monypeny, Seigneur de Concressault, ex-patriot Scot and close advisor to Charles VIII of France.
	Giles Daubeney, 1st Baron Daubeney, fought for Henry Tudor at Bosworth. Led the army in relief of Exeter during the Warbeck rebellion.
	Jean le Sauvage, President of the Council of Flanders. Employed by Philip the Fair of Burgundy, step-grandson of Margaret of Burgundy, but also acted as emissary for Maximilian I, King of the Romans and Holy Roman Emperor.
	Katherine Gordon, daughter of the 2nd Earl of Huntly, married to Perkin Warbeck/Richard of York.
	Richard Harliston, former Governor of Jersey. Fought on the Yorkist side at Bosworth and Stoke.
	Roderigo de Puebla, Spanish Ambassador to England for the court of Ferdinand and Isabella of Spain.
	Roger Machado, Richmond Herald, Clarenceux King of Arms and diplomat under Henry VII.
	Rui de Sousa, Lord of Sagres, Councillor to João II of Portugal.
	Rowland Robinson, ex-patriot Scot and emissary to James IV of Scotland on behalf of Margaret, Duchess of Burgundy.
Other Participants	Tom, a Year 12 pupil.
	Beth, a Year 12 pupil.
	Mr Gates, history teacher.
	Two members of the public, nominated to make informal comments.
	Court Usher.

SCENE 1

A School Corridor

Tom	Do you think he'll buy it? An idea to do something about Warbeck?
Beth	No idea, you never know which way the old Bill will jump. Hopefully he'll be interested. Anyway, we'll soon know, there he is coming down the corridor.
Beth	Mr Gates, sir, do you have a minute?
Gates	Yes, if it's quick. I've got Year 11 on the Tudors in about fifteen minutes. Divorced, beheaded, died and all that. What is it?
Tom	Well, Beth and I both, quite randomly, chose to do our EPQ[2] on Perkin Warbeck as this was a bit of a side-show in our Wars of the Roses module, but it seems to have piqued both our interests.
Gates	Yes, Simnel and Warbeck, the two great pretenders. [*sings*] I'm the original Ch-Ch-Ch Tudor, I said this crown ain't big enough for three of us and had one slayed.
Beth	Well, claimants. Pretenders is a pejorative way of putting it; most people read that term as implying they were false. Anyway, glad to see you know your Horrible Histories.[3]
Gates	Pejorative. Nice Word. Dictionary for breakfast, was it?
Beth	Ha, ha!
Gates	So, what conclusion did you come to?
Beth	Well, I don't think he was false.
Gates	OK, so I'm guessing, Tom, you don't agree?

Tom	You're right. I came to the opposite conclusion, which makes things interesting, doesn't it?
Gates	Did you really disagree that much?
Tom	We looked at it in completely different ways. For me, the whole affair was a European power struggle that Warbeck became part of, a pawn in a battle of international diplomacy. Speaking of pawns, I know you like Chess Club as much as I do, so let me give you an analogy you'll appreciate. Warbeck was a black pawn. Not an important one, not the king or queen's pawn that enters the battle from the outset, fights hard, dies young. No, more a knight's pawn, held back, used in the long game. As the pawn moves down his file, he becomes vulnerable, needs the protection of the knights, rooks, and bishops. As he gets closer to the eighth rank, he becomes more dangerous, but he is still a pawn. Deep in white territory, it is also more dangerous for his protectors, who retreat, fearful of being over-exposed. The pawn only becomes a success if he reaches the eighth rank and gets crowned …
Beth	A queen!
Tom	Analogies only go so far, you know I mean king. Anyway, this is something the white king will never let happen, and come what may, the pawn must go. That was the game played by the crowned heads of Europe with Warbeck as a pawn.
Gates	Very eloquent, poetic almost.
Beth	Well, that's what you get if you do English Literature and Drama as well as History at A-level. If he did a science, he'd look at things differently.
Gates	Ouch!

Beth	Well, it's illogical. He starts from the end and works back to the beginning. He sees a pawn on knight 7, then assumes it started on knight 2.
Tom	g7 and g2 you mean.
Beth	Whatever.
Gates	But it could have started as either the bishop or rook's pawn, is that what you mean?
Beth	Exactly. Henry knew the outcome he needed – Warbeck was an imposter. He worked back to a starting point in Tournai which gave credibility to the story he was telling. It doesn't mean it was true. It doesn't mean that's where Warbeck really came from.
Gates	OK, so what's your take on it then?
Beth	Well, why is it assumed Warbeck was an imposter? It's because Henry told us he was, and he told us he was because he also implied, without ever categorically stating, that Richard III had killed the two princes, Edward IV's sons. Thanks to Shakespeare that narrative has gone largely unquestioned for centuries. Now that historians take a more objective look at the events of the time, they have a more open attitude. I'm not saying Richard doesn't have blood on his hands, it's more that we just don't know.
	Next, forget the names of the two so-called imposters during Henry VII's reign – Lambert and Perkin. Think of them as Lionel and Phillip, say. They go from being jokes to being credible.
	Once you remove these two prejudices from your mind, things look a little different. Start from the beginning, not the end, analyse the facts, data if you want to call it that, and your view might change.
Gates	Sparks really are flying. So, what do you propose?

Beth	Well, since we have all the references and our opposing opinions, we wondered if you thought a debate on Warbeck might be something the Year 12 History group might be interested in. We thought it could take the form of a trial, in which Tom and I act as council for and against, you could act as judge and we'll get others in the class to act as witnesses and jury.
Tom	We'll script their responses to the questions based on what we learnt researching our EPQs. We'll each put the best case we can and see which way the class decides. I reckon we can do it after school if there is enough interest. There are enough roles that the whole class can participate in one way or another.
Gates	OK, I'm intrigued. Sounds like a good idea, I'd like to see what the class makes of all this. Send me a list of characters and I'll set it up for the History group after school next week. Now, I must rush. [*sings*] Now, I'm the original Ch-Ch-Ch Tudor …

SCENE 2

A Classroom

Court Usher	All rise, John de Vere, Earl of Oxford presiding.
Oxford	Be seated and bring in the defendant. You are charged with falsely claiming to be Richard, Duke of York, second son of the late king, Edward IV, of raising rebellion in our land and acting treasonably against our rightful king, Henry VII.
Worsley	M'Lord. My I approach the bench?
Oxford	Certainly, but I fail to see what can be at issue here as the trial has hardly begun.

Worsley   The charges against my client are incompatible. If the Prosecution prove he's a boatman's son from Tournai, then he's not English and can't be guilty of treason. If he is who he says he is, which I will try to prove, he is innocent of all charges because he is the late king's son. The case should be dismissed as, whoever wins, my client is innocent of the charges as you have presented them.

Oxford   Well, firstly it's up to you to prove your case. If you fail, only then will we worry about the legal niceties. This young man has caused this country and our king nearly a decade of unrest. I'm sure if the Prosecution succeeds, then we'll find something to charge him with to put an end to this debacle once and for all. There is a lot at stake here, so let's get on with it.

For the benefit of the court, the case for the Prosecution will be made by the Archbishop of Canterbury, John Morton, who was with our lord, King Henry, in exile in Brittany and has been rewarded by King Henry as the nation's leading prelate.

For the Defence is, rather bravely I might add, William Worsley, Dean of St Paul's.

Worsley   Bravely. That's an interesting way to put it. It is true that I supported the defendant in 1494 and was tried and attainted for high treason.[4] Fortunately for me, clerics can't be executed and the king preferred I pay a fine – it won't surprise you to know it was a heavy one – and I was subsequently pardoned. There is nothing I can say or do in this court that the king does not already know about, so I will defend the prisoner to the best of my ability and without fear.

Oxford   Thank you for that, Dean.

Prosecution, make your opening statement to the jury.

Morton   This is a very straightforward case.

In 1483, after the death of Edward IV, his eldest son, also called Edward, was to be crowned king of England.

He wasn't. His uncle, Richard, Duke of Gloucester, usurped the throne under the false claim that the sons of the late king were bastards.[5] In order to secure his fragile hold on the crown, a hold that few supported, he had the said Edward, along with his younger brother, Richard, Duke of York, murdered.

There is no doubt about this. Rumours were rife of their murder all over Europe.[6] In late summer, it was reported the boys were seen less and less playing in the grounds of the Tower of London. The boy's physician, Dr Argentine, was the last of their servants to be dismissed, and he reported that Prince Edward was, and I quote, 'like a victim prepared for sacrifice, he believed that his death was imminent'.[7] The boys were never seen again. The usurping king never refuted the suggestions they were dead. He could have produced them at any time to quash the rumours, but he didn't. Why not? Because he couldn't.

Therefore, the man in the dock can't be the second of the late King Edward's sons, Richard, Duke of York, because the said duke is known to be dead. Furthermore, we will show that the defendant, Perkin Warbeck ...

Worsley   Objection!!!

Referring to the defendant as Perkin Warbeck is prejudicial to my client's defence. It simply reinforces the Prosecution's assertion in the eyes of the jury without evidence. It is up to the Prosecution to prove he is Perkin Warbeck.

Oxford   Sustained.

Unfortunately, archbishop, you will have to find an alternative way to describe the man in the dock. Defendant, perhaps?

Morton   We will show that the 'defendant' is a boatman's son from Tournai in Flanders who has been groomed to impersonate the late Richard, Duke of York.[8]

Worsley   Objection!!! There is no proof that the Duke of York in question is dead.

Oxford	Sustained.
	Archbishop, you will have your chance to prove this point in cross-examination, but not before.
Morton	We will show that the 'defendant' is a boatman's son from Tournai in Flanders who has been groomed to impersonate 'Richard, Duke of York' by various crowned heads of Europe to ferment trouble in our realm: Charles VIII of France, James IV of Scotland, Maximilian I of the Holy Roman Empire but, above all, the diabolical Duchess of Burgundy, Margaret. All had an axe to grind with our beloved king and all of them in one way or another used the defendant against us, a pawn in a battle of kings and queens. But their support was a sham, and it came to nothing. When it came to support that counts – men at arms – there was none, that's how shallow and manipulative their support was.
	After many years fooling these great heads of state and enjoying to the full their hospitality – why wouldn't a boatman's son make the most of the good life on offer? – he finally showed his true colours in Cornwall over a year ago. No fighter of Plantagenet stock he, running from the king's army at the first sight of battle. No son of the warrior Edward IV.
	But now we have him and can end the fiasco. It won't be difficult. We have it in the defendant's own words, his confession made at Taunton in 1497. He is condemned by his own pen. He gave us the full story, indisputable details of his family and his life, the life of a boatman's son, not the son of a king.
	God pronounced judgement on the field of battle. Our Gracious Lord Henry knows he is the rightful king. Do what you must do. Return a verdict that you accept the pretender is a boatman's son and not, as he claimed, the living son of Edward IV. Only then can justice take its course and England put behind it the threat of war.
Oxford	Dean Worsley, your opening statement for the Defence, please.

Worsley

This is far from the open-and-shut case the Prosecution would have you believe.

There is no proof either of the two sons of Edward IV are dead, even less that they fell victim to the malice of their uncle Richard, the late King Richard III. No witnesses have ever come forward to shed light on their fate, which is quite remarkable given the lengths to which the current king has gone to find them. Surely, if the boys were murdered in the Tower somebody would have spotted something amiss and been only too ready to come forward and earn the new king's gratitude and a nice reward as well. Nobody. Nothing. No bodies have ever been produced. No evidence of a crime. The rest of King Edward's family, Queen Elizabeth Woodville and her daughters – yes, that means our current queen and the late dowager queen – came to terms with King Richard, hardly the action of a mother towards the murderer of her sons, a sister to her brothers' killer.

The supposed death of Edward's sons in 1483 cannot be taken for granted and used as proof that my client is not who he claims he is.

We will take apart the confession for the fabrication it is. We will demonstrate the implausibility of tutoring a foreign boy to a level that could fool the great and the good of Europe for nearly a decade.

We will show that, despite the lack of men at arms in Cornwall, support for my client never faltered. Not James of Scotland, not Maximilian and certainly not Margaret of Burgundy. Charles of France may have wavered, but he had his own ever-changing agenda in all this. Besides, what do you expect from the French?

The Prosecution made much of the defendant being a pawn in a European power struggle. But they didn't tell you that King Henry has his own political reasons for needing Richard, Duke of York, dead, and indeed, anyone claiming to be him dead. If this Richard lives, then he, not Henry Tudor, is the rightful King of England. The king himself repealed *Titulus Regius*, the act that made the two boys bastards and Richard III king, so that their sister, Elizabeth, now his wife and our queen, was not tainted with bastardy. The problem for King Henry in doing that was that he would only have a claim to the throne if both sons of King Edward were truly dead. His claim is wafer thin anyway, but with either boy alive it's non-existent.

Nor did the Prosecution mention that Henry is in the process of arranging the marriage of his son, Arthur, to Catalina – Catherine, as she is known in England – daughter of King Ferdinand and Queen Isabella of Spain. These careful sovereigns won't move on marriage until all claimants to the English throne have disappeared, which is why the king needs my client dead. The Earl of Warwick, son of Edward IV's brother, the Duke of Clarence, also with a better claim to the throne than our king, can't have long for this earth either.

Morton

Objection!

There is no proof that the Earl of Warwick's life is threatened,[9] and it harms our case to suggest otherwise. It paints the king in a malicious, manipulative light, which we all know isn't true.

Oxford

Sustained.

But don't be so presumptuous as to tell the court how they should view the king's character. Continue, Dean.

Worsley

In the absence of two dead bodies, Henry needs victims that can be shown to be false to support his claim that Edward's sons are dead. He did this in 1487 with Lambert Simnel, and he needs to do it again now.

My client is the intended victim, and we accept a Warbeck family of Tournai in Flanders does exist – but my client is not their legitimate son.

The supposed confession is a falsehood and was forced out of him under duress.

With the witnesses we will bring forward, you will find that assertions about this young man fall apart as a tissue of false claims necessary to justify the legality of the current monarch. Look beyond what the Prosecution want you to believe about dead princes, what the king needs you to believe to justify his reign, and see the improbability of their case for all it is.

Oxford

This is a complex and unique case which we will conduct in a unique way to make the arguments easier for the jury to follow. All the witnesses have been sworn in and they will shortly introduce themselves. Counsels will then examine their knowledge of the defendant through the various stages of his life, allowing the competing arguments to be made. Each of the witnesses has their own knowledge of the defendant to share with the court. The Jury will then be able to judge the claims of both parties as they develop.

It will not surprise the Jury that the crowned monarchs of France, Spain, Scotland, Portugal, Burgundy and the Holy Roman Empire, who are involved in this case, have refused to be cross-examined. Each has sent a representative to speak on their behalf.

Would counsel then call each of their witnesses and ask them to introduce themselves to the court.

Morton

The Prosecution calls Giles Daubeney, 1st Baron Daubeney, who will speak on behalf of our king, Henry VII.

Baron Daubeney, for the benefit of the court, would you describe your relationship to the king

Daubeney

Despite my initial support for Richard, Duke of Gloucester – I attended his coronation as King Richard III – I was never comfortable with his usurpation and the murder, sorry, disappearance, of Edward's sons. I supported the Duke of Buckingham's rebellion in 1483 and when this failed, I went into exile in Brittany with Henry Tudor, as he was then.

I fought for Tudor at Bosworth and was rewarded by him in 1486, being made Master of the Mint.[10] In the same year I was made both Lieutenant of Calais and a baron. Since then I have served him faithfully.

In 1497 I was in command of the army the king sent north to confront a possible invasion by King James IV of Scotland, but was recalled south when the Cornishmen rebelled. I was then in command of a force which went to confront the so-called pretender's army after the siege of Exeter.[11]

Morton   The second Prosecution witness is Roger Machado, Richmond Herald.

Machado   My name is Roger Machado. I am of Portuguese extraction but have lived and worked in England for many years. I served King Edward IV and was present at his funeral in 1483. For personal reasons, I left England for a while thereafter, but then joined the exiled Henry Tudor through the help of Thomas Grey, Marquis of Dorset. Before Bosworth, I was made Tudor's personal officer at arms, Richmond Herald. Since Bosworth, I have been made Norroy King of Arms and in 1494 Clarenceux King of Arms. I have served as diplomatic emissary for the king on several occasions since then.[12]

Morton   The next witness we have asked for is Roderigo de Puebla, Spanish Ambassador to England for the court of King Ferdinand and Queen Isabella of Spain.

de Puebla   *Buenos dias.* I am Roderigo de Puebla, a lawyer and diplomat. I first came to the English court in 1487 and stayed five years. I helped to negotiate the Treaty of Medina del Campo in 1489, which arranged the marriage of Catalina, daughter of the King and Queen of Spain, to Arthur, son of King Henry VII and Prince of Wales. I was less successful in bringing about a marriage between Joanna of Aragon and James IV of Scotland. I returned to London as Spanish Ambassador in 1495 in an effort to engage your King Henry in the Holy League of Nations against Charles VIII of France.

Morton   Also from the Iberian peninsula we call Rui de Sousa, Lord of Sagres, Councillor to João II of Portugal.

de Sousa	*Bom dia.* My name is Rui de Sousa, I was ambassador to the court of the late King Edward IV in 1482 on behalf of João II of Portugal, to whom I am a close friend and confidant. I helped negotiate the Treaty of Tordesillas between my country and Spain over the exploitation of newly discovered lands in the New World. I was present at the testimonies given at Setubal in 1496 which are relevant to the current proceedings.
Morton	Finally, on behalf of Charles VIII of France, we call Alexander Monypeny, Seigneur de Concressault.
Monypeny	I am Alexander Monypeny, an ex-patriot Scot and son of William Monypeny, who was a long-time diplomatic servant to the French kings.[13] I am myself, now, a close advisor to King Charles VIII of France. I have led embassies overseas on his behalf and I was responsible for the care of the defendant while he was in France in 1492.
Morton	Those are all the witnesses called by the Prosecution m'Lord.
Oxford	Witnesses for the Defence.
Worsley	We call Jean le Sauvage, President of the Council of Flanders.
le Sauvage	I am employed by Duke Philip the Fair of Burgundy, step-grandson of Margaret, dowager Duchess of Burgundy, but I also act as emissary for Maximilian I, King of the Romans and now Holy Roman Emperor. In 1490 I was made a member of the Council of Flanders and have been its President since 1497.
Worsley	We next call Roland Robinson.
Robinson	Like the Seigneur de Concressault, I am also an ex-patriot Scot. In the past I have acted as an emissary to King James IV of Scotland for Margaret, Duchess of

Burgundy. I served to carry messages between Burgundy and Scotland and have become well-acquainted with the court of the Scottish king.

Worsley

Both myself and the Prosecution would have liked Edward Brampton to appear before the court, but he has, conveniently you might think, found himself too indisposed to come to London. We have agreed with the Prosecution that Richard Harliston appear on his behalf, though this will clearly put limitations on what information either of us can glean with any certainty.

Morton

Brampton has information on the defendant that is relevant to both counsels. He is, however, a man who has served both kings, Richard III and Henry VII, and seems to have decided that it would be in his best interests not to be questioned under oath.

Oxford

Accepted. Will Richard Harliston briefly inform the court of his history and his relationship with Brampton?

Harliston

Your Lordship, I am former Governor of Jersey and I fought on the Yorkist side at Bosworth. I also fought at Stoke in 1487, as, indeed, did Rowland Robinson.

While I was Governor of Jersey, Brampton held the equivalent position in Guernsey. I knew him well up to the time he left Flanders for Portugal in 1487.[14]

Morton

Despite this witness's obvious leanings we have accepted him as there is little alternative. We will be using the testimony of Rui de Sousa to tell us about Brampton's questioning and the evidence he gave at Setubal in 1496.

Oxford

I believe we have also sworn in Katherine Gordon, wife of the defendant, who may be called. She is, however, under no obligation to testify and is legally allowed to withhold, at her discretion, any evidence that may incriminate either herself or her husband. Is that clear to both counsels?

Both Counsels   Yes, your Lordship.

Oxford   Prosecution, call the first witness.

Morton   Baron Daubeney.

I want to begin by exploring the fate of the two sons of King Edward IV. How can you be so sure these sons, Edward V and Richard, Duke of York, are dead?

Daubeney   It was widely known. Dominic Mancini, the Italian working for Angelo Cato, the Archbishop of Vienne, who was in London in 1483 until shortly after the usurper was crowned, wrote in his report that the princes 'day by day came to be observed more rarely through the lattices and windows of the Tower of London up to the point they completely ceased to be visible'.[7] He was a spy. He was paid to know these things.

Morton   So, that's it? Nothing else?

Daubeney   On the contrary. The court of Burgundy was told the boy Edward had said to his brother 'it would be better if you and I learned to die, because I believe I know well that we will not be in this world much longer'.[15]

The Chancellor of France, Guillaume de Rochefort, said in January 1484 that the boys had been murdered, expressing his horror at the event.[16] News also appeared in the *Danzig Chronicle* of 1483.[17] There were many other, more lurid, rumours of the boys' deaths, but these seem to be our enemies enjoying themselves at our expense by exaggerating a true story.[18, 19]

Then their physician, Dr Argentine, who was the last to see the princes, reported to Mancini that Edward was 'like a victim prepared for sacrifice because he reckoned that his death was imminent'.[7]

Even Edward Brampton, a staunch Yorkist, said they were dead when he gave testimony at Setubal in 1486, as we will no doubt hear later.[20]

Morton	So, it was just in the courts of Europe that these rumours abounded? Surely this means nothing; it is in their interest to ferment trouble.

| Daubeney | It wasn't just abroad. The town clerk in Bristol noted 'this year', that is between September 1483 and September 1484, 'the two sons of King E. were put to silence in the Tower of London'.[21] |

Then there's the Crowland Chronicler, a knowledgeable insider reporting to the Abbot at Crowland, who wrote of a rumour in August or September 1483 that the two boys had died 'by some unknown manner of violent destruction'.[22]

| Morton | But you never found the bodies? |

| Daubeney | No, but then King Richard was, if nothing else, cunning. Some say he buried the bodies inside the Tower, and he did appoint a new Mason of the King's Works, Thomas Danyell, and a new Chief Joiner, John Jerveys, to the Tower in July 1483, which is highly suspicious, especially when he didn't make these appointments official for over a year.[23] |

Personally, though, I doubt this burial in the Tower is true. My guess is he dumped the bodies so the fishes could feast.

| Worsley | Objection! We don't want guesswork in this trial. |

| Oxford | Sustained. |

Jury, disregard that last comment by the witness.

| Morton | What about during King Richard's reign – what was the reaction of the leading nobles? |

| Daubeney | Well, look no further than the Duke of Buckingham. He had become his closest ally and been well rewarded, but then even he turned against him. He rebelled in late 1483 but bad luck and bad weather thwarted his attempt to bring justice to the land. |

But he wasn't alone. All over the south of England there was rebellion against the king, which he only put down by bringing in his henchmen of the north. Even that didn't help him in the long run, as every southerner despised those uncouth northerners.

Morton   Did King Henry search for the boys?

Daubeney   Of course, but to no avail. But then, as I said, King Richard was no fool when it came to malice. If the boys were alive, why didn't he produce them to quell the rumours? Because he couldn't.

He needed them dead otherwise he couldn't be king. Nobody believed in the story that the boys were bastards because Edward was already contracted in marriage when he married the late dowager queen, Elizabeth Woodville.[5] They even tried to claim his brother, King Edward IV himself, was a bastard.[24] Ridiculous nonsense. Richard of Gloucester had his eye on the crown from the day his brother died and he was prepared to do anything to get it.

Morton   So, to summarize. When the two boys were no longer seen playing in the Tower gardens, rumours swirled around the country and around the courts of Europe that the boys were dead. King Richard was widely believed to have had the boys killed to cement his position on the throne. He had motive and opportunity and no shortage of men who would do the evil deed. It isn't surprising that the leading nobles and men of all classes in the south of England rebelled against him.

The evidence may be circumstantial, but there is so much of it that it must be true. Am I right in my summary?

Daubeney   Exactly.

Morton   No further questions at this time, but we reserve the right to bring the witness back at a later stage.

Oxford   Granted.

Dean Worsely for the Defence, do you have anything you wish to ask?

Worsley   Most certainly I do.

Baron Daubeney, let's face it, your so-called evidence is wafer-thin. Even your sources can't be trusted to be accurate.

Isn't it true, for example, that the Crowland Chronicler wrote that the boys were alive at the time Edward of Middleham, son of Richard III, was made Prince of Wales in September 1483, which contradicts any assertion the boys were dead by this time?[25]

Daubeney   Anyone can make a mistake, especially about dates. It doesn't alter the fact that the Crowland Chronicler and Mancini thought they were dead. 'When' is less important than 'if'.

Worsley   Let's leave what foreigners think and concentrate on events closer to home.

Isn't it true that Richard, Duke of Gloucester, was a loyal brother to King Edward – **the** most loyal brother? Hadn't he stuck by his brother in exile, fought at his side at Barnet and Tewkesbury, kept peace in the north for a decade on behalf of his brother and never once did anything to suggest malice towards the king's family?

Daubeney   He never really liked Elizabeth Woodville. Apart from that you are right. But when the prospect of the throne appeared upon his brother's death, he systematically and brutally removed his opponents – Earl Rivers, Richard Grey, Lord Hastings. He effectively imprisoned young Edward before he could be crowned and then tricked the queen into releasing her youngest son into his care, if you can call it that. He was hell-bent on becoming king from the minute he heard his brother had died.

Worsley   Well that's your opinion, but others would say differently.

Let's concentrate on the two boys, as that is what is relevant to this trial. If King Richard had the boys killed, why did Queen Elizabeth Woodville and her daughters leave sanctuary and make good with the new king? He gave her a good pension – better than she received from the current king[26] – promised to find husbands for her daughters and all were welcome at court.

Daubeney   She had no choice. It was either that or the rest of her life in sanctuary.

Worsley   Are you really telling the court that a woman would happily socialize with the man who murdered her two young sons?

Daubeney   If she had to.

Worsley   Didn't she persuade her son by her first marriage, Thomas Grey, to return to England from Brittany, where he had been in exile with the now king, Henry Tudor? Doesn't this tell you she had no axe to grind with King Richard?

Daubeney   But he never did come back, did he?

Worsley   Only because Tudor stopped him. And from there afterwards, Tudor never trusted Grey, did he?[27, 28]

Isn't it the case that King Henry was paranoid about the fate of the boys from the minute he took the crown? He failed to find any evidence in the aftermath of Bosworth, and even in 1494 – yes, nearly a decade later – he was still searching.

Didn't he send Thomas Lyneham to Middleham and Sheriff Hutton in that year, still searching for clues in Richard's old strongholds?[29]

Daubeney   If you say so. I don't know.

Worsley   With no proof, why did King Henry send the captain of his guard, Sir Charles Somerset, to Burgundy in March 1495 with an offer to show dowager Duchess Margaret the tomb of young Richard, something that was clearly impossible?[30]

Daubeney   I guess he was trying anything to break her belief in the boy she was grooming.

Worsley	I would suggest he was desperate.

No further questions of this witness, but I would like to explore the disappearance of the two sons further with Richard Harliston.

Richard Harliston, you knew Edward Brampton. Tell us first a little about him.

Harliston	Duarte Brandão, as he was originally, was a Portuguese Jew. There are several interesting stories about why he left – many would say fled – Portugal for England in 1468, where he stayed at the house of the Jews in London, the Domus Conservorum. He converted to Christianity, changed his name to Edward Brampton and, as was the custom for converted Jews, became the godson of King Edward IV. He served the king, was well rewarded, and this continued through the reign of King Richard III. Brampton did well for himself but was always careful. He always looked after himself first. He managed to be absent from Bosworth, then deciding that Flanders was a safer place to be after August 1485.

Worsley	It would have helped the court had he been here to answer questions in person.

Harliston	It doesn't surprise me he's not here. He left Flanders in a hurry in 1487, then returned to London in 1488. Quite why he thought it was safe then I don't know after his long association with the House of York. I know he played host to Richmond Herald, who is with us now, when he was in Lisbon in 1489 and then was pardoned by King Henry the same year.[31] What he did to gain Henry's favour I don't know, but I guess after that he decided he'd had enough of England.

Worsley	Yes, we'll return to Brampton's involvement with Henry later.

For now, I want your comment on the following. In 1484, Brampton was paid £100 for unspecified services to the late King Richard.[32, 33] What do you know about this?

Harliston	Not much, I'm afraid. James Tyrell received an even larger sum – £3,000, I think – about the same time.[34] Both of them had shipping connections, notably with Flanders but with the Channel Islands as well, where Brampton was Governor. I assume it was related to this, but I can't say how.
Worsley	You knew Brampton was Governor of Guernsey for a period, about the time you were governor of Jersey. Is that correct?
Harlison	Yes, he was made governor in August 1483 for life, but it all ended just a few months later, in late January 1484, when Thomas Rydley became governor.[35]
Worsley	So, in the months when our king says the boys disappeared, King Richard appoints Brampton, who had served the Yorkists loyally, to the governorship of Guernsey for life, brings it to an abrupt end five months later, then pays him the huge sum of £100 for unspecified services. What do you make of that?
Harlison	I know what you are implying, but I can't shed any light on the matter. Brampton kept his cards close to his chest. All I can tell you is that the king, Richard that is, was very unsettled by an attempt, possibly more than one, to remove the elder boy from the Tower in the summer of 1483, shortly after his coronation.[36, 37]
Worsley	So, the fact that my client is linked to a family in Flanders isn't surprising?
Harliston	No, it's the most obvious place the boys would be sent for safe keeping.
Worsley	It wasn't just Brampton who may have played a role in the survival of the late king's sons, was it? Sir James Tyrell, as you've already mentioned, was paid a large sum for unspecified services to King Richard.[34] What can you tell the court about him?

Harliston	Well, he was loyal to King Richard, he was Master of the King's Horse, but he was absent from Bosworth as he was Lieutenant of Guînes in France in 1485. As far as I know, he has had nothing to do with the prisoner.[38]
Worsley	What about other members of the wider Tyrell family?
Harliston	I hardly need to tell *you* that his cousin, Sir Thomas Tyrell, another Tyrell who had served the two kings, Edward and Richard,[39] was part of the group arrested at the time of the Stanley plot in 1495.[40] Another cousin, Elizabeth Darcy, was the mistress of the royal nursery for King Edward IV and Queen Elizabeth Woodville, so would have had charge of both sons, but predominantly the younger one, Richard.[41] There were even rumours that the dowager queen lived with her sons at the Tyrell household at Gipping in Suffolk, with the permission of King Richard, but as far as I know that's all they were rumours.[42]
Worsley	So, in summary, the wider Tyrell family, including Sir James, the loyal servant of Richard III, knew the sons of Edward IV well, and at least one of them was active in support of my client in 1495.
Harliston	That is correct. In fact, I'm amazed that Sir Thomas Tyrell got off without penalty from his association with the Stanley plot. He clearly stated that King Edward's younger son, Richard, had survived,[43] which is far more than Stanley did.
Worsley	He certainly suffered less than some of us. I think your comments on both Brampton and Tyrell during the reign of Richard III will have given the jury pause for thought concerning the fate of the two princes. Richard Harliston, one final question. You fought at Bosworth. You held the island of Jersey for several months in the siege of late 1485.[44] You were clearly a Yorkist sympathizer. You fought at Stoke[45] for the pretender called Lambert Simnel, you supported the pretender now in the

	dock and were with him at Deal when he first tried to land on these shores.[46] Why did you continue your support after Bosworth when the Yorkist cause, and apparently the sons of Edward IV, were supposedly long dead?
Harliston	I have been pardoned once by King Henry for my past,[47] and I doubt he will do it again.[48] All I am prepared to say is that a man doesn't put his life on the line – not once, but twice – without good cause.
Worsley	Thank you. No further questions for now.
Morton	Isn't it the case that pretenders to the throne would emerge from Burgundian Flanders whether or not the boy or boys were there? Doesn't the Duchess of Burgundy hate the Tudors to the extent that she would take any opportunity to instigate trouble for King Henry, with or without a real claimant?
Harliston	Well, she does hate him.
Morton	Thank you, that will be all from me for now.
Oxford	Would the two counsels please approach the bench for a moment?
	I am surprised that since we are exploring the fate of the late King Edward's two sons, neither of you wants to take this opportunity to bring as evidence the prisoner's letter to Queen Isabella of Spain, where he writes that his brother was murdered in the Tower while he was spared.[49]
Morton	In fact, my opponent and I did discuss this issue before the trial began and we agreed it was evidence that neither of us thought helpful and would, in any case, only confuse the jury.
Oxford	I'm sorry; I'm not sure what you mean.
Worsley	Well, as well as the small errors – for example, he stated he was 9 when he was actually 11 – the story is

unbelievable. He had to say his brother was dead because if not, then he, the older brother, Edward, is the rightful king, not my client.

Morton I share my colleague's concerns. Why indeed kill one boy and spare the second? It beggars belief that someone who murders one boy will suddenly have a crisis of conscience and spare the second. Why leave the only witness to a murder alive? The story is nonsense. If one was killed, then both must be dead, as we have been trying to prove.

Oxford So, am I right in thinking that for one of you, his letter has one murder too many, and for the other, it has one murder too few?

Morton I think that sums it up for both of us.

Oxford Well, it's clear as mud to me, so I guess we spare the jury and move on.

I think we will now move on to evidence concerning the man known as Perkin Warbeck's early life, in the years before his emergence in Cork in 1491. Archbishop, would you like to begin please?

Morton Roger Machado, Richmond Herald. I know you have acted as a diplomat for the king for many years, but it is your knowledge of the last days of the defendant's freedom I wish to ask you about. I want the jury to know exactly who the man in the dock is, and why not hear it in his own words?

Worsley Objection! The witness can't be questioned unless he wishes to be so, which I can tell you he doesn't.

Morton We have no intention of giving that man a platform to lie any more than he has already. He has confessed, remember?

Oxford Jury, disregard comments about the implication the defendant is a liar.

Continue, Archbishop.

Morton	Roger Machado, you were at Taunton in 1497 when the defendant was brought from sanctuary at Beaulieu Abbey to face the king, correct?
Machado	I was. He was first brought to Taunton and then moved to Exeter.
Morton	And you have full knowledge of the confession made by the prisoner?
Machado	I do. It was a confession given freely, no matter what others may say.
Morton	Summarize for us, in your own words, what was in that confession concerning the boy's family and upbringing.
Machado	He admitted he was born in Tournai in Flanders; his father was Jehan – John – Osbeck and his mother Kateryn de Faro, his grandfather Deryck Osbeck. After his grandfather died, his grandmother remarried to a Peter Flam, who was a Receiver in Tournai and also Dean of the Boatmen on the River Scheldt. His father was also a boatman. He says he had an uncle, John Stalyn, who lived in the parish of St John's in Tournai. He lived for a time with Stalyn and his wife, whose name was Joan or Jane.[50]
Morton	That's a lot of detail.
Machado	In fact, there's more. He listed neighbours and school masters, so many individuals you couldn't make it up.[51]
Morton	And how do you know all this is true?
Machado	You can go to Tournai and check it all out. The records are there, the people, the places he names, they all exist.[52]
Morton	So you don't doubt that the defendant really is from Tournai and a boatman's son, and not the Duke of York?

Machado	Absolutely. He's an imposter. He even wrote a letter confessing everything to his mother, asking her for money to help bribe his guards into making life easier for him.[53]
Morton	Thank you, that will be all for now.
Worsley	Before we explore the confession more fully, let's just stay with his parents and the letter to his mother for a moment. How did she respond?
Machado	She didn't.
Worsley	A mother, who hasn't seen or heard from her only son in over a decade, hearing that he is in the custody of the King of England for impersonating a member of the English royal family, probably under threat of execution, and she ignores it? Some mother!
Machado	I guess she was ashamed of him. Maybe she never received the letter.
Worsley	In 1496, didn't King Charles VIII of France offer to get Warbeck's mother and father from Tournai and send them to England? Surely this would have sorted the matter?[54]
Machado	Did he? I don't know.
Worsley	Isn't this the truth, *Señor* de Puebla?
de Puebla	My king and queen certainly offered a similar service, as they knew *Señor* de Sousa, who is with us today, had met the sons of King Edward when he was ambassador in London and could make an identification, but it was rejected. They were surprised, as this was an easy way to settle things.[55]
Worsley	Let's move on. I'm sure we will return at some point to why opportunities to identify my client as an impostor

by people who knew him were ignored. For now, can we focus on the confession?

King Henry was writing about a Warbeck from Tournai in 1493,[56] but we know that the man in the dock left Flanders in 1487. I don't believe my client went around telling all and sundry since he landed in Cork that he was from Tournai, so what made the king's emissaries hunt in Flanders for his heritage in the first place?

Machado   I don't know. I only know King Henry has spies everywhere.[57]

Worsley   I put it to you that he has been looking for a surviving son of King Edward ever since 1485 because he knows they are not dead, and that includes looking in Flanders.

Machado   No, they are dead.

Worsley   Really?

Isn't it true that King Henry had spies chasing my client all over Europe from as early as 1485? He knew Flanders was a likely hiding place for the sons of the late king, Edward IV, so was looking there from the time he came to the throne.

Machado   Flanders is always hostile as long as Duchess Margaret is alive, that's all I know.

Worsley   I put it to you again that King Henry suspected at least one of the sons of Edward IV was alive from the minute he won at Bosworth.

Machado   No.

Worsley   That his spies searched high and low in Flanders, and in 1487, when they were getting too close, my client was forced to flee to Portugal.

Machado   No.

| Worsley | And King Henry got wind of this and sent envoys to Portugal – yourself included in 1489 – to run him down. This was before the name Perkin Warbeck ever emerged. |

| Machado | Yes, I was there in 1489, but to present the Order of the Garter to the king.[58] |

| Worsley | But you were there for seven weeks. It must have been the longest presentation ceremony in history. |

| Machado | I was away for a long time but was in Portugal only about a month. I landed in Laredo in northern Spain as I had business with the king and queen of that country in Burgos.[58] |

| Worsley | Only a month in Portugal? That's still plenty of time to snoop around for information. |

| Machado | I stayed a month. It would have been discourteous to have left any sooner. |

| Worsley | Indeed, indeed, and very convenient for you. You weren't the only emissary sent to Portugal, were you? In 1487–88, Sir Edward Woodville twice passed through Lisbon.[59] Sir Edward Woodville – Richard, Duke of York's uncle – someone who would recognize him if he saw him. |

| Machado | I believe he was on his way to fight the Moors. |

| Worsley | By travelling through Lisbon and not disembarking in northern Spain? Or is it that he just likes being on a boat? |

| Machado | You will have to ask him about that. |

| Worsley | King Henry seems to have developed a sudden and inordinate interest in Portugal after 1487. Is this why my client disappeared for at least a year after arriving in Portugal, to throw Henry's spies off his scent? |

| Machado | I've no idea what the defendant was up to when he was in Portugal. |

Worsley	And after 1491, when my client had left Portugal for Ireland, King Henry suddenly lost complete interest in Portugal.[58] Why was that?
Machado	He had more import things to deal with. Portugal was unimportant compared to France, Spain and Burgundy.
Worsley	I put it to you again: King Henry had heard the likelihood that at least one of Edward's sons was alive, and after failing to find him in King Richard's old haunts in the north of England in 1485, he sent spies to Flanders. He pursued the boy to Portugal, where he learnt enough about the so-called Perkin Warbeck to start writing a confession for him as early as 1493. He found out that Richard, Duke of York, had been hiding in Tournai, so King Henry put together a family history, turned it into a confession and all that remained was a signature.
Machado	You may think that, but it's not true. Why would the son of a King of England hide with a boatman?
Worsley	Let me remind you that I ask the questions.
Oxford	Dean, far be it for me to tell you how to conduct your defence, but aren't you straying from details of the prisoner's confession?
Worsley	My apologies. Richmond Herald, the defendant didn't write that confession, did he? By 1493, King Henry had already arranged for the confession to be presented,[56] and he just added more details as his spies unearthed them.
Machado	No, that isn't true.
Worsley	In that case then, I'm sure at some point you will explain to us how this boatman's son became fluent in English. For now, I'd like you to explain how he became a proficient clerk.

Machado	I've no idea what you are talking about.

Worsley	The confession is littered with legal terminology. When did a boatman's son 'depose' his confession,[60] or use phrases like 'the foresaid Town of Tournai', 'within the abovenamed Town' or 'the water or river of Scheldt'?[49] He must have been very well educated somewhere if he wrote his own confession.

Machado	Maybe he was so ignorant it required – how shall I put it? – adjusting, so it could be understood in a court. I was about to add 'if needed', but the king's foresight was evidently justified by our presence here.

Worsley	The confession was written by King Henry's clerks and my client forced to sign it, isn't that the case?

Machado	Certainly not. No force was used.

Worsley	I didn't say it was. It wasn't necessary, for you also had his wife and child in your custody.

Machado	So?

Worsley	You said the information in the confession could be verified by the Tournai records?

Machado	Yes.

Worsley	So, is it not then the case that the confession could have been fabricated using this freely available information?

Machado	Yes, but it wasn't. King Henry had spies all over Europe checking on rumours of an imposter; the records simply show that the confession was true.

Worsley	So, then, let's now turn to the details of the confession and the Warbeck family history. Indeed, is it Warbeck, a French Warbecque, a Dutch Weerbecke, Osbeck or even Warboys, as once appeared in one of the king's letters? [61, 62]

Machado	Clerks make mistakes. All these names are pretty much the same.
Worsley	Let's just say that's the first of many mistakes they seem to make. Henry should hire better staff. So, the defendant's mother was, according to his confession, Kateryn de Faro.[50, 62]
Machado	Yes.
Worsley	But in the Tournai records, it's Nicaise or Caisine.[52] Are you telling us that this man doesn't know his mother's name? Or is this just another clerical error? Number two by my count.
Machado	I've no idea. Perhaps it's the clerks in Tournai who made a mistake.
Worsley	In his letter to his mother, the defendant is alleged to have expressed sorrow at his father's death, but the records suggest his father didn't die until 1498, after the letter was written. Clerical error number three, perhaps?
Machado	Categorically no. The king did have information which said Warbeck's father was dead shortly before the time of the prisoner's capture, so he probably heard it for the first time from the king.[61, 63]
Worsley	Ok, so what can you tell us about his sister Jehanne, who, he wrote, died from plague in Tournai?
Machado	Nothing. You seem to know as much as I do.
Worsley	Then it will no doubt surprise you to hear that according to Tournai records, Jehanne is alive, married and still living in Tournai.[52, 53, 64]
Machado	Perhaps there were two daughters named Jehanne; one dies young, the other lives.[65]

Worsley	Or that there is no record of plague in Tournai from 1425 to now?[53, 64]
Machado	Perhaps there was plague in some of the surrounding area which came into Tournai but didn't become widespread.[66] Maybe she was just seriously ill, something other than the plague. Maybe so ill Warbeck only thought she had died. You choose.
Worsley	The confession states his father had a job as Comptroller in Tournai.
Machado	Yes.
Worsley	It's a pity then that no such job exists.[67] And his grandfather, Peter Flam, was employed by Tournai both as a Receiver and also Dean of the Boatmen.
Machado	Yes, the family were in the business as boatmen, as you know his father was.
Worsley	Whoever wrote the confession, then, didn't know that the two jobs were incompatible. You couldn't hold both at the same time. One looked after the interests of the workers, the other the interests of the city.[67]
Machado	Well then, he must have held them at different times.
Worsley	Clerical error number six – or is it seven? – by my count. They do seem to be piling up.
Morton	May I just cut in briefly? Was this Peter Flam his grandfather or his godfather?[67]
Machado	I don't know. If Peter Flam was his grandmother's second husband, then there would have been a large age gap between them, so godfather seems more likely. That might explain why the confession was inaccurate about the jobs Flam held. I mean, when he held them.

Morton	Thank you for clarifying that point.
Worsley	I don't see much clarity myself, but maybe the jury are smarter than me. I have three final questions for this witness. Firstly, why does the confession tell us nothing about how the prisoner was taught to be fluent in English, and secondly, how he seems word-perfect on the court of King Edward IV? All we are told is that he was, apparently, taught to learn English and taught what to do and say.
Machado	It must have been Atwater, Taylor and Poytron, the sympathizers who recognized him on the quay at Cork.
Worsley	Some teachers! Surely the confession alone would not have been enough to satisfy the king. Why didn't he use one of the many people still at court who had known Edward's sons to question him? If he is an imposter, surely it would be easy to ask him questions he couldn't answer.
Machado	I can only assume that the king felt he had all he needed in what the prisoner confessed.
Worsley	Finally, why was a confession needed at all? The other pretender, Lambert Simnel, wasn't required to write and sign a confession when he was captured, was he? It's not like our king to need a confession to administer his justice, is it?
Machado	Simnel didn't cause the trouble the defendant did. There were people all over Europe who needed to be convinced. Of course, King Henry could have just told them, but surely everyone can see it's better if the whole truth comes from the Pretender's own mouth.
Worsley	I think we have laboured the confession and letter enough. There are more minor errors in the confession I could dwell on, identified by people who know Tournai better that I do. Small discrepancies, but not the sort of thing a

native of the city would get wrong.[58] However, I believe the story is clear enough, so it is for the jury to decide on its authenticity. There is enough truth in these confessions that can be proved, so there is no doubt that such a family existed. But there are far too many errors of detail that a true son would not have got wrong. So, I put it to you: the defendant was fostered by the Warbeck family as a way of hiding him from the opponents of King Richard III ...

Morton

Objection!
This 'fostering' is conjecture for which there is no proof.

Oxford

Sustained.
Defence must either prove it or withdraw it.

Worsley

Richmond Herald, you have excused numerous errors in the defendant's confession as being clerical errors, mistakes due to fatigue, stress, even when he is talking of his own life, his own family, his own friends. Yet in the period from 1491 until his capture in late 1497, there is no record of him making *any* mistakes when asked questions by *anyone* who met him about the person you claim he was impersonating. These were people who knew the court of King Edward IV, of King Richard III, all of whom could speak perfect English? But no mistakes. How do you explain the difference?

Machado

It just shows how well coached he was to fulfil his role.

Worsley

Thank you, for now.

Oxford

Questioning will now turn to further aspects of the prisoner's life up to 1491. Archbishop, would you begin?

Morton

Baron Daubeney, Richmond Herald, I'm not sure which of you is best placed to answer my questions. What do we know about the early life of Perkin Warbeck?

Daubeney

What we know comes from the prisoner himself and what he put in his confession.

| Machado | Perhaps I should answer this, as I was there when the confession was made.

He told us in some detail in fact. At some point while he was young – I've no idea how old he was then – he went with his mother to Antwerp to live with his cousin, John Steinbek or Steyn or something like that, so he could learn Flemish. |

| Morton | So what language did he speak normally? |

| Machado | Well, Tournai was probably mainly French-speaking. The Scheldt is the border between Picardy and the Burgundian low countries. |

| Morton | So he went to learn Flemish – why? |

| Machado | Well, he seems to have been training for work in the textile industry, so he would have needed Flemish to work in the markets, deal with traders, that sort of thing. |

| Morton | So, he was no fool, and apparently good with languages? |

| Machado | It seems so. |

| Morton | Continue the history, please. |

| Machado | He spent about a year in Antwerp but was forced to return to Tournai because of the wars in Flanders. He was then taken under the wing of a merchant called Alex and a man called Berlo who worked for him. Together they went back to Antwerp, where he stayed for about five months in a house next to the English Merchants Hall. Apparently, he stayed more due to illness than anything. He seems finally to have arrived in Middelberg around Christmas 1486, again lodging with another merchant.[50] |

| Morton | Does this tell us, then, he was learning a trade in textiles? |

| Machado | It looks that way. |

| Morton | And he lived next to the English Merchants Hall, possibly learning some English? |

| Worsley | Objection! Speculation. |

| Oxford | Sustained.
Move on, archbishop. |

| Morton | And then what happened to him? |

| Machado | The house in Middelberg was opposite that where the wife of Edward Brampton was staying, so it seems he joined the Brampton household and then went with them to Portugal, around or after 1487. |

| Morton | Rui de Sousa. You were with Brampton when he gave his testimony at Setubal in Portugal in April 1496, on what he knew about Warbeck.[20] Tell us, is this account of how he came to know Warbeck true? |

| de Sousa | Yes, that's what he said. I'm sure you would also be interested to know that Brampton also stated that Richard, Duke of York, and his elder brother, Edward, had been killed by Richard III. |

| Morton | Really! That arch Yorkist, servant of two Yorkist kings, and he admits Richard had the boys murdered? |

| de Sousa | That's what he testified. |

| Morton | To be clear for the jury, Richmond Herald. In your opinion, the evidence leads to the prisoner being a young man making his way in the world of textiles, and not one of Edward IV's sons, whom Brampton, a Yorkist all his life until Bosworth, testified were murdered in the Tower of London. |

| Machado | That is where the evidence points. |

| Morton | Thank you. I don't think I need ask you anything more for now. |

| Worsley | I think we can leave the Taunton confession behind us for a moment. We have already explored how reliable it might or might not be. For now, I am more interested in what Brampton had to say at Setubal and its veracity. *Señor* de Sousa, this, then, would be the Edward Brampton who was pardoned by King Henry in 1489, correct?[69] |

| de Sousa | I didn't know that, but then I don't know Brampton all that well. He has – how shall I put it? – something of a colourful history here in Portugal. Rumour has it he fled Portugal in 1468 because he killed somebody, but I don't know if that's true or not.[31] |

| Worsley | In the French version of Warbeck's confession, my client apparently stated that he in fact stayed in Tournai and was expensively educated. He was taught music, maybe the organ, and Latin as well.[70] This is also the testimony of Brampton at Setubal, isn't it?[20] |

| de Sousa | That may be true. Brampton certainly said as much. |

| Worsley | Brampton also testified at Setubal that the boy's father was named Bernal.[20] Did anyone else ever claim this? |

| de Sousa | No, not at Setubal. |

| Worsley | Nor did the prisoner in his confession. So much for how much Brampton really knew.

What we have is one confession and many different and conflicting variations from witnesses. Is there any truth in all this? It's a pity only the copy sent to France still survives, not the one originally circulated for people in this country to read.[50] Don't you agree, it seems there are at least two quite different versions about the prisoner's upbringing? |

| de Sousa | It would seem so. |

| Morton | Excuse me interrupting, but doesn't all this just tell us he was intelligent, well-educated and good at languages? |

Something that is entirely relevant to his role in the great deception.

de Sousa   Maybe.

Morton   You also seemed surprised a boatman's son would learn music. Did you know that Gaspar van Weerbecke, who must be somehow related given his name, was a leading musician at the court of the Duke of Milan?[71]

Worsley   Objection!
Unless the archbishop can be more specific about the link to the Warbecks of Tournai, then this line of questioning is irrelevant.[72]

Oxford   Can you, archbishop? If not, let the Defence continue.

Morton   I'll pass.

Worsley   If I may continue then, perhaps without interruption, archbishop?
Didn't Brampton claim in his testimony at Setubal that Warbeck only spoke French? No comment about him being multi-lingual?

de Sousa   That's not what he testified, but he did say the boy seemed to prefer the company of other French-speakers, which suggests this was his preferred language, which is hardly surprising. Maybe he spoke to others; I don't know.[73]

Worsley   *Señor* de Sousa, I find this all very confusing. We have Warbeck the aspiring merchant who travels widely within his country learning his trade, while at the same time, he seems a gifted academic and musician who never left his home town. They both can't be correct, can they?

de Sousa   You never know, it's possible they are both correct. Maybe he started learning music, got fed up and moved on. Literally. Don't you know any young men who think they know best?

Worsley	That's as maybe, but it still seems that the confession is, well, inconsistent, shall we say.

Let's turn to other aspects of the confession. We have heard that my client is, so the Prosecution would have us believe, the only son of Jehan, John, a boatman. Since when did a working man like that aspire to have his son become a musician and pay good money to make it happen? Or why did he let the boy's mother take him off to be a wool merchant and then abandon him to others? Who would take over the boat business when Jehan died? Does any father want to see everything he has worked to achieve just get cast aside when he dies?

de Sousa That's life sometimes.

Worsley I suggest to you that these two paths, whichever you believe he took – or even if, as you say, both are true – seem to be a result of parents who really don't care that much about their supposed only son. Parents who care so little they don't respond to a letter from their son in captivity. More the actions of guardians rather than parents, or not even relatives at all?

Morton Objection!
This is all supposition.

Oxford Denied.
Supposition it may be, but I want to hear what our Portuguese visitor thinks.

de Sousa He thinks nothing. It is folly to try to understand how families behave. I don't understand my own, let alone a stranger's.

Worsley I think we have heard enough about my client's – how shall I put it? – varied upbringing.
Perhaps, then, we can now continue briefly with his departure from Portugal and arrival in Cork.
Señor de Sousa, from what you heard at Setubal and the testimonies given there, what can you tell us about the young man's time in Portugal and his reason for leaving?

de Sousa	From what I have heard, he left Brampton's household fairly soon after arriving in Portugal and went to work for a man named Pero Vaz da Cunha, a knight from a well-to-do family highly respected at the Portuguese court. A merchant and seaman as well, I believe.[31]
Worsley	And my client was often at sea in the service of da Cunha?
de Sousa	Apparently he was sailing around the coast of Senegal for a period, but I couldn't say exactly where, when nor why.
Worsley	Just so it's clear to the jury, he was in Portugal for over three years, but a lot of that time he was in the employ of a man named da Cunha and was, for a period, not actually in Portugal – coincidentally during a time when King Henry's spies, sorry emissaries, were visiting the country. Keeping out of their way, one might think.
de Sousa	I don't know exactly when he was at sea with da Cunha and if that was at the same time as we received emissaries from England. If the two did coincide, it wasn't your client's doing, it was just how it happened.[74]
Worsley	Do you know *why* he finally decided to leave Portugal?
de Sousa	It's not clear. Some say after his African adventure he simply had a taste for travel, wanted to see other countries …
Worsley	So he chose Ireland?
Member of Public	That must have pleased the Irish Tourist Board.
Oxford	Quiet! The public are here to listen, not provide a running commentary.
de Sousa	All I can say for certain is he left in 1491 with a Breton merchant named Pregent Meno. I think if you ask Richmond Herald, that's what he says in his confession. Brampton testified he wanted a boat

back to Flanders but missed it, so instead took another going to Ireland.[20]

Machado	I can confirm that in his confession he said he wanted to see other countries.
Worsley	The boat he took, this was the boat of Pregent Meno, a Flanders silk merchant?
de Sousa	Yes.
Worsley	So, a silk merchant takes his silk to sell in wind-swept, rain-soaked Ireland? Quite the businessman, wouldn't you say?
de Sousa	Maybe he was blown off course.
Worsley	And is it correct that the boy left the ship, in wind-swept, rain-soaked Cork, wearing the very same silk garments?
de Sousa	It seems that is what got him noticed. Not unreasonable. If you want to sell something, you advertise it.
Worsley	What happened next?
de Sousa	He was recognized by some men there.
Worsley	Some men?
de Sousa	I think he was more specific in his confession.
Worsley	Richmond Herald?
Machado	He named a number of Yorkist sympathizers: John Atwood, Hubert Burke – both Irishmen – John Taylor, Stephen Poytron – both English, I think – for example.[50]
Worsley	Thank you. *Señor* de Sousa, what happened to the Breton Meno after he left Cork, do you know?

de Sousa	The records have it that Meno and his boat were captured by King Henry's men after they left Cork and were on their way to Flanders. They followed him in a boat named *Anne of Fowey*.[75, 76]

Worsley	Remarkable, isn't it? Out of the blue, the young man named Warbeck turns up, by chance, in the Yorkist-sympathizing part of Ireland. He wears bright but totally inappropriate clothing for the country but, surprise surprise, it gets him noticed. By whom? Yorkist sympathizers. Hardly surprising, since letters sent to the Earls of Desmond and Kildare alerted them he was on his way.[77, 78] This was no random chance. This was a prearranged meeting. People who knew his true identity had been working towards this for years.

Morton	Objection! Speculation.

Oxford	Sustained. Jury, disregard those last remarks.

Worsley	And despite the fact we have been continually assured by the archbishop that our King Henry had no idea Warbeck existed in 1491, let alone was in Portugal, they seem to know almost immediately he had arrived in Cork from there and captured the boat he came in. Remarkable. I assume Meno was punished for his actions?

de Sousa	On the contrary, he did very well by the king. By 1494 he had been made Constable of Carrickfergus Castle in Ireland, he was granted lucrative trading deals, received regular payments from King Henry and came to be referred to as his servant.[75, 79]

Worsley	Carrickfergus, eh? So, he became the king's spy on the route between Scotland and Ireland?

de Sousa	I couldn't comment as I've no idea where this Carrickfergus is.

Oxford	I think, Dean, we should give the Prosecution a chance to make their case at this point.
Morton	I'd like to address Baron Daubeney, if it please the court. Baron, the Defence claims the arrival of the defendant was prearranged, expected by men who already knew who he was. Is that how you see it?
Daubeney	Certainly not. They first thought he was the Earl of Warwick, son of the Duke of Clarence.
Morton	The one Lambert Simnel claimed to be?[80]
Daubeney	Yes, him. And, by the way, he – Warwick – was in the Tower of London in 1487 and he's still in there now.[81] Then they claimed he was Richard III's bastard son, John of Gloucester.
Morton	How do you know all this?
Daubeney	It's in his confession.[50] He denied being either of these men of the House of York to the Mayor of Cork, John Lewelyn. But then, in his confession, he stated that they then said he was the second son of Edward IV and that seems to have stuck.
Morton	They?
Daubeney	Atwood and Taylor.
Morton	Why the Duke of York?
Daubeney	I can't say. For sure, he wasn't in the Tower of London; well, not unless you count as a corpse. He looks a bit like King Edward, maybe that was it.
Morton	Tell us what they did with the boy now they had their hands on him.

Daubeney	Well, the first thing was to teach him English and to start to pass on what they thought he needed to know about the court of King Edward IV.
Morton	That can't have been all that much, as men like Atwood and Taylor were not part of the king's inner circle.
Daubeney	No, but they could make a start. Certainly, they could teach him enough to get by until they could get him to the Duchess of Burgundy, who was the duke's aunt. She could do the rest. And, don't forget, he was on a ship with Brampton from Flanders to Lisbon; he would have probably picked up a few things then. Brampton was never one to play down whom he knew and how he knew them.
Morton	Surely the good people of Cork knew instantly he wasn't English from the fact he couldn't speak English. Even his French accent would have given him away.
Daubeney	The Irish down there don't speak English; it's only in the Pale where civilization exists. They don't know the language and wouldn't know one accent from another.
Morton	But it was there in Ireland that he was taught fluent English?
Member of Public	Well, Tom's been doing French since he was 11 and he still can't get beyond '*Je m'appelle Tom, je suis* blah blah blah'.
Oxford	Quiet in the public gallery!
Daubeney	He was good at languages. We've heard already he left Tournai to learn Flemish. He must have picked up some Portuguese while he was living in Portugal, even some English on the ship from Brampton. It's no surprise to me he could also learn English easily.
Morton	Finally, Baron, the Defence seems to think King Henry's men were tracking Meno's boat from Portugal to Cork,

and that's why they ran him down so quickly after he left Ireland. What do you say to that?

Daubeney   They clearly underestimate the king's network of spies, especially in Ireland. What is the saying: keep your friends close and your enemies closer? He has spies everywhere there might be Yorkist sympathizers. It's hardly a surprise to me that they were in Cork and had a boat at the ready to bring messages to London. In this case, they just used it to chase Meno down.

Morton   Thank you, Baron. That is all from me for the moment.

Worsley   So Baron, he was the Earl of Warwick and John of Gloucester before being Richard, Duke of York. Of course it's true, it's in his confession. I think we've explored the accuracy of the confession enough already for the jury to know how to treat such information.

Let's talk instead about the 'imposter', as you call him, and how he was groomed.

He says in his confession he was forced to learn English against his will.[50] Do you seriously expect us to believe that someone reluctant to learn, who already had a strong French accent, could fool the continent, including the person he claimed was his own aunt, for nearly a decade that he was a native English speaker?

Member of Public   I bet the teachers here could name a good few of us lot that fall into the 'won't learn, can't learn' category.

Oxford   This is my last warning! If the public won't remain silent, I'll clear the court.

Daubeney   Well, he did. Duchess Margaret believed what she wanted to believe, so he didn't need to fool her, she fooled herself.

Worsley   Really, Baron? I don't think she was a fool. She managed to steer her country through years of turbulence after her husband died and while her step-daughter, Mary, a minor, was Duchess.[82]

Besides, it wasn't just his spoken word either, was it? Look at all the letters he wrote. To Spain, for example, stating 'it pleased the Divine Clemency that the lord, having compassion on my innocence, preserved me alive.'[49] A fluent speaker would be happy with that turn of phrase. Or in his will in 1495, where he writes, 'given the uncertainty of human destiny … the conviction that one condones their iniquity'.[83] How many more examples would you like to hear? Hardly beginners' level English, wouldn't you agree?

Daubeney

He got somebody to write them for him, clearly.

Worsley

Presumably somebody else dictated them as well and he was not involved at all. Just like his confession, you might say.

Morton

Objection!
There is no proof the confession was anything other than his own.

Oxford

Sustained.
Jury, disregard the Dean's last comment.

Worsley

Then let me put my point another way. If Duchess Margaret – I'm assuming you think it's her who cooked up this whole plot – wanted an imposter, why not use an English boy? One less thing for him to learn; just coach him about Edward's court and his upbringing. Surely choosing a foreigner as the imposter was just asking for trouble?

Daubeney

Well, there weren't many English boys in Burgundy to choose from. Besides, he does look a bit like King Edward.

Worsley

Thank you for pointing that out.
So, Baron Daubeney, Margaret finds a boy from Tournai – not even the part of Burgundy she had any connection with, as it's French – and decides to turn

	him into the late King Edward's younger son. Isn't it interesting, ladies and gentlemen of the jury, how often we get the same excuse why he gets chosen: because he looks like King Edward. Hasn't it occurred to you, Baron, that he looks like King Edward because he is his son?
Daubeney	No.
Worsley	I'm finished with this witness, m'Lord.
Oxford	I believe we now move to the prisoner's travels around Europe, starting with King Charles VIII of France – and no comments from the public about the French Tourist board, please.
	I think we have questions for Alexander Monypeny, *Seigneur* de Concressault and close advisor to Charles VIII of France.
Worsley	*Seigneur* de Concressault, you are close to King Charles VIII and one of the men who was responsible for looking after my client while he was in France in late 1491 until he left for Burgundy in 1492. Correct?
Monypeny	Correct.[84]
Worsley	As an ex-patriot Scot, you were an obvious choice to lead a contingent from France to the court of James IV in Scotland in the summer of 1491, with a view to bringing back an embassy from the Scots.
Monypeny	It was always a pleasure to visit the land of my birth, but not to stay too long. The weather doesn't suit me anymore.
Worsley	What was the purpose of the embassy between Kings James IV and Charles VIII?
Monypeny	It was a great matter, that's all I know.[84]
Worsley	Nothing more?

Monypeny	I'm not at liberty to discuss matters of state.
Worsley	But you do know that the French king sent men – Atwater, Taylor, Poynton – to Ireland about that time?[85]
Monypeny	Yes, but he didn't tell Taylor very much about why he was going. At least, I assume he didn't. Taylor thought he was going to raise support for the Earl of Warwick, or so he said in a letter to his friend John Hayes back in England.[85-87]
Worsley	Perhaps this explains why he said the boy was the Earl of Warwick when he first saw him in Cork?
Monypeny	Maybe.
Worsley	But would it be wrong to suggest that Atwater and companions met my client at Cork purely by chance?
Monypeny	I believe it would be wrong to suggest that.
Worsley	How did King Charles react when he found out that my client had arrived in Ireland?
Monypeny	He sent men to get him.
Worsley	Men?
Monypeny	Louis Lucas, the naval commander, and Stephen Frion.
Worsley	Frion?
Monypeny	Stephen Frion was a Yorkist sympathizer. He had served Duke Charles the Bold and his wife, Margaret, in Flanders, and he was part of Duchess Margaret's entourage when she briefly returned to London in 1480. He served both Kings Edward IV and Richard III, and indeed King Henry until he found it necessary to flee back to Flanders in 1489.[88]

Worsley	So Frion, who had spent several years in Burgundy serving Duchess Margaret, went to Cork on behalf of Charles VIII? Doesn't this link France, Burgundy and possibly Scotland in the Warbeck affair long before our King Henry brought the name Warbeck to the world's attention? And suggest that the boy's arrival in Cork was no accident.
Monypeny	That's something only the three monarchs know for sure.
Worsley	But from what you have said, Frion is certainly somebody who might have recognized the Duke of York from his visit to London in 1480. Is that why he was sent, because he would recognize him?
Monypeny	I don't know if he was high enough up in the Flanders delegation to meet with King Edward's sons in 1480, but it's possible.
Worsley	Ok. So, why was King Charles so interested in this boy?
Monypeny	The French king had one preoccupation in 1491: Brittany. He wanted it, and what was in his way were the troops sent by King Henry to support the Duchy. King Henry owed the Bretons – he had spent years in exile there before Bosworth. King Charles saw anybody who threatened King Henry as useful. My enemy's enemy is my friend, as people say.
Worsley	But he didn't keep the boy, *le garçon* as our king loves to call him, very long.
Monypeny	No, he solved the Brittany problem by marrying Duchess Anne of Brittany, much to the annoyance of Maximilian of Burgundy, to whom she was, at the time, betrothed.
Worsley	And at any time during the months he was in France, did he, my client, give any cause, any evidence, any suggestion that he was not a native English speaker with knowledge of the Plantagenet court?

Monypeny   No.

Worsley   So even after just a short period of language tuition, he was fluent enough in English to play the part. Quite remarkable.

But what about his manner? Royalty know how to behave in court, the etiquette at meals, how to address people, that sort of thing, things a boatman's son couldn't possibly know. Were there any flaws in my client's behaviour on that front?

Monypeny   Not that I am aware of.

Worsley   Thank you.

Archbishop, your witness.

Morton   King Charles wanted someone who could make life difficult for King Henry. Did he care if the pretender was real or fiction?

Monypeny   No, certainly not.

Morton   You are Scottish. You still have a strong accent. Everyone else around the boy was French. How could they tell when somebody was speaking native English? Were they all acquainted with the range of accents across our land?

Monypeny   No, they couldn't know and cared even less.

Morton   In other words, he wouldn't have needed faultless English to fool the French court?

Monypeny   I object to the suggestion the French court could be 'fooled', but I concede your point.

Morton   Furthermore, you have said that *le garçon*, as the king called him, behaved faultlessly in court, something a boatman's boy would not know how to do. But perhaps I could ask *Señor* de Sousa; didn't he spend time around the court of King João II while he was in Portugal, observing how court people behaved?[20]

de Sousa   As I've already testified, he was servant to Pero Vaz de Cunha, maybe for about three years, and da Cunha moved in high circles. I can't say if his servant was formally trained, but he would have seen enough of how others acted in the company of the nobility.

Morton   Thank you.

Seigneur de Concressault, I think you told us that among those sent to Cork to bring the boy – apologies, the young man - back to France was a Stephen Frion, someone who was well acquainted with King Edward IV's court. Surely the long sea voyage back to France would have been ample opportunity to coach the boy how to behave in the presence of royalty?

Monypeny   It would have been only a few days at sea, and besides, I doubt Frion was sufficiently an insider to King Edward's closest circle to be able to teach him much.

Morton   But he could have taught him something. I think you have given us more than enough to explain why the prisoner's behaviour at court fooled – sorry, deceived – Charles VIII.

Moving on, Kings Henry and Charles made their peace with the Treaty of Etaples and le garçon was on his way out of France? No promise of undying loyalty from King Charles to the boy?

Monypeny   There was no big fanfare, no big parting of the ways; he just left.

Morton   He knew his time was up in France now that the French king had no more use for him and had no need to back his cause?

Monypeny   It certainly looked that way.

Morton	That's clear: King Charles just used the Pretender until he had no more need of him. Thank you, no more questions.
Worsley	Just one small point regarding the treaty you mentioned between the two kings, Henry and Charles. It was signed in November 1492, but a codicil that the two parties would not aid each other's traitors and rebels wasn't added until mid-December. Is that correct?[89]
Monypeny	That's what the record shows.
Worsley	Enough time between the treaty and its codicils for my client to leave France before King Charles would break the treaty, wouldn't you say? It doesn't sound like he was kicked out, more that it was just politics and the French king was making it as easy as possible for my client to move on.
Monypeny	I guess it takes lawyers quite a while to get the paperwork written. The slower they are, the more money they make – isn't that right, Mr Lawyer?
Worsley	I'm not a lawyer. No more questions for this witness, m'Lord. After leaving France the prisoner arrived at the court of Duchess Margaret of Burgundy, so perhaps I can call Jean le Sauvage to explore these aspects of the case?
Oxford	Unless the archbishop objects, then go ahead.
Worsley	Jean le Sauvage, you worked closely with the Duchess of Burgundy?
Le Sauvage	Yes. I became a member of the Council of Flanders in 1490 and am currently its President. I now work primarily for her step-grandson, Duke Philip the Fair, but over the years I have also served Duchess Margaret and her step-daughter Mary's husband, Maximilian, current Holy Roman Emperor.

Worsley	When the defendant arrived in Burgundy from France in 1492, was Duchess Margaret surprised by this?
Le Sauvage	She gave that impression.
Worsley	So, she had no idea he, that is Duke Richard, was alive?
Le Sauvage	Apparently not.
Worsley	Did that surprise you?
Le Sauvage	Not really. If King Richard had wanted to hide the boys in Burgundy, then his sister's court would have been too obvious. She had very little to do with Tournai, which seems to be where he came from, as it's a French city, although the Bishop of Tournai is a close friend of hers. So, if she knew anything, my guess is it was very little. I was not at the centre of things in 1483 so I can't comment as fully as you would like, but it certainly appeared she was unaware of what had happened to the boy after 1483, so his reappearance in France in 1491 must have come as something of a welcome surprise to her.
Worsley	But she was in no doubt it was her nephew?
Le Sauvage	If she had any doubts she didn't show them. In a letter to Isabella of Spain, she only spoke in positive terms about knowing him instantly.[90]
Worsley	According to the Prosecution, it was over the next few years that she tutored the boy so he could act the part of Richard, Duke of York. Is that what happened?
Le Sauvage	Frankly, it wasn't possible. She left England in 1468, five years before he was born. She only visited England once during the boy's lifetime, for about three months in 1480, but even then she didn't reside at court.
Worsley	No? Where did she lodge?

Le Sauvage	Coldharbour in Thames Street. King Edward had it refurbished for her at some expense.[91, 92] I believe it's the king's mother, Lady Margaret, who uses it now.
Worsley	So, her knowledge of the household of Edward IV during the boy Richard's lifetime was extremely limited? That is, she simply wouldn't know how he was brought up, who his friends were, what he liked doing, every day matters like that?
Le Sauvage	Yes, that's why she couldn't have tutored him to impersonate Duke Richard. She didn't have enough first-hand knowledge. Not enough, anyway, to fool anyone who knew him well.
Worsley	Like the women he claimed were his sisters, for example, if they had ever met? Particularly Queen Elizabeth, that is?
Le Sauvage	Just so.
Worsley	I'm sure we will return to the question of why King Henry never gave his wife a chance to prove my client is not her brother at a later point in this trial. But let's be clear, in her conversations with the young man he never gave Duchess Margaret any concern that he was simply a boatman's son from Tournai?
Le Sauvage	No. It isn't just how you look and what you know. It's about how you behave. You have to behave like a prince as well as sound like one.
Worsley	There was no shortage of visitors from England to Burgundy to see the boy in the flesh, so to speak. People who did know the court of King Edward IV during Duke Richard's lifetime. People who wouldn't have bothered to support someone they knew was dead. Did any of these men point out mistakes he made in conversations with them?
Le Sauvage	No.[93]

Worsley	Not even Robert Clifford, who took part in the tournament when Richard, then Duke of York, was married to Lady Anne Mowbray in 1477 and knew him well? Didn't he come to Mechelen in 1493 and didn't he acknowledge the boy was who he said he was? Wasn't he convinced from first sight?[94]
Le Sauvage	Yes. At least, that was the impression he gave.
Morton	I must interject here or the jury will be misled. Isn't it true that Clifford was a spy, and retracted his comments in support of the prisoner after his exposure of the Stanley plot, something we'll come to shortly, no doubt?
Oxford	The witness may answer, but I must ask you to stop there. I'm sure you will want to question other witnesses, better placed than *Monsieur* le Sauvage, about who knew what in this country, at a later stage.
Morton	Very well, but please answer my question *monsieur*.
le Sauvage	I heard that he had given information to King Henry in 1495 concerning plots in England in support of the accused, but I don't know what was said or how true what he said was. I believe subsequent to this he was given a pardon for past indiscretions.
Morton	Thank you, and apologies to the court for my abrupt intrusion into the defence questioning.
Worsley	Isn't it remarkable how many men who told King Henry what he wanted to hear then received pardons? Brampton, Meno, Clifford. No matter, as the Judge has said, I'm sure we will return to the issue of Master Clifford at a later point. Can we return to my client's appearance for a moment? We can all see the mark over his eye, surely this must be an incontrovertible sign of who he is? Either Richard, Duke of York, had such a mark or he didn't. Which is it? If he didn't, surely somebody who knew him would

recognize instantly he was an imposter? And can anyone plotting to put an imposter on the throne of England seriously believe they could use someone with such a clear outward sign of his falsehood?

le Sauvage   I didn't know Richard, Duke of York, when he was in England so I can't comment. But nobody else who saw him thought fit to raise this point.

Worsley   In summary, the duchess recognized her nephew from the outset and she never wavered in her support?

Le Sauvage   No. She wrote to Spain stating as much.

Worsley   Yes, we'll come to the letter to Spain in due course, I'm sure.
   And Emperor Maximilian, how did he react to the boy's arrival?

Le Sauvage   They were of similar age, so they seemed to become friends very quickly. He treated Duke Richard with great respect.

Morton   Objection!
   I must protest about the continual reference to the prisoner as Duke Richard. If I can't call him 'Warbeck' …

Oxford   I'm going to deny that objection.
   In the case of *Monsieur* le Sauvage, since he only knew him as Richard, I'll allow him to continue with that address. The witness may continue.

Le Sauvage   The two of them, Richard and Maximilian, went to Vienna together in 1493 to the funeral of Maxmilian's father, Archduke Frederick III, and Duke Richard was treated like royalty. He went to the funeral at Stefankirche in the company of the kings of France, Hungary and Sicily.[95, 96]

Worsley   This is the same King of France that we have been told by the Prosecution kicked Warbeck out of his kingdom when he had no further use for him?

Le Sauvage	Yes, King Charles VIII.

Worsley	Continue.

Le Sauvage	The two, that is Emperor Maximilian and Duke Richard, spent at least eight months in each other's company around this time.

Worsley	And in all this time, the emperor never heard or saw anything that would make him doubt the young man's identity?

Le Sauvage	No, Maximilian's support didn't waver. He was persuaded to let King Henry to join the Holy League against King Charles VIII after King Charles invaded Italy in 1495, even though King Henry made it a condition that the emperor dropped support for Duke Richard. Though he signed the paperwork agreeing to your king's inclusion, under considerable pressure I might add, he added a codicil to the agreement exempting himself from withdrawing support for York.[97] He then wrote to the Pope in the same year, in support of his step-mother, Margaret, who was asking him to remove ex-communication orders on Richard and his supporters.[98]

Worsley	What about the supposed marks on the boy's body that he said confirmed who he was. *Señor* de Sousa, can you tell the court what you know of these marks so the court understands this line of questioning.

de Sousa	Only what one of King João's heralds, a man named Tanjar, testified at Setubal in 1496. He seemed to have known the defendant when he was in Portugal, and on a trip to Flanders he met a man who claimed to be the boy's father. To verify if this was the truth, Tanjar asked the man what distinguishing features the boy had, to which the man replied 'a mark on his face under his eye, an upper lip that was raised up a bit, and another on his breast'.[20]

Worsley	Thank you.
	Monsieur le Sauvage, did Emperor Maximilian then seem convinced by these marks that you've heard described?
Le Sauvage	Yes, he was quite open about this. He even seems to have seen that mark which is hidden to our eyes.[99, 100] If Maximilian really did see this hidden mark, then he can have been the only one to do so, except perhaps Duke Richard's wife, Lady Gordon.
Worsley	There will be more questions but that is all for now. Thank you.
Morton	Let's begin by looking at motive. Duchess Margaret would have supported anybody she thought could make life difficult for King Henry, real or imposter, wouldn't she? It really didn't matter what he looked or sounded like.
Le Sauvage	Yes, she hates King Henry and the part he played in the downfall of the House of York.
Morton	And Emperor Maximilian. Isn't it the case that he had his own motive for supporting the prisoner …
Le Sauvage	Yes, but …
Morton	Let me finish. The motive being that in return for his support, Maximilian was made heir to the kingdom of England should the prisoner die on the throne and childless.[101]
Le Sauvage	It was a fair deal. Burgundy had, for years, laid claim to the English throne through a line originating with Isabella of Portugal, the grandmother of the emperor's wife, Mary.[102] Duke Richard had nothing to lose. He was young and could expect to father a son.
Morton	Let's move on and talk about the prisoner's arrival in Flanders.

If Margaret had only seen this young man on a few occasions before he arrived in Flanders, how could she possibly recognize him? He could be anybody, couldn't he?

Le Sauvage   It's true she had only seen him briefly and that was when he was only 7, so you could be right in what you say. However, others before me have noted how much like the late King Edward he looks.

Morton   You say Margaret couldn't have tutored him because she didn't have enough first-hand knowledge of her brother's household, but doesn't this also mean she couldn't argue with anything the boy told her?

Le Sauvage   To some degree, yes. But to be completely believable and never say anything that would betray himself, I doubt it.

Morton   He could have been schooled by others though, couldn't he? We have already heard mention of Stephen Frion, who went to Ireland to fetch him at the behest of King Charles VIII. He had been at King Edward's court; couldn't he have tutored the boy?[88]

Le Sauvage   Well, he had more knowledge to impart than the duchess, that's for sure.

Morton   You say both Duchess Margaret and Emperor Maximilian supported the prisoner, but words are cheap. What about money?

Le Sauvage   Margaret gave him 8,000 crowns.[103, 104]

Morton   That's a paltry sum. Didn't she pay 20,000 crowns for a gold chain for her step-grandson's christening? [104, 105]

Le Sauvage   Or you could say she was especially generous to Mary's son as she was so fond of his mother.

Morton   And the emperor? My sources tell me he was broke and all he did was try to get others to give financial support.

Le Sauvage	Partly true. There isn't a monarch in Europe who doesn't claim to be broke, and Maximilian was no exception. He did try to get financial backing from the likes of Duke Albrecht of Saxony[106] and others, but he also took out a large loan of over £12,000, most of which was to support the duke's invasion fleet.[107]

| Morton | It doesn't sound to me enough to make an invasion succeed. It's nothing compared to the seasoned German troops under Martin Schwartz that Margaret organized in support of Lambert Simnel in 1487,[108] but the jury can make up their own minds. |

That will be all from me for now with this witness.

| Worsley | If I may, your Lordship, just one more question. Emperor Maximilian's support for the first pretender, the so-called Lambert Simnel, was luke-warm, was it not? |

| Le Sauvage | Yes, it was Duchess Margaret who supplied the support: German mercenaries, money, ships. Her stepson-in-law Maximilian was more concerned with events in Brittany, a possible French invasion, his proposed marriage to Anne of Brittany. His mind was elsewhere.[109] |

| Worsley | But the emperor did give continued support to my client four years later, and for quite some time at that. Did he learn nothing from the failure of the Simnel rebellion? That backing imposters would lead only to ignominious defeat and a waste of money? |

| Le Sauvage | Apparently not. |

| Worsley | Thank you. I'll leave it to the jury to make their own conclusions as to why that might be. |

| Oxford | Since we are on the theme of support for the pretender's cause, perhaps we could turn our attention to support for him in this country. |

Dean, do you want to begin?

Worsley	Baron Daubeney, let's talk about Robert Clifford, a name that has already cropped up in these proceedings. He was at the Duke of York's wedding to Anne Mowbray in 1478, was he not?
Daubeney	Yes.
Worsley	In early 1493, Clifford crossed to Burgundy. In Mechelen, even though he was now a young man, Clifford would still surely recognize him one way or the other? We have the famous marks, so at least the visible one should have told him all he wanted to know.
Daubeney	He may have said he recognized him as the duke,[94] but that doesn't mean he was telling the truth.
Worsley	In 1493, after he had seen him, he came back to England to raise troops on his behalf. Correct?
Daubeney	He was certainly back here plotting, but with Clifford you never knew his motives.
Worsley	It was in March 1493 that Clifford met with Sir William Stanley. Yes? [110]
Daubeney	I'm not good with dates, but I believe so.
Worsley	For the benefit of the Jury, this is the same Sir William Stanley that, to all intents and purposes, put King Henry on the throne. Is that a fair comment?
Daubeney	He led the charge that resulted in the usurper Richard's death at Bosworth, if that's what you mean.
Worsley	When Lord Clifford met Sir William Stanley in March 1493, after he had seen my client in the flesh and been convinced he was Richard of York, he brought Sir William into the plot. He then sent Lord Clifford back to Burgundy with the promise that he, Stanley,

would join forces with whatever troops my client could muster. Sir William Stanley seemed a true believer to me.[110]

Daubeney   That's your opinion, but that's all it is.

Worsley   You are sceptical that Lord Clifford truly didn't recognize the boy as Richard, Duke of York. So, on his return to England in 1493, are you suggesting he was acting to provoke Sir William into a false plot? Why would King Henry do that? Why did he distrust Stanley so much?

Daubeney   Who knows how the king thinks? Until this matter of the pretender is settled, I think he mistrusts everyone.

Worsley   Late in 1494, Clifford had returned to England and was pardoned by King Henry. Correct?[111]

Daubeney   That date I do recall.

Worsley   He was arrested on his return, then almost immediately pardoned. So, it was Lord Clifford who ratted on Sir William Stanley to save his own neck?

Daubeney   He was hardly likely to go to the scaffold without trying to get himself freed.

Worsley   A month or so later, Stanley and other plotters were executed.

Daubeney   Yes, Stanley was executed for treason.[110, 112]

Worsley   Can you explain to the court why such a staunch supporter of King Henry, winning his crown for him, should turn against him?

Daubeney   He didn't. I believe he said that if he was certain the young man was King Edward's son, then he wouldn't take arms *against* him. Nothing about taking arms *for* him.[113, 114]

Worsley	Typical Stanley, always keeping his options open.
	But he was prepared to accept the possibility a son was alive. Doesn't that tell us there was, in 1495, still no proof King Edward's sons were dead?
Daubeney	No. Stanley supported King Edward, not King Richard or even the Duke of Clarence. He fought for Edward at Blore Heath, Towton and Tewkesbury, but not for Richard at Bosworth or Simnel at Stoke. He thought he deserved more from King Henry for his role at Bosworth, but the king never gave him the peerage he craved.[115] My guess is he saw an opportunity to advance himself through the boy in Flanders – as you said, the Stanleys like to keep their options open. Unfortunately for Sir William, he got found out backing both horses in the same race.
Worsley	But at his execution, he never recanted his support for the defendant.[112]
Daubeney	He wasn't the only one taken in by the lie.
Worsley	Thank you, baron. I will leave it at that for the moment.
Morton	Baron Daubeney, am I right in thinking that Clifford was, at one time, a Yorkist?
Daubeney	Well, he was initially, but after Bosworth he became King Henry's Chamberlain of Berwick and fought for the king at Stoke in 1487.[116]
Morton	I see. So, after 1487 he was a supporter of the present king. Is it not then the case that Clifford was, all along, King Henry's spy in Mechelen?
Daubeney	It is quite likely. Our king likes his spies.[57, 117]
	Clifford was paid £500 in January 1495 not long after he was pardoned, so he must have done something to earn that reward.[118]

Morton	So, he would have needed to convince people – Duchess Margaret and the defendant, I mean – he believed in their cause?
Daubeney	It would be the only way he would get information. It's what spies do.
Morton	So, the fact that Lord Clifford appeared to believe the prisoner was who he claimed, this meant nothing.
Daubeney	I would agree. Nothing.
Morton	And his so-called conspiracy meetings with Sir William Stanley and others, these were consistent with an infiltration into the Yorkist ranks to see who could be trusted by the king and who couldn't. Isn't that the case?
Daubeney	I would say that's perfectly likely.
Morton	Thank you.
Oxford	If we are finished with questions about Robert Clifford …
Worsley	Just one final one, if I may. Baron Daubeney, if Clifford was, all along, acting as Henry's spy, why did he need a pardon in late 1495?
Daubeney	You would have to ask Clifford that.
Worsley	An interesting answer, if I may say so. Perhaps, m'Lord, I may continue with the witness about other aspects of the Stanley plot?
Oxford	Of course.
Worsley	Was Sir William Stanley the only one Lord Clifford plotted with?
Daubeney	I don't know.

Worsley	How about Lord Fitzwalter? Sir James Tyrell and his cousin, Thomas? Thomas Langton, Bishop of Winchester? John Kendal, prior of the Order of the Knights of St John of Jerusalem and one of the king's trusted servants? Sir George Neville? Any of these names ring a bell?[119, 120]
Daubeney	They ring a very faint bell. Churchmen, politicians ... dreamers. None of these could raise an army or fight for a crown. They are nobodies ...
Oxford	The witness needs to show some respect. The man asking him questions is one of those who you deem 'nobodies'.[4] Continue.
Daubeney	As for Neville, a bastard son of the Kingmaker's line, not worthy to be called 'Sir'. You have to accept the fact that nobody, apart from Sir William Stanley, was of any significance. If he had lived, history may have been different, but thank God he didn't.
Worsley	In 1493, well before the Stanley plot, Humphrey Savage tried to rouse Londoners into supporting the man claiming to be Richard, Duke of York.[121] Does the name 'Savage' mean anything to you?
Daubeney	Remind me.
Worsley	John Savage commanded one flank of the Tudor army at Bosworth. I fail to see how that could escape your memory.
Daubeney	You said Humphrey Savage.
Worsley	Humphrey was John's brother. The Savage family were supporters of King Henry after Bosworth, and the brothers were maternal nephews of the Stanleys.[122] Pretty close to the king's inner circle wouldn't you say? And at least one of the Savages believed the young man in Flanders could be who he said he was.

Daubeney	That hardly makes support for Warbeck widespread, does it?
Worsley	No, but King Henry did execute fifty-five men from twenty-four different counties – I repeat, twenty-four – after the failed Deal landing in 1495, didn't he? [123]
Daubeney	He did what he had to do.
Worsley	So, support for the invasion was, evidently, country-wide?
Daubeney	Fifty-five men from twenty-four counties hardly qualifies as 'support' to my mind. Besides, none of them were of any status.[123]
Worsley	No further questions, m'Lord.
Oxford	Archbishop, I understand you want to question *Señor* de Puebla about the involvement of the court of Spain in this affair?
Morton	I certainly do. Roderigo de Puebla, the court of Spain received a letter from Duchess Margaret of Burgundy in 1492 telling them of the arrival of, in her words, 'Richard, Duke of York'.[90] Did either King Ferdinand or Queen Isabella believe her?
de Puebla	Certainly not. It was a joke. Duchess Margaret claimed to have recognized the boy instantly, but this is hard to believe as she hadn't seen him for over a decade. My queen wrote back and told her she doubted his claim. The Spanish royal family would not be taken in like some others were.
Morton	But they did try to persuade the pretender to, well, let's say 'just give up'?
de Puebla	They did. They sent my colleague Don Pedro de Ayala to Scotland, but why they trusted that worthless aristocrat,

who knew nothing about diplomacy and everything about having a good time, I don't know.[124, 125] Don Ayala was to offer money, a pension and ships to bring the defendant to Spain, but he failed. He tried to trick him by telling him Scotland and England were about to sign a peace treaty, which would have been the end of his hopes. He still failed.[126, 127]

Morton Will you explain to the court why Spain was so eager to get hold of the pretender?

de Puebla I had negotiated a treaty with King Henry in 1489, the Treaty of Medina del Campo, whereby Prince Arthur, the king's eldest son, would marry Infanta Catalina, the daughter of my king and queen. But they were wary. Why send your beloved daughter to a country that hadn't stopped fighting itself for half a century when there was a crazy young man on the loose trying to stir up yet more trouble?

Morton So, you wanted him out of the way so the marriage could go ahead without any worry that King Henry and his son would be involved in yet more domestic wars?

de Puebla Absolutely. We want peace with England so her ships would leave ours alone. We want a united Holy League so that King Charles of France has to keep himself to France. While northern Europe is still worried about wool and war, my sovereigns can see the future. We have more interest in digging holes in the ground to find gold in the New World than digging graves for dead soldiers.

Morton So there was never any support for the pretender from Spain, no acknowledgement he was really a royal?

de Puebla Never.

Morton Thank you.

Worsley You say your country never acknowledged the young man as a royal?

de Puebla	Never.
Worsley	But in the secret correspondence between the monarchs and their ambassadors, yourself included, they called him the Duke of York.
de Puebla	We don't have such secret messages …
Worsley	You do and they are in code.
de Puebla	If they are in code, how do you know what they say?
Worsley	Because we have broken the code.
de Puebla	Impossible.
Worsley	We all have codes. Nobody writes to their ambassadors except in code. It's part of the game. What we in England do better than anyone is crack codes. Mark my words, the Tudors will be famous for it one day.[128, 129]
de Puebla	I don't believe any of this.
Worsley	Well, let me help you by telling you what you claim not to know. There are two sections, code names for important people and code names for people who aren't.
de Puebla	Really???
Worsley	Yes, and code name 'DCCCCVII' is the Duke of York, or Warbeck as you say they only ever called him. He's in the royal code list between Duchess Margaret of Burgundy and King Alfonso of Naples.
de Puebla	This is a joke.
Worsley	I'm afraid not. The other list, persons not belonging to royal families, doesn't mention a Warbeck. How do you explain that?

de Puebla	I won't even try because I don't believe you. You are making all this up.
Worsley	I can assure you I'm not. The fact is that King Ferdinand and Queen Isabella called him Warbeck when they were happy for anyone to read the letter and the Duke of York when they wanted things kept secret. Hiding their true instincts, perhaps? So, which should we believe is true?
de Puebla	That's up to you. I don't believe any of this story you've told us about secret ciphers, and neither should anyone else.
	Frankly, I don't know what my sovereigns truly believe, but it doesn't matter. For all of us across the continent, the man in the dock is just a pawn. For King Henry, he was an irritation; he wants him dead whether or not he is a duke. Duchess Margaret might believe in him, but either way it suits her purposes because he's making life difficult for England. The rest of us don't care either way, we just want him gone because he makes European diplomacy more complicated. You won't get a true answer out of any of us because we either don't know or don't care.
Oxford	I think on that very honest but depressing note we will move on.
	The only witness we haven't heard from is Roland Robinson, who can answer questions about the involvement of King James IV of Scotland in this affair.
Worsley	Perhaps, Rowland Robinson, you can tell us how my client came to be in Scotland at all.
Robinson	In the summer of 1495, an invasion force left Flanders and first tried to land at Deal in Kent. This was easily defeated, and I think you have already heard a witness comment that around fifty-five men were captured and executed.[123]
Worsley	But the prisoner was not among those who landed?

Robinson	No, he seems to have waited on a ship to see how things would unfold.
Worsley	Doesn't this smack of cowardice?
Robinson	Caution, for certain. But then it's probably standard practice. Don't forget, the then Henry Tudor did the same thing in 1483 when he tried to land at Poole.[130] It was a good decision on his part, as King Richard's men were waiting for him. He turned tail and headed back across the Channel. So, if the prisoner was worried he may have been betrayed and a trap was waiting for him, you could say he took a prudent approach.
Worsley	What happened next? Did he act like Tudor and sail back where he came from?
Robinson	No, the ships sailed on to Ireland and attempted to take Waterford. Not the smartest move by whoever suggested it, as this was one city that was staunchly supportive of King Henry.
Worsley	So, what was left of this invasion fleet eventually sailed to Scotland?
Robinson	For about three months I have no idea where your client was, but then, yes, he did sail for Scotland. And he was welcomed with open arms by King James IV. He gave him a good pension, clothes and, of course, a wife.
Worsley	King James, then, was quite wealthy, spending all this money on a stranger who turned up out of the blue?
Robinson	Well, firstly, James was not wealthy, so the amount he spent on his guest was a little surprising.[131] However, while 1495 might have been when the two men met for this first time, I wouldn't call them strangers.
Worsley	I think you'll have to explain that last remark, for the jury's benefit as much as the rest of us.

Robinson	King James of Scotland and Margaret, Duchess of Burgundy, were in contact about five months after he came to the throne in 1488. I believe another witness here today led a large mission, at least forty people, from Duchess Margaret to Scotland in late 1488.
Worsley	Would that be you, Richard Harliston?
Harliston	Yes. Richard Ludelay of Ireland and myself, in fact. We were, I am led to believe, the first overseas mission to visit the new king.[132]
Worsley	What was the purpose of this mission?
Harliston	I think my fellow witness, *Seigneur* de Concressault, has already answered a question like this. Like him, I can't divulge matters of state.
Worsley	I understand. Rowland Robinson, perhaps you can tell us then if this was an isolated communication between the two countries at that time, 1488?
Robinson	No, it certainly wasn't. There were numerous letters passing between Scotland, Flanders and Ireland at that time. There might even have been letters – secret they must have been – to England.[133]
Worsley	And that was it until 1495?
Robinson	No, I believe a herald travelled from Ireland to Burgundy as early as 1490 and passed through Scotland on his way, for which he was paid by King James, but I don't know the reason for this detour.[134] I also know the prisoner wrote to Scotland in 1491 when he was still in Ireland with the Earl of Desmond. Apparently, King James might even have been expecting such a letter.[135]
Worsley	Is this in any way related to the failed landing at Deal?

Robinson	I was not party to the detailed plans, but I believe there were to be simultaneous uprisings in Ireland and England, along with an invasion from Scotland, with the aim of dividing King Henry's forces.
Worsley	But this never happened?
Robinson	Yes and no. There was an invasion, though not much of one, from Scotland. The border chiefs acted too soon, probably looking for quick rewards.[136] The Stanley plot in England was uncovered and dealt with, and any unrest in Ireland would have had minimal impact. I think the failure at Deal was just part of this ill-fated plan.
Worsley	And so, after the failed attempt to capture Waterford, my client found his way to Scotland and was received in some splendour by King James, at Stirling I believe?[137] And soon after was married to Lady Katherine Gordon?
Robinson	Yes, Stirling. And it was a quick courtship, most unusual for marriages between royals.
Morton	Objection! We only have proof that one of them was royal, and even that is weak.
Oxford	Sustained. However, I must also ask the jury to disregard the final comment on the ancestry of the prisoner's wife until such time as the Prosecution can offer proof questioning it.[138]
Morton	I will, indeed, bring proof in time, but for now, I'll let the matter rest.
Worsley	Roland Robinson, please continue.
Robinson	However you describe it, the marriage was soon after he arrived in Scotland. I can't believe that it was love at first sight and nothing would stand in their way, though as far as I know they were devoted to each other. It just seems like another pointer to much earlier

Right: Figure 1. Henry VII, the first Tudor king of England. For the first fifteen years of his reign, he was plagued by the spectre of Yorkist claimants to his throne.

Below: Figure 2. Keyford Rectory, Frome, Somerset, home of the Twynyho family. It is no longer extant.

Remains of
KEYFORD NUNNERY,
Built 708.

Above: Figure 3. Farleigh Hungerford Castle, home of George, Duke of Clarence, and his wife, Isabel, at the time Ankarette Twynyho started in their employment.

Below: Figure 4. Warwick Castle, home of George, Duke of Clarence, his wife, Isabel, and children Margaret and Edward at the time of the birth of their second son, Richard.

Figure 5. Cardinal John Morton, who joined Henry Tudor in exile in Brittany and went on to become his Lord Chancellor and Archbishop of Canterbury.

Figure 6. The coronation of Lambert Simnel in Dublin, showing Lambert on the shoulder of William Darcy of Platten, a man of reputedly great physical stature.

Figure 7. Edward V, depicted in a stained-glass window at St Matthew's Church, Coldridge, Devon.

Figure 8. Perkin Warbeck, sixteenth-century copy by Jacques Le Boucq of the only known contemporary portrait of him.

Figure 9. Margaret, Duchess of Burgundy, sister to both Edward IV and Richard III and aunt of the two 'princes in the tower', Edward and Richard. She was a staunch supporter of both Yorkist pretenders.

Figure 10. Maximilian I, Holy Roman Emperor, who was a steadfast supporter of Richard of York/Perkin Warbeck, even after he was held captive by Henry VII.

Figure 11. James IV, King of Scotland, who gave both home and a bride to Richard of York/Perkin Warbeck. His support wavered as the Pretender's attempts to regain his throne faltered.

Figure 12. Charles VIII, King of France, was the first European monarch to welcome the Dublin Pretender, but his support waxed and waned with political expediency.

Above: Figure 13. Wedding portrait of Queen Isabella of Castille and King Ferdinand II of Aragon. Their main concern was removing all threats to the Tudor dynasty to allow the marriage of their daughter, Katherine of Aragon, to Arthur, Prince of Wales, to go ahead.

Right: Figure 14. Elizabeth Woodville, dowager Queen of England and mother-in-law to Henry VII. From the time the Simnel rebellion was announced by Henry VII, she spent her remaining years isolated in Bermondsey Abbey.

ELIZABETH VXOR
EDWARDVS IIII

Left: Figure 15. Jean le Sauvage and his wife, Jacqueline de Boulogne. Le Sauvage was emissary for Maximilian I, King of the Romans and Holy Roman Emperor.

Below: Figure 16. St Rumboult's Cathedral, Mechelen, burial place of Margaret, Duchess of Burgundy, and physician John Clement.

communication between the duchess and King James. Marriages between high-ranking people don't happen overnight; they are in essence strategic and these things take time.

Worsley   You mean the wedding was already arranged before my client left Flanders?

Robinson   I can't confirm that, but the speed with which it all happened suggests it's a possibility.

Worsley   How did King James and his guest get on?

Robinson   Just like the relationship between Emperor Maximilian and the prisoner. They were of similar age and got on well.

Worsley   So was an invasion of England eventually agreed, in support of my client's claim to the throne of England?

Robinson   Yes, though it didn't get very far, despite the fact King James raised a reasonably strong force.[139]

Worsley   Why not?

Robinson   Several reasons.[139] First, King Henry had support from some of the Scottish nobles who were favoured by the Scottish king's dead father and who wouldn't support his son. John Ramsey, 1st Lord Bothwell, the dead king's favourite,[140] the Duke of Ross and the Earl of Buchan, to name but three.[139]

Second, King James had eyes on only one prize: Berwick. In fact, at the outset the troops were only paid for two weeks' service.[141] If he won Berwick and saw signs of support for the 'son of Edward', he might have gone further. The accused, on the other hand, while he anticipated support from northern barons such as the Nevilles, Dacres, Lovels and Herons,[142] felt he would have most solid support in the west around Carlisle, from families such as the Skeltons.[143]

Worsley	And this never materialized?
Robinson	No. To make matters worse, the Scottish troops ran amok, much to Duke Richard's disgust. He saw the victims as his English subjects and was back in Edinburgh within a couple of days. The presence of German and French soldiers in his army, and the general distrust of all things Scottish, didn't help rally support from the English.[144]
Worsley	Are you saying there was support from outside Scotland for this invasion?
Robinson	Yes. Duchess Margaret sent over about sixty German men at arms in two boats, and our friend here, *Seigneur* de Concressault, was also present.[139]
Worsley	*Seigneur* de Concressault, is this true?
Monypeny	Yes, but King Charles sent me to mediate between the two sides.[139]
Worsley	What was King Henry's reaction to this threat from the north? Did he take it seriously?
Robinson	Seriously enough to offer his daughter in marriage to King James, though this was rebuffed.[145]
Worsley	How did this failed invasion affect the relationship between King James and my client?
Robinson	It certainly cooled.[146] They saw far less of each other, but King James didn't react like the French king, Charles VIII, and get rid of him. He still paid his pension, even though he was broke and the prisoner stayed in Scotland another ten months.
Worsley	Did King James begin to doubt the true identity of my client?

Robinson   I can't answer that for certain. I think he was more disappointed in his fighting spirit than anything. James was a bit hot-headed himself in that respect, and anyone not as aggressive as himself would have failed to find his favour. Besides, after marrying Lady Gordon it was natural that these two spend time together, so inevitably he would spend less time with the king. There was, so far as I know, nothing in the way York acted or spoke that gave cause for concern. And, of course, he gave him a close relative as a wife.[147] It would be a lucky boatman's son indeed who was given that beauty, I can tell you.

Worsley   If King James was as short of money as you say, why did he turn down the offer of 100,000 crowns from Charles VIII to hand over my client? Surely if he doubted his identity this was more than a good price! [148]

Robinson   I can assure you that if I was in the same position as King James and doubted the identity of someone who might really be a commoner, I'd have jumped at the money.

Worsley   Since we have reached a point in the affair when my client leaves Scotland, I will end my questions for this witness for now and allow my colleague the Archbishop time to ask questions.

Morton   Rowland Robinson. You say you got to know the King of Scotland and his court well from your time there on behalf of Duchess Margaret of Burgundy, so will you please give the court some background to this king.

Robinson   He came to the throne in 1488 when he was only 15, after a group of nobles had assassinated his father, James III. The new king, James IV, was a bit headstrong, as many young men are. He wanted to make his mark on the international stage and because King Henry continued to support the faction that had backed the dead king, there was inevitable hostility between the two countries. Berwick was, as ever, a potential flashpoint. Berwick to Scotland is like Calais to the French – a permanent reminder of the fact another country still has an unwelcome foothold on their land.

Morton   I may be wrong here, but this sounds like a familiar story. A Flanders story at that. A grudge against the English king, and a disgruntled monarch who takes any opportunity to destabilize his opponent's kingdom. King James, like Duchess Margaret, didn't care about York or Warbeck; it was just another way of unsettling our King Henry, wasn't it?

Robinson   Well, I'll give you a Flanders answer to your Flanders story. Like Duchess Margaret, he hated King Henry and certainly would take any opportunity to get at him. That doesn't mean the prisoner wasn't who he said he was.

Morton   But King James did use the accused for his own ends, didn't he?

Robinson   Yes, he certainly wanted something in return for his support, but then which monarch can you name that acts as a charity?

Morton   So, what were the king's terms for supporting his guest? What did he want in return for the money he was spending?

Robinson   Berwick, for sure, and money back when his friend was King of England.[149] Not that much different really to how the emperor dealt with him.

Morton   And it was the Scottish king who ran the invasion, decided where to attack and so on?

Robinson   Yes, King James was definitely in charge. The problem was that the two men had different agendas. One was playing a long game to be King of England, the other a short game to recapture Berwick. As I've already testified, some of King James's soldiers were only retained for a couple of weeks,[141] so a full-scale invasion was never the main goal as far as he was concerned, not initially at least.

Morton   Finally, when the pretender did leave Scotland, he must have had the king's support for his future plans – an army, a fleet, everything an invader needs to unseat a sitting monarch.

Robinson   Not quite. Just an unarmed ship and no soldiers.[150]

There was something final about the whole affair. James paid the last instalment of the pretender's pension early and there were presents for Lady Gordon.[151] There was, though, a plan to invade England a second time when the defendant invaded England, but it was up to him to raise troops, which is why I assume he headed for Ireland.

Morton   Just one ship, nothing more?

Robinson   Yes, one ship named *The Cuckoo*.[150]

Morton   Well, if that doesn't sum up this whole shambolic attempt to unseat a lawful king, then nothing does. No further questions of this witness.

Oxford   We are now at the point at which the prisoner reaches these shores. I think, Dean, you wish to start the questioning.

Worsley   Richard Harliston, you were with the invading army at Deal. What can you tell us about my client's actions after leaving Scotland in 1497?

Harliston   As you know, I left your client's side after Deal …

Worsley   Why was that?

Harliston   I could see the game was up. There was no plan, no cohesion, nobody in England after the death of Sir William Stanley to rally support. There was support, but nobody of any stature to organize it. Lord Fitzwalter, George Neville, they simply didn't have enough clout.

I went back to Duchess Margaret. I had risked enough in the Yorkist cause by that stage.

Worsley   But my client carried on?

Harliston   Yes. Even when things failed to go his way with the invasion from Scotland, he carried on.

I think he left King James's court for Ireland and ended up in his old haunts in Cork, where Atwater, whom he had met in 1491, was still active. Sir James Ormond, who had resisted King Henry's pardon, was killed in an ambush a week or two earlier, and unfortunately, he was just about your client's only supporter. Henry had turned almost all the other lords, chieftains – whatever they called themselves over there – to his favour. On top of that, there was a famine in Ireland, so it was not the best of times to raise a fighting army.[152]

Worsley   But he carried on regardless?

Harliston   I believe at this point the Spanish were offering him ships and a pension to give up. Didn't the Spanish Ambassador already testify to this?

Worsley   *Señor* de Puebla?

de Puebla   This is true. There were ships waiting off Kinsale, but he ignored them.

Worsley   Why then, Richard Harliston, did he carry on, heading for Cornwall, not Spain?

Harliston   I don't know. There were rumours of a rising in Cornwall, but it's hard to know if this was because of the prisoner or he just thought he could use it as an opportunity. Either way, anyone could see the chance of success was negligible.

Worsley   Was there any kind of plan?

Harliston	Maybe, maybe not. King James led another invasion to coincide with the Cornish rising,[153] so this may have been another attempt to split King Henry's forces, but the two events weren't coordinated; and anyway, both these risings were over before the Pretender landed in Cornwall. As I said before, their plan lacked the necessary coordination to have had any chance of success.
Worsley	So, in your opinion, an imposter would have taken the money and run at this point.
Harliston	If I was that imposter, it's what I would have done.
Worsley	Roland Robinson, you were involved in all this; is this how you saw it?
Robinson	I must agree. I was with the Pretender when he landed at Whitesands in Cornwall, and I took this news to King James. But it was too late. The king was already on his way home after another short-lived invasion of England's north. As was I, after that. I could see there was no chance of defeating King Henry. It was time to face reality, not a dream.[154, 155]
Worsley	Thank you all. That's enough from me for now. Archbishop ...
Morton	Baron Daubeney, can you give us your perspective on all this.
Daubeney	I was sent north to meet the second Scottish invasion, but my force wasn't needed. The Earl of Surrey had already confronted King James and his army, and the Scottish king reacted in his typically hot-headed manner.
Morton	That being?
Daubeney	He challenged Surrey to a fight, single combat, with Berwick – always Berwick – the prize. Of course, Surrey

had more sense than to accept, so King James turned tail and headed home.[154]

Morton

So, what did you do?

Daubeney

The Cornishmen had risen and were heading for London, so I was recalled to meet that threat.

Morton

Which you did successfully?

Daubeney

Yes, with a little help.[156]

Morton

And these Cornishmen, they proclaimed the Pretender as king?

Daubeney

No, they weren't interested in him. It was all about taxes, you know, the thing peasants always complain about. They resented the money being raised to spend on the war with Scotland, which was nothing to do with them and at the other end of the country.

Morton

How did King Henry react to the prisoner's landing in Cornwall?

Daubeney

He was very relaxed. He knew this was the last chapter of this sorry tale. The Cornish rising was an irritation, but was dealt with well before the Pretender landed. Apparently, about 3,000 men joined this second Cornish rebellion, but they were low-status ruffians, not soldiers.[157]

King Henry was at Woodstock when the landing took place, but he knew from past experience the Pretender was no fighter. The king was on home ground. It was just a question of time.

Morton

You say about 3,000 common men joined him, but what about those who landed with him? How many men were there, and how many ships?

Daubeney

By reports, there were three ships and no more than about eighty men.[158]

Morton	Yes, but what about support from Duchess Margaret of Burgundy?
Daubeney	None.
Morton	From Emperor Maximilian?
Daubeney	None.
Morton	From King James IV?
Daubeney	None.
Morton	King Charles VIII?
Daubeney	Certainly not. He was desperate for King Henry not to join the Holy League against him. The last thing he would have done was antagonize our king. In fact, as I think has already been testified, he tried to bribe the Scots to let him have the prisoner so he could hand him over to King Henry and win his favour.
Morton	So much for the prisoner's support. Hardly an army befitting a king, was it?
	I don't believe I need question you further. I think everyone is aware of the failure of the invader to take Exeter due to heroic defence by those loyal to the king, the prisoner's flight from the battle – as usual – and his capture at Beaulieu Abbey. I think that brings us to the prisoner in captivity, unless, Dean, you have questions?
Worsley	I do just have one or two small points to raise.
	Baron Daubeney, you mentioned the part played by diplomacy and the Holy League in determining the French King Charles's support for my client.
Daubeney	Lack of support, you mean.
Worsley	Yes, but is it not also true that other countries – Spain, for example, but more importantly Flanders – wanted

King Henry *in* the Holy League, so they also had a reason for not sending troops in support of the invasion? They balanced the chances of success of toppling King Henry against winning his support against the French king, and decided the latter was the better option. Isn't that the case?

Daubeney   Possibly.

Worsley   After the failed Deal landing, Emperor Maximilian agreed to let King Henry into the Holy League,[159] which the king would only join on condition all support for my client was dropped. Does this also signal a lack of support for the invasion on the emperor's part, or were there any caveats?

Daubeney   I can't answer that. Ask le Sauvage.

le Sauvage   I believe a caveat was inserted to the effect that all was agreed, but, and if my memory serves me, words were added to the effect 'except for what we may wish to be done to the same King of England in the cause of Prince Richard, Duke of York, if divisions and disputes arise between them'.[97] I think you have already asked the Spanish Ambassador about this exemption clause. They knew about it.

Worsley   The Holy League wasn't the only reason for Emperor Maximilian to hold back in support of the invasion, was it?

le Sauvage   Things were difficult economically in Flanders at that time. We needed to re-establish the wool trade with England, so trade talks were reopened on this front after Deal. The emperor's son, Duke Philip, was more flexible than his father. He agreed to clauses in the trade deal which included not helping each other's enemies.[97, 160]

Worsley   Thank you.

Baron Daubeney, returning to events after the landing, tell me what you know about the siege of Exeter.

Daubeney	Another military failure by the Pretender. The Earl of Devon, Edmund Courtenay, and his son, William, fought off all attempts to take the town and the Pretender left with his tail between his legs.
Worsley	You make it sound like a heroic defence, which I'm sure it was, but in the end, the earl and the Pretender came to an arrangement, didn't they? If the invaders withdrew, the earl would not pursue them.
Daubeney	So?
Worsley	The earl's son, William Courtney, was married to Princess Catherine of York, sixth daughter of King Edward IV and so potentially the Pretender's sister. Did she persuade her father-in-law to negotiate a truce? Was she uncertain about her brother's fate in 1483? Could she have worried that it was her brother that her husband and his father were fighting?[161]
Daubeney	No. Definitely no. The Courtenays fought bravely. There was no evidence, not even a rumour, of capitulation on their part.
Worsley	So you say. You confronted my client and his army outside Taunton, after the siege of Exeter had been lifted.
Daubeney	Correct.
Worsley	Do you often offer challenges of single combat to a boatman's son? Somewhat beneath you, I would have thought, and certainly headstrong, very like King James IV, wouldn't you say?
Daubeney	I did it at the king's request.[162, 163]
Worsley	So let me rephrase the question then. Does *the king* often offer challenges of single combat to a boatman's son? Or does this imply the challenge was to somebody of similar noble status?

Daubeney	It meant nothing of the sort. It was a means to an end. We all know who would have won that contest. It would have brought things to an end without further loss of our soldiers. The king was, as always, being merciful and wise.
Worsley	Then we come to the point at which my client met capture. I have already explored the so-called confession with Richmond Herald, so I will move on to another matter. The archbishop can return to the subject of the confession again if he so wishes, but I thought he would have realized by now that wouldn't help his case.
Morton	Objection!
Oxford	Sustained. The Jury will make up their own minds on the validity of the confession, not you, Dean.
Worsley	My apologies. Perhaps I can ask you to tell us a little of how Lambert Simnel, another pretender, was treated after he was captured in 1487?
Morton	Objection! What relevance is this?
Oxford	Let's see, shall we?
Daubeney	He was given a job befitting his status, in the king's kitchens, I believe.
Worsley	And after the Deal landings, what happened to the men who were captured, the pretender's soldiers?
Daubeney	They were hanged, naturally.
Worsley	So perhaps you can explain to the court why the so-called imposter, the man in the dock, was treated so differently? Why wasn't he executed immediately? Or at least put to some demeaning work befitting of a boatman's son?

Daubeney	King Henry was merciful. He promised him his life if he left sanctuary. Richmond Herald will attest to that, for he was there.[164, 165] The evidence is before your eyes that he kept his word. Besides, unlike Simnel, this pretender had a wife and child with him.[166] That touched our gracious king.
Worsley	Really? Richmond Herald, tell us of the prisoner, which he now was, and his arrival at Taunton. How was he dressed?
Machado	He was still playing a part even then. He dressed himself in gold, the fool.[165]
Worsley	How often does the king allow the son of a boatman to enter his presence dressed like royalty?
Machado	That was a mistake I won't allow to happen again.
Worsley	How often does the king pay for a boatman's son to have a tailor to make clothes for him? King Henry did assign him a tailor, didn't he?[167]
Machado	The clothes were rough and ready, not court finery.[167]
Worsley	How often does the king pay for a boatman's son's horse to be fed?[167]
Machado	It means nothing. He paid for a horse for his Spanish fool to ride with him when necessary.[168, 169]
Worsley	My client may have been a prisoner, but seems to have been allowed rather a lot of liberty, wouldn't you agree?[170] How often, for example, does the king let a boatman's son walk and ride freely about the palace parks, such as at Sheen?[171]
Machado	He could never escape; he was always watched.
Worsley	How often does the king take a boatman's son as part of his entourage when he takes the court to the country?[172]

Machado	He paraded him around to show his people he was nothing, a captive.
Worsley	You may see it that way, but I think from the treatment afforded my client in captivity that more of us should claim to be King Edward's son and get captured.

The king let his captive see his wife regularly as well, didn't he? |
Machado	Never at night.
Worsley	I put it to you, Richmond Herald, that once captured, your king soon realized that he wasn't in possession of a boatman's son but his own brother-in-law and treated him as accordingly as possible without looking foolish.
Machado	Never. You may think a horse and clothes gave him special treatment, but he was paraded around as if he were no more than a servant, just like Simnel.
Worsley	The fact of the matter is that King Henry didn't know what to do with his prisoner when all logic says he should just have executed him. Isn't that true, *Señor* de Puebla? Wasn't Spain getting tired of all this hesitancy?
de Puebla	Indeed. In fact, I wrote to my sovereigns asking them to – how can I put it diplomatically? – advise King Henry on what to do with his prisoner, as he didn't seem to know.[173] Even eight months after capturing the person who had made his life so unbearable for a decade – what was holding him back from doing what we could all see was necessary and inevitable? We were all getting tired of this cloud hanging over the royal marriage between Infanta Catalina and Prince Arthur.
Worsley	What, indeed, was holding him back? Wouldn't we all like to know?

So now we come to probably the most crucial series of questions, one I have just touched upon. |

There is a prisoner before us who claims to be the Duke of York, King Edward's son. There are people who are even now in King Henry's court and who knew this Duke of York when he was younger.[174] What did they make of the prisoner when he was brought to London? Oliver King, the Bishop of Bath and Wells, for example?

Machado   I don't believe he gave an opinion.

Worsley   Andrew Dymock, who was the late Earl Rivers's lawyer, and who must have seen both of King Edward's boys, did he make comment?

Machado   Not that I'm aware of.

Worsley   Dr Argentine, the physician who attended both princes in the Tower of London, was he asked if there was any resemblance between the boy he knew and the prisoner?

Machado   I don't think so.

Worsley   Sir James Tyrell, Governor of Guînes, who would certainly recognize the Duke of York as he was well-known to both King Edward, who knighted him, and King Richard?

Machado   I think he is still in France.

Worsley   The names could go on. We could even ask my opponent, the counsel for the Prosecution, what he thinks, as he too knew the Duke of York when he was young, but I won't put him on the spot.

What amazes me is that there isn't a list of people queuing up to confirm to King Henry the prisoner is nothing like the young boy they knew.

Machado   But nobody said he was the missing son either.

Worsley   What would have been the consequences for anyone who was prepared to say 'this is the Duke of York? Oh, and by the way, he is the rightful king'?

Machado	I think you can guess.
Worsley	So, I think we agree that it's no surprise nobody was prepared to acknowledge the prisoner as who he said he was. Who wouldn't want to retain a link between their head and their shoulders? But I am astonished you can't name people who confirmed what the king thought.
Machado	I'm sure there were, but neither I, nor you apparently, know about them.
Worsley	There is one person who we haven't mentioned, who above all could resolve this question. So, please tell the court why the current queen, Elizabeth of York, has never been allowed to meet the prisoner and call him the imposter you say he is.
Machado	The king wouldn't ask his queen to tell him what he already knew.
Worsley	We have heard from other witnesses of these famous three marks, marks on his body which my client claims would prove beyond doubt to anyone who knew him and saw them that he is who he claims he is. A person such as the queen, his possible sister, who would have known him since birth and seen him as nature intended, why wasn't she asked to make the ultimate judgement?
Machado	The king would never demean or humiliate his wife by asking her to look at the semi-naked body of a boatman's son.
Worsley	Or he feared the worst. No further questions, m'Lord.
Morton	*Señor* de Sousa, perhaps I can ask you, someone with no stake in this affair, the same question. You met the youngest son of the late King Edward IV when you were ambassador to London and you gave testimony on this matter at Setubal in 1496.[20]

de Sousa	That is correct.
Morton	To be clear. You saw the young prince in London sometime after 1481 when you arrived as Portuguese Ambassador,[175] and again some years later when he arrived in your home country. Based on these sightings, what did you testify at Setubal as to the identity of the man now in the dock?
de Sousa	He was not the boy I saw in London, singing beautifully with his mother and sisters. That boy was far more handsome than the one that came to Portugal. Nor is he the one that is before us now.
Morton	Thank you, ambassador.
Worsley	*Señor* de Sousa, you were ambassador to King Edward so you had many official dealings with him?
de Sousa	That was my job.
Worsley	But it was hardly your job to socialize with Queen Elizabeth and her children, so how often did you see the prince 'singing with his mother and sisters'? You are very specific about this meeting, so it seems this can't have been a regular event.
de Sousa	I did not see them often, but it was so memorable that it sticks in my mind.
Worsley	Now tell us what makes your memory of a servant boy in Portugal so clear that you also remember that so vividly?
de Sousa	I saw him at a court celebration. He was a page to Pero Vaz da Cunha, as has already been testified, and was dressed in a gown of silk. That was what made him noticeable.
Worsley	Does the sight of a page in a silk gown at a celebration gathering really fix itself so clearly in your mind that,

	nearly a decade later, you can say with certainty of recollection that he was not the boy you saw – and rarely saw, I might add – as a 7-year-old in London some fourteen years earlier?
de Sousa	Yes.
Worsley	I must say, your powers of recollection are quite remarkable for a man of such advanced years. May I ask, what age were you then, about 60?[176]
de Sousa	I refuse to dignify that comment with a reply.
Worsley	Finally, one thing that still bothers me. In a letter from the Spanish monarchs to their ambassador, *Señor* de Puebla, here with us, they suggested that they could send you, *Señor* de Sousa, to make an identification as you had seen the boy only two years before he arrived in Portugal.[177] Given that Warbeck arrived in Portugal in about 1487, doesn't that mean a least one of Edward's sons was still alive in 1485?
de Sousa	I think I have a better memory than my Spanish friends, despite my age.
Worsley	A selective memory, perhaps? No further questions of this witness, m'Lord.
Morton	I have listened patiently to the cross-examination concerning who may or may not have recognized the prisoner from his time in King Edward's court. But this line of questioning is a two-edged sword. Richmond Herald, at Taunton in 1497, was the prisoner asked to identify anybody who the Duke of York should have been able to recognize from before 1483 – people well-known to the King and Queen at the time?
Machado	There were over twenty nobles present when the prisoner was paraded before them. Some he certainly would not have known well enough to remember, but among them

were three who he should have done: his half-brother, Thomas Grey, Marquis of Dorset; John, Earl of Arundel, his cousin and of similar age to himself; and John Rodon, a servant who attended his bedchamber.[178]

Morton   And he didn't recognize any of these three?

Machado   None of them.

Morton.   Thank you. Your witness, Dean.

Worsley   Let's be clear, Richmond Herald. King Henry asked my client to remember people fourteen years after he first saw them at the age of 7. A boy of 7 who was more interested in his games than the people around him, and certainly not people twenty years older than himself like Thomas Grey, or a mere servant like Rodon. I should have thought it astonishing if he remembered any of them.

Machado   You might, but the rest of us didn't. He didn't even stop to think, he just said he didn't recognize anyone.

Worsley   This is the same man who had just confessed, if I can call it that, to being Perkin Warbeck. He could hardly claim then that Perkin Warbeck knew the Marquis of Dorset, could he?

Machado   No, but as far as the king and everyone else at Taunton were concerned, all aspects of his questioning were consistent. He said he was Warbeck and he behaved like Warbeck.

Worsley   I think he was trying to save his skin.

Morton   Objection! The Jury is not interested in what counsel for the Defence thinks.

Oxford   Sustained. Jury, disregard the Dean's last comment.
              I think we have now come full circle in this 'who knew who?' tit for tat. It is time to move to the last few months

of the prisoner's captivity, the months leading up to this trial. Archbishop?

Morton I'm happy to let the defence take the lead here.

Oxford Dean, then, it's your prerogative.

Worsley Baron Daubeney, my client made two attempts to escape, is that correct?

Daubeney The first time was in June of last year, 1498.

Worsley He seems to have just walked out – maybe with the help of a ladder to escape through a window, or a door left unlocked? Is that what happened?

Daubeney Firstly, it would be true to say he was hardly a prisoner. That is, kept in a jail. You have already heard that King Henry showed him mercy and confined him in some comfort. Then he was helped to escape by two of his guards, Smith and Jones, and two others, Kebyll and Sherwin, who had some skill with locks, but it only took four days to recapture him.[179]

Worsley It all seems a bit too easy. What punishment did these men receive for their part in the escape?

Daubeney They were let off without punishment. The king just thought they were fools and deserved leniency.[180]

Worsley There seems no end to the king's mercy. Nonetheless, the Spanish thought King Henry had arranged the escape, didn't they? [181, 182]

Daubeney Why would he do that? It's unbelievable. The Spanish must be mad.

Worsley Perhaps because he needed an excuse to execute him, since he doesn't seem to have found one so far, despite the confession. We could be forgiven for thinking he couldn't yet execute his brother-in-law, and needed another pretext.

Daubeney   Why do you keep on with this false pretence he was the king's brother-in-law? He isn't. He is an imposter who the king could execute at any time.

For certain, the Spanish were getting impatient, but when King Henry transferred the prisoner to the Tower of London they seemed satisfied it was all coming to an end. And, I might add, not before the prisoner had been humiliated in the stocks in public view, where he repeated his confession.[170]

Worsley   King Henry could execute him any time, so why is he still alive and in the Tower seventeen months later?

Daubeney   Punishment.

Worsley   More indecision, I would say.

Daubeney   You are entitled to your opinion, however misguided.

Worsley   Then there was a second escape plan, in August of this year, which is the reason we are all now at this trial.[183, 184]

This one is even more remarkable. It involves the Earl of Warwick, who has also been a prisoner in the Tower since 1485 and has been described as 'dim witted',[185] and my client, who has hardly shown any great competence in organizing anything, along with a number of ordinary citizens with no influence at all. And what were they planning? Apparently, to seize the Tower, steal everything they could lay their hands on in the Treasury, then explode barrels of gunpowder to cause confusion. The plan seemed to involve killing the king and making either Warwick or my client monarch in his place. I would guess they told them different stories as to who would be king to rope both of them into the conspiracy.

I put it to you that all this is total fantasy, not a real escape plan, just another ploy put together to generate an excuse to execute the two men who stood in the way of finalizing the marriage of Prince Arthur and Infanta Catalina of Spain.

Daubeney

You are right, it was a plot that had no chance of success, but that simply tells you the level of support your client, and indeed the Earl of Warwick, has. Nobody with any sense would believe such a plot could succeed, nor would it have any popular support. The country knows who its king is and wants to keep it that way. The men involved in this foolishness were all long-time adherents to the Plantagenet cause. Henry had no part in any of this.[183]

Worsley

The plot was discovered and retribution taken. Yes?

Daubeney

Most certainly. Unlike the prisoner's last escape, most of those involved within the Tower were executed.[186] So much for you believing these men were put up to instigate a plot for the king's ultimate benefit.

Worsley

It merely tells me these men were gullible. And, I note you say 'most', not 'all' those involved were executed. I believe Thomas Strangeways, one of those guarding my client, has been pardoned. A 'strange way' indeed for the king to act, unless he was in the man's debt for services rendered.[187]

But I agree, the executions were widespread this time. King Henry seems finally to have made his mind up on what he had to do to make the Spanish marriage a reality.

Daubeney

I'm glad you agree that he did act decisively. There are now just the two outstanding convictions that are needed to put an end to this sorry and troublesome affair.

Worsley

It will be up to the Jury to decide that, at least in the case of my client.

The attempted Tower plot at least shows that support for the Pretender within England hadn't completely evaporated. But what about the European support after his capture in 1497? Rowland Robinson, how did King James IV react?

| Robinson | The Treaty of Ayton was agreed after the prisoner had left Scotland but before his capture. It seems King James had already made his mind up about the success, or rather probable lack of it, of the Pretender's hopes. By the treaty, King James would marry King Henry's daughter, Princess Margaret.[188] |

| Worsley | So, the Scottish king had completely given up on the pretender's cause? |

| Robinson | Not entirely. He insisted on a clause, much to King Henry's displeasure, maintaining safe haven and safe conduct for Duke Richard, as he called him, and his supporters as he had previously promised.[189, 190] King Henry was not happy with this and the last I heard he had sent Norry, King of Arms, north to have this clause removed from the agreement.[191] |

| Worsley | Jean le Sauvage, how did Duchess Margaret of Burgundy and Emperor Maximilian react to my client's capture? |

| le Sauvage | It was the emperor who was most incensed. He wanted me to come to London to negotiate the accused's release. He gave me 10,000 florins to bargain with. I was also to forcibly tell King Henry that if he executed his prisoner he would be executing his own brother-in-law.[192] I thought this was quite a brave move, as his son, Duke Philip, was more inclined to let things pass. He was not as involved with the accused as his father, and besides, he wanted to improve trade with England.[193] There must have been some interesting father–son discussions about all this. |

| Worsley | This bribe was, however, clearly a failure? |

| le Sauvage | Yes, but in fact it wasn't my fault. I work for Duke Philip, not the emperor himself. It was Duke Philip's wish I remain in Flanders, so one of his councillors, Jean Courtville, went in my place.[192, 194] |

| Worsley | Thank you. That is all from me for now. |

Morton	Jean le Sauvage, I noted you avoided answering the Dean's question of how Duchess Margaret reacted, so please enlighten us.
le Sauvage	She was really quite ill at this time.[193] She had sent the Bishop of Cambrai over to England, seemingly to talk trade but also to visit her 'Richard' and find out how he was faring.
Morton	This was at the time when the accused once again confessed that he was an imposter?
le Sauvage	Yes.
Morton	And that Duchess Margaret was well aware of this?
le Sauvage	He said she knew everything. Or at least, that's what *Señor* de Puebla, who was also there, reported. But then, there is more than one way to interpret that.[195]
Morton	*Señor* de Puebla, is this true?
de Puebla	It is.
Morton	Did Duchess Margaret ever write directly to King Henry?
le Sauvage	I think you already know the answer to that. According to de Puebla, and it's only his word we have for this, she did write apologizing for her behaviour, asking the king to pardon her and assuring him of her obedience.[196]
Morton	*Señor* de Puebla?
de Puebla	Again, it is true.
Morton	So, *Monsieur* le Sauvage, she finally faced the truth?
le Sauvage	Maybe. But holding to her belief wouldn't have helped her cause at this stage in the game. Making a confession might have been her best bet for saving her 'Richard's' life.

140

Morton	I have no further questions for this witness.
Oxford	I think that concludes our cross-examinations, unless either counsel can state otherwise.
Morton	M'Lord, I would like to call Lady Katherine Gordon.
Oxford	You may, but let me repeat the warning I gave at the outset of this trial. Not only is this witness not obliged to answer your questions, but I will not allow either of you to encroach on her privacy and good name. You may begin, archbishop.
Morton	Lady Katherine, you are a close relative of King James IV of Scotland?
Gordon	I am.
Morton	And it was widely seen as a mark of King James's belief in the accused's lineage that he should marry him to a close relative.
Gordon	I believe it was viewed that way in some quarters.
Morton	But you aren't that closely related to your king at all, are you?
Worsley	Objection! It is not the role of this court to question the genealogy of the witness, who is of noble stock.
Oxford	I believe this may have some bearing on the case so I will allow it; but be careful, archbishop, you are treading on thin ice. Objection overruled.
Morton	Your mother was Elizabeth Hay, the Earl of Huntley's third wife, who was only related back to the Scottish crown by six generations – six generations – from King Robert II, not, as some people say, by his second wife, Annabella Stewart, who was the daughter of King James

I. Hardly the close association with the crown of Scotland which some would have us believe. [97]

Oxford

There is no need to respond to that statement, Lady Katherine. The archbishop has made his point.

Tread carefully, archbishop, I won't tolerate personal questions of this sort any further.

Morton

You were at Exeter when the prisoner made his confession. How did you react to finding out you had married a commoner?

Worsley

Objection! There is no proof he is a commoner.

Oxford

Overruled.

He was presented to Lady Katherine as a commoner, so it's reasonable to ask how she reacted.

Gordon

It was hard to take after all we had been through together. It was all very emotional. I wept bitterly. But then, he was a prisoner of the king, so who knows how true his confession was? Richard – my husband, I should say – had warned me that if he was captured a confession would be drawn out of him. One that would suit his captors. [198, 199]

Morton

That will be all. Thank you

Oxford

Dean.

Worsley

First, let's just end the archbishop's line of questioning with something less personal. I hope that will be acceptable to the court.

Lady Katherine, can you please tell the court, were there any other female members of the royal family available to be betrothed to the man who is now your husband?

Gordon

None.

Worsley	So there was nobody of higher rank in Scotland that King James could have offered in marriage, nobody superior to you in standing or lineage?
Gordon	In my opinion, no.
Worsley	Thank you. Now, let me turn to some less hurtful questions about your family. Your father, Lord Huntley, is currently High Chancellor of Scotland?
Gordon	He is.
Worsley	That makes him a close associate of King James and highly trusted by him?
Gordon	Of course. My father is the most powerful man in Scotland below the king.
Worsley	I think that made you a bride any man would be proud to take. Tell the court, has your father ever, but particularly over the last year since the prisoner's capture, raged against you for marrying the defendant?
Gordon	No.
Worsley	Members of the jury must make up their own minds, but from what you have told us, King James would not have married you below your station, whatever the archbishop may have tried to imply. Now, since you have been at King Henry's court, tell us how he has treated you?
Gordon	I must confess I have been treated exceptionally well.
Worsley	But you are a lady-in-waiting to Queen Elizabeth, are you not? Isn't that demeaning?
Gordon	On the contrary, it's a position of considerable importance. I rank highest among the ladies assigned to wait on the

queen, and I rank after only the queen, her mother and the two infant princesses, Margaret and Mary,[200] among the ladies at court.

Worsley

So you are treated like nobility, someone worthy of a noble marriage, not as a prisoner?

Gordon

As I said, I have been treated well. The king has assigned me six servants,[171] the normal number for a duchess, so I have no complaints. One of them is probably a spy …

Morton

Objection!

Oxford

Overruled.
Don't take us for fools, archbishop, of course one of them is a spy.

Worsley

You are allowed to meet with your husband, quite freely?

Gordon

Yes, except at night, for obvious reasons.

Worsley

Yes, King Henry has enough pretenders to the throne of England without adding yet more.
    But I am still puzzled. You are nobility, your husband is a commoner, so why does the king think you need his company?

Gordon

Given who he believes my husband is, I don't know. The archbishop would no doubt cite it as another example of the king's kindness.

Worsley

And the king was again merciful in making you a lady-in-waiting to his wife and queen. The two of you must have had some interesting conversations?

Gordon

We had much to talk about.

Worsley

I'm sure you won't tell us about private conversations, so I won't ask. Let me ask you this instead – did you ever see the queen in the prisoner's company?

Gordon	Never.
Worsley	Did you ever ask her if they had met?
Gordon	I never asked and she never commented.
Worsley	What about her two sisters, Princesses Cecily and Anne? They were also at court as ladies-in-waiting to the queen, like yourself. Did they ever meet your husband?
Gordon	Not that I know of.
Worsley	Isn't that remarkable? If there was one sure way of settling this matter, it would have been to let the sisters of Richard, Duke of York, any one of the three, see him and confirm he is not their brother.
Gordon	You make it sound so easy. I'm glad for their sake they never had to do this.

What if they had to tell the king he was their brother? They wouldn't dare. Could they lie convincingly? I don't know. Can you imagine what the king would do if he thought any of them believed he was their brother? |
Worsley	But surely King Henry is so confident in his prisoner being an imposter he has nothing to fear?
Gordon	Maybe he's not as confident as he makes out. Who knows?
Worsley	What about you, may I ask? How confident are you in your husband's identity? I notice that you haven't annulled your marriage, something you are entitled to do as your husband took you, according to the Prosecution, under a false name.
Gordon	When I married I took vows. I see no reason to break those vows, but perhaps the verdict of the court will change that.[201]

Worsley	We have heard from other witnesses that my client claimed he had three distinctive marks on his body which would confirm who he was. I'm sure his sisters would be aware of these marks, if indeed they exist.
	As his wife, you must also have seen the marks hidden to others …
Oxford	Enough!
	I will not allow questions of an intimate nature to be put in an open court. You have strayed into territory where even the archbishop feared to tread.
	Now, if you have no further questions, I think it's time we allowed this good lady some privacy.
Worsley	Thank you, Lady Katherine, that is all I wish to ask.
Morton	I have no further questions either, m'Lord.
Oxford	In that case, Prosecution, would you present your summing up?
Morton	We have heard a lot of testimony, mainly the Defence mounting attack after attack on the identity of the prisoner as claimed by our king. But when it comes to reaching your decision, there are only two questions you need to ask yourselves.
	Firstly, in 1485, were the two sons of King Edward IV alive or dead? This is by far the most important question, because if you agree with the case we have presented, that these two unfortunates had met their death at the hands of their uncle, King Richard, then you need go no further. Any second question as to who it is that stands before you in the dock becomes redundant. If, on the other hand, you remain to be convinced on this matter, only then do you need to consider the identity of the accused man standing trial.
	So, let me begin with the important question before you. Were the two sons of King Edward IV alive or not in 1485? I cannot deny that the evidence is anything other than circumstantial that they were dead. If it were

otherwise, if we had bodies to show you of two innocent young boys cut down in the prime of their youth, then we would have done so and this sorry decade of falsehood would never have taken place. But we cannot. What we have done is present an overwhelming body of circumstantial evidence that leads inexorably to just one conclusion, the malice of King Richard III, his usurpation of the throne and the murderous end to his two nephews.

We have heard from Baron Daubeney that news of the boys' death was widespread. It was reported by the Crowland Chronicler, who was near the centre of government and who had no political axe to grind. We heard the news reached Bristol and was noted in the mayor's calendar there. And all over Europe it was the talk of every court, whose members were astonished at the barbarity of the usurper. And who can blame them? Didn't we all recoil at the news? These murders will go down as the greatest shame in our history. They will never be forgotten.

There was only one man who could dispel these rumours and that was the usurper, King Richard himself. Just ask yourselves how you would behave if your neighbour slandered your reputation over what you could prove to be a falsehood. Would you sit there and do nothing, allowing your reputation, and by implication that of your whole family and household, to be dragged through the mud? Of course not! You would present your accusers with the proof which would vindicate your good name. But what did King Richard do? Absolutely nothing. You must now ask yourselves, 'why not, why didn't he produce the boys for the world to see?', and you will come up with only one answer – because he couldn't. The boys were dead.

Cast your minds back to 1483 and the reaction of the country to the new king's coronation. Was he widely acclaimed as the nation's saviour? No, he was greeted with rebellion, one in which even his most ardent supporter, the Duke of Buckingham, God rest his soul, finally turned against him. Was his reign one of peace and prosperity? No, the threat of rebellion and invasion was ever-present, until, mercifully, our king, Henry Tudor, came from exile to relieve us of our misery. So, we may have nothing but circumstantial evidence, but in the final reckoning, there is one who is certain of the truth: God gave his verdict on the usurper and his crimes on the field at Bosworth. Ask yourselves, members of the jury, do you know better than him?

We now turn, for those who still need convincing, to the second question I mentioned: the identity of the man in the dock. This is immaterial if, as I believe you will, you have accepted that the Duke of York was dead by 1485. Is the accused a boatman's son from Tournai? Certainly, as he confessed himself. The evidence is there in the Tournai records, everything he told us can be backed up by the available written evidence; you only have to take a boat over the Channel to read the papers for yourselves. It is true that there are inconsistencies in the confession, but who hasn't made mistakes when their life is threatened? And as for the so-called errors in the confession, which are nothing more than variations in spelling, the precise words used and so on – do these clerical failings, for that is what they surely are, detract from the substance of the confession? For when you strip away these minor contradictions, you are still left with a history that is both verifiable and believable. In short, it is the truth.

The Defence has made much of the way the king has treated both the accused and Lady Katherine. This is simply a mark of his mercy. As well as his kindness and prudence, never forget the humiliation to which he has subjected the imposter: being led through the streets of London when he was brought from Cornwall, in the stocks at both Westminster Hall and then Cheapside after his attempted escape.[170, 202] You should also ask yourselves why the king has allowed the Lady Katherine to keep such close company with his queen, who the Defence would have you believe is her sister-in-law. Would the king really allow the two to consort, plot perhaps, if he truly believed the accused was his brother-in-law? No, the king had nothing to fear and no reason why he should not treat the Lady Katherine with the kindness and respect her position deserves. Fate has dealt her a cruel hand; it is the least the king can do now to make her life better.

Finally, you must ask yourselves why it is that we are here today. It is because our enemies abroad have spent a decade using this boatman's son as a pawn in a European power struggle, a bargaining chip to gain influence with our king or, more often, influence against our king, led, of course, by the implacable hatred of Margaret, Duchess of Burgundy towards the man who put an end to the Plantaganet dynasty.

But what did all these machinations finally add up to? Forget the royal treatment afforded to the pretender while he revelled in being the centre of attention and a lavish lifestyle unimaginable to a boy from Tournai. Forget that he fooled rulers across the continent into supporting him with warm words. When it came to the ultimate challenge, how much support was he given? Remember the testimony of Rowland Robinson: the self-styled King Richard IV landed in Cornwall with three ships and about 100 men. Some invasion force! The support for the prisoner was words, not warships. The French King Charles VIII, the Scottish King James IV, Emperor Maximilian and even Margaret, Duchess of Burgundy, finally came to their senses and left him to his fate.

You have no choice, given the evidence we have presented. The man in the dock is Perkin Warbeck, a boatman's son from Tournai and nobody else. He has committed crimes against our country and you have no choice but to find him guilty and may God have mercy on his soul.

Oxford

Defence, would you present your summing up to conclude this trial.

Worsley

Thank you my Lord.

The Prosecution case is based on two clear points and two points only, so let's begin by examining them closely.

Firstly, according to the Prosecution, the man in the dock cannot be Richard, Duke of York, because he is dead. But we have no proof whatsoever that that is the case. Yes, there were rumours, but from where did those rumours, in the main, originate? From courts hostile to King Richard III is the simple answer. Malicious rumours of a usurping king and child murderer were nothing more than that: rumours. Rumours to be played to advantage wherever needed.

No bodies have ever been found, and of course, it's possible that this could be because these were well hidden, but there is no certainty here: it equally points to the boys being alive. However, the arguments concerning Elizabeth Woodville, her forgoing of sanctuary and acceptance of a place at King Richard's court for her and her daughters, are hardly the actions of a mother towards the murderer of her sons. It is for you, members of the jury, to decide in this matter. Would any of you consort with the killer of your children?

In reaching your conclusion about the fate of King Edward's sons, consider this: what is indisputable, and frankly astonishing, is that in the fourteen years since the Battle of Bosworth, not a single witness has come forward to offer any clue as to the boys' fate. Just think about it. Despite the rewards and favours that would follow, nobody, nothing. No noble lord, perhaps a supporter of the late king, wishing to re-establish himself under a new regime. No lowly servant who noticed something amiss in the Tower of London in the late summer of 1483. Nobody, nothing.

King Henry's own actions – continually searching for evidence, paranoia about the man in the dock, the hesitancy over convicting and sentencing him after he was captured – all point in one direction: King Henry had no idea if the princes[203] were dead or that his prisoner wasn't really his brother-in-law.

We can't be sure when King Henry started seeking information in Flanders about King Edward's sons, but with no bodies or evidence of their death beyond rumour, he must have worried that King Edward's sons were alive. Quite reasonably, he assumed Flanders was the most likely hiding place for at least one of them. Did his spies close in on Perkin Warbeck, which was why he not only fled to Portugal but then went to ground – or perhaps I should more accurately say to sea – for much of his four years in that country, to wait for the trail to go cold? But the king still pursued him, and through Edward Woodville's time in Lisbon flushed him out and brought him on to the world stage via the gateway of Cork.

It wasn't by chance that he was taken to be the Duke of York by a bunch of Irish barbarians who wouldn't have a clue what this duke looked like; it was a prearranged meeting in a Yorkist stronghold, a steppingstone for his re-emergence on the world stage to claim a crown that was his by right.

Leave aside the rumour and conjecture. What evidence we have points to a living Duke Richard.

Secondly, we have to consider the evidence from both the testimonies made at Setubal in Portugal and by the prisoner himself at Taunton. The picture they paint of Perkin Warbeck is of a boatman's son who roamed the world seeking his fortune and became the unwitting instrument of political intrigue.

But what are the facts? Everything said by those testifying at Setubal was already known by 1496; the witnesses who gave evidence were just telling King Henry what he already knew – and what he wanted to hear. Claims by the Spanish monarchs that *Señor* de Sousa saw the prince in London two years before he landed in Portugal were not brought to your attention by the Prosecution because it is an inconvenient fact which undermines their case that the boy was already dead in 1485.[177] On the other hand, and this may be the reality, *Señor* de Sousa's aging memory may not be quite all he claims it to be. Can you really rely on the evidence of, and I'm sorry to have to say this, an old man, that the prince he saw at age 7 singing with his mother and the young man he saw at least five years later are different people?

Sir Edward Brampton's testimony at Setubal is totally unreliable. We know that he looked after himself first and was always happy to bend with the wind. You must ask yourself why King Henry pardoned him – what was in it for the king? Brampton claims Warbeck's father was named Bernal, when nobody else does. He claims Warbeck trained to be a musician, when nobody else does.[70] So why should you believe Brampton when he says the king he once served loyally had his two nephews killed?

For the final part of the case against my client as presented by the Prosecution we have the confession at Taunton. Can I, for the benefit of the jury, summarize the implausibility of the prisoner's confession? Apparently, this 'Warbeck' was a joiner's son from Oxford, taken to Ireland by a priest and taught the ways of court so he could impersonate a king. He was supported by the Duchess of Burgundy, from where he sailed to Ireland to gather support before invading England at ...

Oxford

Stop, stop! What are you talking about?

Worsley

I'm sorry, I do apologize to the court. I seem to have got my notes mixed up and am telling you about the earlier pretender, the so-named Lambert Simnel.[80] It's easy to get the two pretenders mixed up when their stories are so similar. Anyone could be forgiven for thinking the king was using the same tried and tested method to discredit my client as he did with Simnel.

Morton

Objection!

Oxford

No need to clarify the objection, it's sustained.
Jury, ignore the last comment from the Defence. I must warn you, Dean, not to play games with the court.
Now continue.

Worsley

What the Defence does not dispute is that a Warbeck family existed – indeed still exists – in and around Tournai, that Jehan Warbeck was a boatman and he had a son called Perkin. We do not know when this Perkin was born, but it was probably soon after the Warbeck marriage in about 1474,[52, 65] making him of similar age to my client. However, and more importantly, what we do not know is whether this son survived.

It must be clear that if King Richard III sent one or both of his nephews to Flanders, they were not hidden in his sister, Duchess Margaret's, court, where their presence would have been obvious. Is it not plausible that one boy was placed in a local family that could be trusted, whilst still under his aunt Margaret's watchful eye?

Leaving aside that the Taunton 'confession' was made under duress, it was clearly written by lawyers in advance and simply presented to the prisoner to sign. It is riddled with inconsistencies which are unthinkable if they were made by the true son of Jehan Warbeck. The outline elements of the story are true, but not the detail. Doesn't this fit with a boy adopted by a family, who becomes an addition to the family but never fully part of it? Ask yourself why the defendant's letter to his mother from Exeter never received a reply. Ask yourself why there are inconsistencies in the Warbeck confession, but never, in the eight years since 1491, has anyone ever found any falsehood, lies or evasion in anything my client said about his life as Richard, Duke of York. The truth is that my client *is* the Duke of York and Perkin Warbeck was the role he played, not the other way around.

Next, let us consider the actions of his supporters. King Charles VIII certainly used the boy to his own ends, either supporting him or denying him, depending on his fluctuating relationship to King Henry. Nothing can be deduced from this other than that we can't trust the French! So, what's new?

King Ferdinand and Queen Isabella of Spain also had their own agenda to pursue, the marriage of their daughter to Prince Arthur, so inevitably sided with King Henry. But, in their secret coded files, they referred to the pretender not as Warbeck but as the Duke of York. Revealing, isn't it?

While it is unquestionably true that all the crowned heads of Europe used my client in their diplomatic struggles, none of this means he was an imposter. Surely you, the jury, would agree that their position was so much stronger if they had a real claimant to the English throne in their hands, not just an imposter?

In this regard, we must briefly touch on the meaning of kingship. A king is God's representative on Earth, divinely anointed and crowned. A king is divinely blessed and approved by his anointing and crowning. Kings do not raise commoners up to be their equal, whatever the diplomatic rewards. It diminishes their God-given status. The Emperor Maximilian simply would not, indeed could not, elevate a commoner to even appear to be his equal, yet that is how he treated him. As did King James of Scotland.

The steadfast supporters – his aunt Duchess Margaret, Emperor Maximilian and King James IV – all never wavered. Yes, there were opportunities for each of them in return for their support, but that support went beyond any return they might expect. In this regard, you need only dwell on the attempt by the emperor to pay a ransom for the prisoner's release *after* King Henry had captured him. You simply don't throw good money after bad; you cut your losses and move on.

If all this wasn't enough to convince you, let me finish by asking you to think about the man himself, his appearance and his character. There is no denying he looks like King Edward – surely it's a family resemblance? We will never know what Queen Elizabeth and her sisters made of him because they were never allowed to get anywhere near to him. Why not? Surely this would have settled matters once and for all. Once more, King Henry was afraid to confront the inescapable conclusion that his prisoner was his brother-in-law and rightful King of England. And it doesn't end there. The monarchs of Spain and France both offered to provide the mother and father of Perkin Warbeck for King Henry, but again he refused. It doesn't matter that these may have been empty gestures; the point is that he didn't want to know, he didn't want to get at the truth once and for all.

My final comment is this. At Deal in 1495, the invasion was thwarted and my client could have given up there and then. After the subsequent failure at the siege of

Waterford in 1497, he could, again, have given up. Ships to take him to Spain waited, along with the promise of an obscure yet comfortable retirement. He could have gone back to Scotland with his wife and lived out his life at the court of King James, and even if the king's largesse became less than it had been, how much better would it have been than the future he would have expected as a boatman's son? He chose none of these easy options. He invaded Cornwall when all the odds were against him. It is not his failure as a military man, something he was never trained for, that you should focus on. It is that he put his life on the line because he knew he was the rightful King of England, Richard IV of England.

I have finished my case for the Defence, m'Lord. The task before you, members of the jury, is to return a verdict that shows you now believe him.

Oxford   I thank both Counsels for their summaries, despite the games the Dean has played in his summary.

Members of the jury should now retire to consider what has been presented. I realize the difficulties you will face in arriving at your verdict. We have few truly reliable facts, much circumstantial evidence and surrogate witnesses who may either not know the truth or are acting to shield what their masters really know.

May God be with you in reaching your verdict.

Ushers, clear the courtroom.

SCENE 3

An Empty Classroom

Gates   Well, let's wait and see what your peers make of all that. Very interesting and congratulations for putting it all together. Very professional, I must say.

So, we just wait now, and that's an end to it. It shouldn't be long.

Tom   You never know, they may have Henry Fonda in there.

Beth   What???

Gates   He's a film buff as well. *Twelve Angry Men*. 1957. Google it.

It will be interesting to read your EPQs. Beth, you dominated the questioning so I assume your report will be much longer than Tom's?

Tom   The trial itself may have given a false representation of that, sir.

My – I mean the archbishop's – summing up for the Prosecution did cut to the nub of the problem. If you believe the boys were dead, then it doesn't matter who the man captured in Beaulieu Abbey was, does it? So, a lot of my EPQ centred on the question of the boy's death or survival.

Gates   You didn't make as much of it as you might in your questioning of Daubeney.

Tom   It's difficult, as neither Daubeney nor any other witness, possibly with the exception of Harliston, could actually shed light on the issue. Besides, the trial was about Warbeck, not Richard III.

Gates   But you must have come to a conclusion given you were prepared to take the side of prosecuting Warbeck as an imposter.

Tom   Yes, I did. I looked at it this way. There are five possible answers to the so-called 'Princes in the Tower' mystery. It could have been Richard III or Buckingham who killed them in 1483. It could have been Henry VII or Margaret Beaufort after 1485, or it was nobody. It's possible that one boy – the elder one – died naturally in 1483 or thereabouts,[204] but let's leave that aside as it only complicates matters.

I ruled out either Margaret or Henry, even though they certainly had motive and opportunity. If they found the boys alive after Bosworth, they – the boys, I mean – had to die or Bosworth would have been a waste of time. The elder boy, Edward, would have had to be reinstated as Edward V. The Tudor motive for killing the boys was, for sure, stronger than the Plantagenet one. But did either Tudor do the evil deed? I doubt it.

Firstly, I don't believe Richard would have been foolish enough to have hidden the boys somewhere in England, somewhere Tudor would have been able to find them easily. Secondly, Henry was paranoid about Warbeck, if not so much Simnel, which suggests he didn't know for sure what had happened to the boys. If this was a bluff to cover his own murderous act, it was a very clever one, but I think that's stretching credibility too far. Finally, surely if Henry had found the boys alive and then had them killed, his best option would have been to immediately produce the bodies as evidence – evidence he had found – that Richard was the murderer. It's what the rumours had conditioned people to expect; no one would have thought otherwise.

Taking the most objective and unprejudiced analysis I could – you see, Beth, even those of us in the Humanities can be objective – I then looked at the case for them being alive, leaving Richard's guilt until last. My problem with them being alive was simply that that means it was a case of Richard kicking the can down the road. At some point, say 1490 or so, when Edward was in manhood, he had every chance of re-emerging as a challenger to King Richard. It's something current politicians wouldn't worry about. In fact, more often than not, can-kicking is government policy, but that's not how the medieval mindset worked. I just couldn't believe Richard would let the problem of a credible challenge to his throne emerge from the shadows at some future date. Besides, hiding the boys for two years would have been no easy task. Thus, I concluded they weren't alive.

After that, once the 'if' question has been answered, the 'who' matters less, at least as far as the Warbeck affair is concerned. Ricardians might think otherwise.

Beth

First, you seem to forget that Henry IV imprisoned the two sons of Roger Mortimer in 1399, sons of the man who

Richard II had once nominated his successor. Edmund Mortimer was about 8 and his brother, Roger, younger; not dissimilar in ages to Edward's boys. Henry V set them free in 1413, and did they immediately challenge his position as king? No, they became loyal supporters, so it is possible to kick the can down the road without consequences.

Second, hiding away is not as difficult as you seem to make out. You remember the Lord Clifford who was killed just before the Battle of Towton in 1461? Well, his son, 7-year-old Henry, went into hiding and only re-emerged in 1485 with the accession of Henry VII. There are all sorts of rumours about where he was for twenty-four years – tending sheep being the most speculative – but the point is he remained hidden.

Tom

But Henry Clifford wasn't heir to the throne and a widely known member of the nobility. I can't imagine the Yorkists went to great lengths to find him.

Beth

Fair point, but what about Henry VI then? He went awol after the Battle of Hexham in 1464. Cheeses don't come much bigger than the king, but he managed to remain hidden by Lancastrians in the north for about a year.

Besides, Edward, Prince of Wales – Edward V if you like – would hardly have been a nationally recognizable face as he has spent almost all his life in Ludlow Castle.

Gates

OK, OK enough. We're starting to drift away from Warbeck. Leaving all that aside, did you, Tom, have a preference, Richard or Buckingham?

Tom

That's a difficult one. It would be fair to say that, up to 1483, Richard had behaved impeccably and held no malice towards his elder brother and family, with the possible exception of Elizabeth Woodville. He did take a legal route to the throne with the pre-contract argument.[5] Even if you doubt the validity of this legal pretext – and let's be clear, it would have been a difficult pretext for the peasants in the street to get their head around – it was still a *legal* claim to the throne. Richard's motive – that the boys had to die for him to be king – is on the weak side but not completely non-existent. We know that his coronation wasn't a universally accepted event and there were efforts to wrest control of the two boys.

Beth

His coronation was attended by all the great and the good, so he couldn't have been that unpopular.[205]

It's also interesting you mention the failed attempt to rescue – some might say abduct – the two princes.[36] That's seems a good reason to me why Richard kept the whole thing quiet *and* kept the fate of the boys a secret. He didn't need any more rescue attempts.

Tom

True, but as far as the coronation is concerned, the nobles could just have been covering their own back or looking for a free lunch.

Back to the point. Arguably, Buckingham had the best motive. He emerged from political obscurity when Edward IV died in April 1483 and allied himself front and centre with the Duke of Gloucester.

Gates

Richard III-to-be.

Tom

Indeed, Richard.

But despite Richard rewarding him beyond his wildest dreams, he turned on him. This could be because he knew Richard had killed the boys, but if he did know this he kept it to himself, which doesn't add up as it was political dynamite. He did, however, have a distant claim to the throne himself – he was a descendant of Thomas Woodstock, Duke of Gloucester and the youngest of Edward III's sons – but only if Richard and the boys were out of the way. The other explanation, that he supported Henry Tudor's claim to the throne, just doesn't hold water. Tudor's claim was even weaker than his own.

So, m'Lord, my conclusion was that the boys were dead, Buckingham was the most likely – but not the only possible – culprit and thus Warbeck must have been an imposter. Case closed.

Gates	If Buckingham did it, why didn't Richard just say so and clear himself?

| Tom | I don't think Richard could risk it. If he claimed a dead man – Buckingham that is – had done it, who would have believed him? All the rumours surrounded Richard, not Buckingham. Richard was seen as the one with a motive. Wouldn't people just think he was covering himself by blaming a man who couldn't answer back?

Essentially, there were two questions to be answered: were the boys dead and who killed them? By blaming Buckingham, Richard had answered the first question – they *were* dead – while leaving the second question unanswered and himself as prime suspect. From his perspective, it was better to leave both questions unanswered. |
|---|---|

| Gates | Fair summary, I would say.

OK, you've made a case for the boys being dead, but you still have to tell us who Warbeck really was, and the difficult issues of his language and court knowledge. |
|---|---|

| Tom | OK, but remember, we are entering the land of speculation here, as Beth will probably agree.

So, to begin what will be a long story, we have the appearance at Margaret's home in Binche in the autumn of 1478 of a young boy named Jehan le Sage. He seems, in 1478, to have been 'about 5'. For the next seven years, until 1485, Margaret's accounts show he was well looked after and educated by a priest named Pierre de Montigny, whose name is consistent with him being from one of Hainault's noble families. There were yearly entries in the accounts for all seven years; it wasn't just a one-off act of charity. So, John the Wise, or maybe John the Good, sounds like it's a familiarity, a pet name for the young boy, doesn't it?[206, 207] |
|---|---|

Gates	So, what's the connection that explains this Jehan's ability to speak English, or was it the priest's job to teach him?

Tom	Slow down, I'm coming to that.
	Edward IV, Margaret's brother, had a jester also named Jehan le Sage, who accompanied Margaret on her voyage to Flanders to get married in 1468.
Beth	A jester named John the Wise? I didn't know the Plantagenets did satire!
Tom	In the summer of 1478, just before Jehan appears at Binche, Edward sent his ship *The Falcon* to Flanders with fifty-two men and two grooms. The purpose is not stated, but it doesn't sound like commerce – why take up spaces with horses? – or spying, as the number of men involved isn't, well, discrete. The horses also suggest onward travel, maybe by someone too rich, too young – maybe both – to walk. In the summer of the same year, 1478, Lord Hastings was paid for having sent men secretly to Flanders to check out if the earlier trip had gone according to plan.[207] So maybe this was young Jehan the Sage on his way from Edward to Margaret and she nicknamed him after Edward's jester.
Gates	Who do you think this Jehan is then?
Tom	Well, this really is speculation, but I'd say there are three possibilities. The first, arguably the most speculative and unlikely, is that he was Edward, Earl of Warwick, son of George, Duke of Clarence.
Gates	Well, that is a bold suggestion.
Tom	Well, it's recorded that around the time of his arrest in 1477, Clarence was believed to have brought a child to Warwick Castle – or at least was thinking about it – to impersonate his son, whom he was planning to send away to safety.[80, 208] What is interesting is that one of the men tasked with carrying out this scheme was John Taylor, our old friend who met Warbeck in Cork.[209] Ireland and Flanders have been suggested as the destinations, with the former being consistent with the emergence of Lambert

Simnel as Edward VI from there, but you can't rule out Flanders.

Beth   But this can't have anything to do with Edward IV and *The Falcon*, can it? If Clarence was looking to protect his son, it was *because* of his brother, not with his brother's help.

Tom   I couldn't agree more.

Also, the Earl of Warwick would have been 3, going on 4 years old in autumn 1478, a bit too young if we accept Jehan was about 5 then. The only reason I mention it is that in the accounts for Margaret's home in Mechelen in 1486 is the perplexing entry of payment for wine for 'the son of Clarence from England'.[210] It might well be just a clerical error, as there is no evidence that the Earl of Warwick had escaped from the Tower, despite rumours at that time.[211]

Gates   Don't you think a surrogate at Warwick Castle would have been noticed?

Tom   It's not impossible that he was unnoticed. The boy was young, not much more than 2, and all the people who subsequently looked after him – Thomas Grey, Richard, Duke of Gloucester, let alone Henry VII – would not have seen much, if anything, of him by 1477. Once the switch has been passed off without question, it becomes accepted and the surrogate becomes embedded in reality.[80, 211]

Gates   OK, so what are your more plausible alternatives?

Tom   That he was a bastard son of Edward IV, which, for a start, would explain the similarity in looks with Warbeck. From here, there are two possibilities. It may be that Edward fathered a child while he was in exile in Flanders during late 1470 or early 1471, but as such he would be a little old – about 7 – in 1478. On the other hand, he may have been a bastard born in 1473 whom we don't know about.

Gates   That *is* speculative.

Tom	Agreed.

All I can suggest is that this was also the year in which Richard, the one who might be Warbeck, was born. If Edward had been playing away while his wife was pregnant, maybe she put her foot down and the bastard child was never formally acknowledged. Then, Edward sends him to Flanders when he's old enough to travel, for the childless, recently widowed Margaret to look after.

Gates	Well it fits, albeit at a squeeze. And it doesn't explain how the boy knew so much about King Edward's court. Even if he had been anywhere near it – and your suggestion includes the idea that Elizabeth Woodville would have opposed this – a boy of such tender years would hardly have picked up much about court protocols.

Tom	Again, agreed, but it's the best I can do.

You do have to admit, though, that it puts the pretender in Margaret's hands much earlier than 1491, so the fact that he played his part in the deception so well, including his ability to speak English, become a lot more plausible.

Gates	But you haven't made a link yet with the Warbecks of Tournai.

Tom	In 1485, boy Jehan and the priest, Pierre de Montigny, disappear from the Binche accounts, never to reappear,[207] so it may be that it was just time for the boy to make his own way in the world. That doesn't link them to the Warbecks, but I'm not the only one with that problem; Beth has it as well. But 1485 is about when our story of Perkin Warbeck and Richard of York begins.

Gates	Yes Beth, it's your turn now to be in the witness box.

If I am to believe your account, then how do you make out the Duke of York ended up as a boatman's son in Tournai? It's hardly a royal hiding place, is it? This seems to be the Achilles heel in the Defence argument.

Beth	It's a fair point, and I don't think we'll ever know the answer. All I can do, like Tom, is make suggestions.

Tom	I'm all ears.

Beth	Well, look at it from King Richard's perspective. His hold on the throne in the summer of 1483 was tenuous. However legally correct he might have been in declaring the sons of Edward IV bastards, it was still a legal technicality. You don't win hearts and minds that way. For most of the population, they wouldn't even understand any of it, a point Tom has already made and it's still debated now.

So, I think Richard wanted a short-term fix, something to buy time to establish himself as undisputed ruler. He couldn't see the Buckingham rebellion coming, nor the shadow of Henry Tudor casting itself across the Channel, but he did know there were people who wanted possession of one or both of the boys to be the focal point of rebellion. He needed to hide them, at least for a year or so. He could then bring them back and treat them well, as we know he did with their mother and sisters.

Gates	I think we can agree with that so far, and with the choice of Flanders, but you'll need more than that to convince either of us about being hidden as a boatman's son.

Beth	Putting the boys in Margaret's court wouldn't solve the problem, as they could still be kidnapped from there. I've said already Richard had good reason to keep the boys' location secret, given that there had already been one attempt to take possession of them. If men were prepared to spring them from the Tower of London, then Burgundy wouldn't put them off. So it had to be more covert.

The biggest problem in hiding someone overseas is the language. The minute you speak, you give the game away, which is why claims that Warbeck was taught English are so hard to believe. Clearly, neither of Edward's sons could speak Flemish, but they did have a second language that might be useful.

Tom	Latin?

Beth	As if Latin was the second language of the streets of Ghent and Antwerp!

No, French you idiot. They must have learned some French by this stage. Admittedly it was less the language of court than in previous times, but it is the other language they would surely have been exposed to. Now Tournai is technically part of France and is French-speaking, even though it's surrounded by Burgundian land. And it's only about 30 miles from Binche, one of Margaret's favourite residences.

Gates

But that still doesn't give us a link.

Beth

OK, so I must admit here I'm speculating. Tournai is also about 35 miles from Cambrai and in the Cambrai diocese, and the Bishop of Cambrai was a great friend of Margaret. In fact, he was her confessor. Mechelen, another of Margaret's favourite residences, is in the same diocese.

Tom

Weren't there rumours she had his child, the bishop's child that is?[212]

Beth

Absolute nonsense, they were both morally above reproach;[213, 214] that was just another rumour put out by somebody, probably Robert Clifford,[215] but it's interesting you bring that up. Hold that thought for a minute or two.

Gates

But a bishop wouldn't know the common folk of Tournai, would he?

Beth

No, but Margaret's almoner, Nicholas Finet, might,[216] and he was a canon in Cambrai. Margaret herself founded several hospitals and schools,[217] so there's a possible link there also.

Tom

That still doesn't give you a link with Richard III.

Beth

Oh, but it does.
The Bishop of Cambrai was Henri of Berghes, who was the brother of John III of Glymes, and both were the sons of John II.[218] Both Johns, but particularly the father, were close associates of Richard III.[219] Possibly the last visitor Warbeck received just before his execution was

from a servant of Anthony of Berghes, who was Abbot of Flanders and brother to both Henri and John.[220] Even their sister was a close friend of Margaret, being supervisor of a training school at a convent in Mechelen.[213] The whole family were seemingly very close to the House of York.

Tom

The bishop and the duchess: come on, I can't hold that thought for much longer; men only have a short attention span supposedly.

Beth

Well, it struck me that Henry Tudor might also be aware of this link between the bishop, Margaret and Edward's son, so he tried to discredit all three of them in one go by suggesting Warbeck was a love child by him. This is what Robert Clifford claimed in 1495 anyway.[212, 215] Obviously untrue, but it was a way of somehow acknowledging any link between the three of them in a totally negative way.

Tom

Well, you've tried to explain away the language issue, but wouldn't the people of Tournai ask who this strange boy was who suddenly appeared in the Warbeck household?

Beth

I agree and I don't have a good answer. We must assume first that there was a boy called Perkin at some point – nobody seems to dispute that – and that he was probably about the same age as the Duke of York. There must have been a reason why the real Perkin disappeared and died – war maybe, or plague, I don't know – but there must have been a credible opening to slot our boy in.

Gates

But I still can't see how people wouldn't have said, 'hang on a minute, he doesn't look like your son'.

Beth

Again, agreed.

Maybe the boy had been gone from Tournai a few years so a change would be expected. The other thing that strikes me, it's not odd but still remarkable, is just how much time Warbeck spent away from his family. He was forever moving around to places where he wouldn't be known, like Antwerp and Middelburg, so that would go a long way to avoiding those difficult questions.

In fact, you ask why a prince would hide as a boatman's son. Well, he was hardly in Tournai with his let's call him 'father', he led a completely different life altogether. That's not all. One source suggests the Warbeck family weren't poor at all. When Nicaise Werbecque sold the family home in 1498, it was bought by the son of a merchant, so must have been a dwelling with some style. Then, when she died in 1513 her will ran to a sizeable 60 by 100cm. OK, a lot of that is probably the usual paying for prayers to be said, but there was enough money left to make various charitable bequests. She doesn't seem that cash-strapped to me.[221, 222]

Gates	Maybe, maybe not. Seven out of ten for effort, I'll give you that.
Tom	But where the Warbecks lived in Tournai was, apparently, a fairly rough part and the father was a violent drunk by all accounts.
Beth	Maybe at one time they were poor. Social mobility is possible, you know, just as your income doesn't determine how placid or aggressive you are.
Gates	Possibly, but …
Beth	There is one other scenario we haven't considered and that is that both of us are, one way or another, wrong about the Tournai connection.
Tom	What!!
Beth	It is possible that the captured Warbeck was who he claimed to be – York – but had nothing to do with the Warbeck family in Tournai.
Gates	Now you do have me confused.
Beth	Well, as far as I'm aware, during the whole period from Cork to Cornwall, Richard, if I can call him that, never said anything about *where* or *with whom* he had

been living post-1483.[223] All we have is his so-called confession, which may or may not be true. Think about the parallels with Simnel. Henry needed a cover story …

Tom

In your opinion …

Beth

In my opinion …, to obscure the truth.

You can't make up any old story, one that's easy to disprove. It must have a veneer of credibility. Simnel coming from Oxford where a Simnel family may have lived, and a Simnel there may have been a carpenter or a related profession, all probably true. On the other hand, too much detail might look good but makes you a hostage to fortune, too many places you can get caught out. So, make the detail fuzzy. We don't know anything definite about Simnel's father or if he was alive at the time of Stoke. It's unclear whether Lambert himself came from Oxford or was taken there, nor who tutored him into the role of pretender. Opportunities to clear up all these points were conveniently ignored. Then we have the priest who may have taught him appear and disappear in the bat of an eye, then another priest of the same surname does the same appear/disappear act after Stoke. Plausible deniability, the lot of it. Warbeck's history is very much the same. Maybe Henry knew Richard was in hiding somewhere near Margaret's home, so he makes up a story involving a family in Tournai, one with some facts that are easy to prove and make the pretender clearly an imposter, but still rough at the edges which leave him, Henry that is, some wiggle room. Warbeck seems to have had parallel lives, both based in Tournai, either a boatman's son moving into textiles or an educated boy good at music. Maybe there were two individuals in Tournai; the first is the real Warbeck and the second is York, with Henry building his story around the boatman's son. It's a point I tried to make in the trial but, not surprisingly, you – sorry, the judge – told me to stop playing games with the court.

The more you think about it, the more plausible this idea becomes. It means there is a grain of truth in all the various testimonies no matter which way they argue and how conflicting they seem. And we don't have to just eliminate whole swathes of testimony just because it doesn't fit whichever narrative we might have chosen. Take Brampton's testimony at Setubal, for example. He claimed Warbeck had been taught music and Latin, something we both dismissed as it didn't fit in with a boatman's son.[70] But if both Warbeck *and* Richard were in Tournai at about the same time, it would make sense.

Gates

OK, all very interesting, but I can see doubt written all over Tom's face.

Anyway, thank you both, I guess on that note of uncertainty we leave it for now.

Beth

Well, not quite. The story continues beyond this trial.

Gates

What?

Beth

Well, there are two things that are, shall we say, open-ended.

As you know, I believe Warbeck was the real deal, but his confession on the scaffold does worry me.[224] For me, it's the weakest part of my case and I'm glad Tom couldn't use this in the trial.

Warbeck would have heard confession, been in a state of grace, so to commit a sin – lying – as his last breath would have condemned him to eternal damnation, something he couldn't – wouldn't – do. If he was of noble blood, he would have believed in a king being God's anointed representative on Earth and would have been deeply religious. Committing a sin as his last act would have been unthinkable.

Tom

So, are you implying that after all we have just been through in court, he was an imposter?

Beth

I didn't say that, I just think it's something that requires more thought.

Tom

Oh dear, here it comes, straight out of left field.

Beth	Possibly, but here goes.

Are we certain that the man who was hanged was indeed Perkin Warbeck as named?

I am convinced Henry had serious doubts about Warbeck's true identity. Why else did he treat him so well after his capture? Why did he need to manufacture an excuse for having him executed? Did he know that his wife had guessed it was her brother he was holding? It's conjecture I know, but isn't it possible that Henry executed someone he said was Perkin Warbeck? It could have been anyone, and, because he claimed the Duke of York was already long dead, this kept the Spaniards happy so that the marriage of Arthur and Katherine could go ahead. The Spaniards wouldn't care if Warbeck was York or not, so long as he was dead.

Gates	OK, but how do you pull this stunt off?

Beth	We know that in all likelihood one of the three physical

signs which linked Warbeck to the Duke of York was his left eye. When the Bishop of Cambrai visited Warbeck in the Tower in 1498, he looked nothing like he had remembered him. At least, that's what de Puebla reported. He said how much altered Perkin was and that he was so much changed he didn't have long to live.[194] Apparently, he had been beaten the previous year and seemed unrecognizable.[224, 225] While I accept this was about a year before the execution,[226] who's to say how recognizable he might have been when he went to the scaffold?

And it might not have been the first time Henry had pulled this stunt. Henry's blind biographer, Bernard André, wrote that at Exeter, Henry's servants had 'mockingly beaten him [Warbeck]',[227] very handy if you intend to parade your prisoner around the country and not let incriminating marks around his eyes give the game away. So, in terms of the hanging, was there a possibility of facial disfigurement so that the use of a doppelganger, beaten around the face, wouldn't be noticed?

Tom

Who in their right mind volunteers to have themselves executed for someone else?

Beth

Henry could have got any convicted criminal from his jails and promised money to their family in exchange for undergoing the fate which would happen anyway. Knowing Henry, he would have found a way that cost him as little as possible; nothing at all if he could.

I think this is just how Henry would think – practical and pragmatic as ever. The Spanish were happy, his wife was happy and so long as Richard-slash-Warbeck kept quiet – and why wouldn't he, as he was hardly going to claim to still be alive for a second time – then it was job done.

Tom

OK, plausible but a bit thin.

Beth

Well, Katherine Gordon's part in all this is interesting. She was very well treated by Henry, except after her husband's first attempted escape, which came shortly after James IV had secured a peace deal with Henry but which still included a clause that allowed safe passage for the pretender's supporters. For almost a year after the first escape attempt, Katherine Gordon was absent from the royal accounts, so it seems she was being punished for something.[228] Did she help her husband in his escape? Does it signify she still believed in him? You probably don't know this, but in her will, Katherine left a small bequest to a Margaret Keymes, who she called 'cousin'. This Maragret was the daughter of Cecily, one of Edward IV's surviving daughters, so to call her 'cousin' implies she still believed her husband was also one of Edward's children.[229]

Her life after 1499 also raises questions. She was still well-treated, but wasn't allowed to leave England, not to go home to Scotland or anywhere else. Why? What danger did she pose? Was it somebody Henry was keeping her from seeing?

What's more, she could easily have had her marriage to Warbeck annulled as he was not who he claimed to be when the marriage was sanctified, but she didn't, nor did she marry again while Henry was alive.

Tom   Yeh, the old lecher fancied her and wouldn't let her.

Gates   Let's keep this clean, please.

Beth   What's more, after 1509 she remarried three times. Don't you think that's odd?

Tom   What, you think that's when Richard-slash-Warbeck actually died?

Beth   Possibly. I confess, it's just as likely as being when Henry, the seventh that is, no longer had a hold over her. Who knows? As I said, it's a loose end that still needs explaining, but I do have a more speculative explanation if you are interested.

Gates   Go on then, it's too late to turn back now.

Beth   Well, let's suppose I'm right and Richard-slash-Warbeck wasn't executed in 1499. What happened to him?

Tom   We don't know, but I'm sure you're going to tell us!

Beth   Have you ever heard of Richard of Eastwell? I thought not.
Well, there was an oral tradition with the Fiches family of Eastwell, Earls of Winchelsea, which found its way into print in the 1800s.[230, 231] To cut a long story short, a Sir Walter Moyle built Eastwick Place in the mid-sixteenth century and noticed that a builder he employed spent his spare time reading, in fact reading Latin texts. When probed about his background, about which he was generally secretive, he told the story that, as a boy, he had been taken to Richard III's tent on the eve of Bosworth and told he was Richard's son.[231]

Gates   Wait a minute. Why have we never heard of this son – a bastard, I assume – when we have heard of two other bastard children Richard owned up to fathering, John and Katherine?[232]

Beth   Well spotted. The suggestion is that this boy is, in fact, the son of Edward IV who King Richard made illegitimate by virtue of *Titulus Regius*. Richard told him that if he won the battle he would acknowledge him, and if he lost, well, the boy should keep all this to himself and disappear.

Tom   And did he?

Beth   Well, one historian[231] has him living in Colchester under the care of the Abott of St John's until the dissolution of the monasteries, after which he somehow ended up in Eastwell.
You may think all this is a bit off-the-wall, but strange things happened in Colchester after 1485. There was a well-known sanctuary in the abbey there, and Francis Lovell and two Stafford brothers – same family as our old friend the Duke of Buckingham of Rebellion fame – holed up there after Bosworth. What's interesting is that Henry Tudor, Henry VII as he now was, paid next to no attention to this sanctuary; indeed, Lovell and his mates were there for six months.

Gates   And you think they took this 'illegitimate boy' there with them?

Beth   It's possible.

Gates   But I still don't see how this links with Perkin Warbeck, which is how this all started.

Beth   As far as I know, this hasn't been suggested by others, though it has been mooted, as I mentioned earlier, that he might be one of the sons of Edward IV, probably the younger boy, Richard. In previous speculation along these lines, Richard of York-slash-Richard of Eastwell was in and around Colchester after Bosworth until he turned up in Kent,[231] which is a long time with no sign of what he was up to. I don't agree with this, so the alternative Warbeck link is my own speculation.

Tom   And the basis for it is?

Beth   First, on 12 February 1512, Henry VIII issued a pardon for a Richard Grey of Colchester, alias of North Creke, Norfolk, yeoman or labourer.[233] Grey was the name of Elizabeth Woodville by her first husband, we have already established a possible link with Colchester *and* he is named as a labourer, as was Richard of Eastwell. Is this Richard-slash-Warbeck still alive after his supposed execution in 1499?

Gates   OK, a possible connection, but far from proven.

Beth   True, but despite all this speculation there is one indisputable fact associated with this Fiche family oral tradition. The parish register for Eastwell records the death of a Richard Plantagenet on 22 December 1550.[231] Fact. Edward IV's illegitimate son was named Arthur Plantagenet before Henry VIII made him Lord Lisle, so for a Yorkist royal bastard to be called 'Plantagenet' has precedent.

Tom   But that's Arthur Plantagenet, not Perkin Warbeck.

Beth   Patience, my boy, patience.
    Although in the trial I claimed Warbeck was error-free in everything he said or did with regard to his identity as Richard, Duke of York, that isn't *entirely* true.

Tom   What!?

Beth   Well, it's not a mistake, really, more you could say a slip of the tongue.
    It is reported by Giles Daubeney that Richard-slash-Warbeck once referred to himself as Richard Plantaganet[234] and, don't forget, he signed off his letter to Isabella of Spain with 'Richard Plantagenet, second son

of Edward IV'.[49] Hardly an error, I would say, but I'm suggesting it may be a very tenuous link to the man now known as Richard of Eastwell. Edward IV's younger son might have taken Richard Grey as his post-1499 alias, but on his deathbed, he wanted to be remembered to posterity as who he truly was, Richard Plantagenet, second son of Edward IV.

Gates
Not so fast there. If this is true, going back to our discussion of Katherine Gordon and her marriages after 1509, what you are saying would make her a bigamist three times over.

Beth
Well spotted, sir, and I can't deny it's a blow to my argument, but not, I suggest, a fatal one.

If Henry did oblige his queen by not executing her brother, he is hardly likely to have made this widely known. It seems to me both plausible and good tactics to allow Katherine Gordon to believe her husband was dead, and it helps cement the end to the Warbeck saga in the world's eyes. Katherine Gordon committing bigamy was hardly her fault, given what she knew.

Gates
… or didn't know, more to the point.

Beth
Exactly. If Henry did go down this route, it hardly makes it into the top ten of Tudor crimes, does it?

Gates
Well, it does tie loose ends together, but by the thinnest of threads.

Tom
So, you said there was a second loose end as well, if Warbeck avoiding death as Richard of Eastwell wasn't enough.

Beth
OK. If you thought the first loose end was whacky, hold tight for the second.

Have you ever heard of Jack Leslau?

Gates
No, should we?

Beth	He was a writer, amateur historian and art enthusiast, interested in the Wars of the Roses, and he did some independent research. He found out that in 1488 a man named John Clement enrolled at University in Louvain, in what is now Belgium.[235] What makes this unusual is that he is the only person ever not to sign against his name in the entry register.
Tom	So?
Beth	Well, Leslau's conjecture is that John Clement was not his real name; he was hiding his real identity.
	Now, there is a painting by Holbein of the family of Sir Thomas More, currently hanging in Nostell Priory in Yorkshire. All the family members except one can be identified, and Leslau claims this is a John Clement, who appeared in More's household during the reign of Henry VIII.
	Holbein had a reputation for hiding messages in his paintings – *The Ambassadors* is the best-known example[236] – and Leslau found elements of the More family portrait which suggested the unknown man – John Clement – was of royal descent. Some of what Leslau claimed is believable, but it does spiral into Dan Brown territory as his theory unravels.[235]
	What makes this John Clement interesting is that he became President of the Royal College of Physicians and is the only President not to sign against his name in the register. Same story again. Spooky or what?
	This Clement died in 1572 and is buried in the royal part of the church in Mechelen, sometimes called Malines, which is its French name, apparently next to the grave of Margaret of Burgundy. Leslau thinks this John Clement is Richard, Duke of York.
Gates	Hold on a minute. Richard was born in 1473, he dies in 1572, making him 99. Totally implausible.
Beth	Absolutely, they can't be the same person. But this is where my theory comes in.

Tom	Deep sigh!
Beth	It seems to me that there are two John Clements, who may or may not be related.[237] The older Louvain JC might be Edward, the elder son of Edward IV. Maybe he saw what happened at the Battle of Stoke in 1487 and decided that was enough of trying to reclaim his throne. Like the physician John Clement, this other JC didn't sign his name in the university register. The lack of a signature suggests this Clement, whoever he was, was also hiding something. Having said this, it would make more sense if this first John Clement was Richard, Duke of York and the two Clements were father and son, which would make sense given the common surname. The problem is, the timeline is ambiguous. We don't know exactly when Warbeck left Flanders for Portugal, but after Easter 1486 is often quoted but without evidence. JC the first could only be Richard-slash-Warbeck if he left Flanders much later, sometime in 1488, after the Louvain registration. Possible, so we can't rule this out, but until somebody turns up a more accurate date for Warbeck sailing into the sunset we can't make a judgement. Let's park the identity of this older Clement for now, because it doesn't easily lead us anywhere as things Warbeck stand.
Gates	Pity, but go on.
Beth	My theory about the Clement in More's household is this. You know Richard-slash-Warbeck had a son.[166] It's fairly well established, but I didn't dwell on it in the trial as it doesn't have any bearing on his father's identity.
Gates	There may have been more than one child. It's speculation, but it has been suggested Katherine Gordon was pregnant when the ships landed in Whitesands Bay in Cornwall, and that she miscarried.[166, 238, 239]
Beth	True, but again a sideshow. What appears to be the case is that the boy we can be fairly sure existed went with her to London after her

husband's capture. According to Wroe, this boy then just disappeared,[171] which takes us to the land of guesswork and hypothesis.

Gates

And clearly you have one.

Beth

I was looking at things from the perspective of Queen Elizabeth.

A man is brought to court who for nearly a decade has claimed to be your brother. He has persuaded many around Europe to believe this, including your aunt. But you are not allowed to see him, to make the key judgement.

So, what do you do? You interrogate the one person who knows him well, his wife, the person who is now your lady-in-waiting. You would ask her what she knew, you would ask about the physical signs that nobody knows about or has seen but would have been exposed in the intimacy of the bedroom. You might look at her one-year old boy and search for a family resemblance.

Tom

He's got a Plantagenet nose, that sort of thing?

Beth

That sort of thing. It seems Warbeck and Edward IV looked alike, at least in the two portraits we have of them.

I'm only guessing here, but if you came to the conclusion Katherine Gordon's husband was your brother, you would realize pretty quickly that his son, your nephew, would be in danger. While Henry hesitated over what to do with the father, wouldn't your instinct coincide with that of the mother and want him away and safe?

Gates

And you are going to tell us what became of him?

Beth

No, but I'll suggest. Where would you send him?

Tom

Flanders?

Beth

In 1496 or 1497, about the time Warbeck's son was born, a room at Margaret's residence at Binche was renamed 'Richard's room'.[240] It wouldn't be a surprise, would it, if

Richard-slash-Warbeck had named his son Richard, after himself?

In 1499, the year Warbeck was executed, Margaret gave funds for the education of an English boy for sixteen years.[241] Now we come back to More and John Clement. Somewhere between 1509 and, say, 1512, a John Clement enrolled at St Paul's School in London.[242] There was probably a school there before, but around 1509 a John Colet established the school which still exists today. The entry requirements were an ability to read and write and some knowledge of classics, things you might expect of the boy if he had spent some time in Margaret's care. What's more interesting is Clement's entry – or rather, lack of it – in the admissions register. Details for these early pupils are sketchy, but you usually get some basic stuff, when they were born, where they come from, their parents' names.

Gates	And I'm guessing none of this exists for Clement?
Beth	Nothing. Zip, zilch, *de nada*. It starts – starts, mind you – with 'he was taken from St Paul's school by Sr Thomas More'.[242] This is probably in 1515, when he accompanies More on an embassy to Flanders. He subsequently goes to university in Oxford and then joins More's household. He even gets a mention in the preface to More's famous *Utopia*.[243]
Gates	And you think the lack of a family background is hiding the fact he was Warbeck's son, raised by Margaret of Burgundy.
Beth	Exactly. No proof, just speculation.
Gates	Well, the dates are about right. Sixteen years after 1499 is 1515.
Tom	And, if he is Warbeck's son and was born in 1496, when he died in 1572 he was 76. Not unreasonable; certainly better than 99.

Beth	One last jigsaw piece, for what it's worth. Clement was buried in Mechelen, in a tomb close to that of his great-aunt Margaret. That wouldn't happen to a commoner, suggesting he was of royal blood, which he was if he was the son of the Duke of York.
Gates	But how do you connect Margaret of Burgundy and Thomas More with this John Clement?
Beth	Guesswork again, I'm afraid, but this is how I see it. Margaret's court was full of scholars. Jean le Sauvage, he who was commissioned to negotiate the release of the captured Warbeck, was one. Another was Erasmus. Erasmus was a friend of Thomas More. He first visited him in London in 1499 and was a close friend until More was executed in 1535. Could that be the connection? Erasmus was also one-time secretary to the Bishop of Cambrai, Henri of Berghes, *and* he knew John Colet of St Paul's fame, helping him find staff for the new school.
	Speculation, I know, but the circumstantial evidence for linking More, Clement and Flanders builds up. The plot thickens, doesn't it?
Gates	Go on then, if there's more, to pardon the pun. It's pointless stopping now!
Beth	Well, interestingly, More took Clement with him to Antwerp in 1515, where he wrote *Utopia*, and during this period he – maybe both of them – visited Jerome Busleyden at Mechelen.[245] Jerome arrived in Mechelen around the time of Margaret of Burgundy's death in 1503, so was probably not acquainted with her, but his older brother, Francis, certainly was. Francis was appointed, by Margaret, as tutor to her step-grandson, Philip.[246, 247] Francis was secretary to Henri de Berghes, Bishop of Cambrai …
Gates	Another one, just like Erasmus! Wasn't he another of Henri's secretaries?

Beth	Exactly. And remember, old Henri was one of Warbeck's last visitors. Francis died in 1502, so was not a direct correspondent with More, but we keep coming back to links between Clement and Warbeck through Henri de Berghes, his secretaries and Flanders.
Tom	You tell a good story, but why would More, a friend of the Tudors – at least until the time they beheaded him – do this?
Beth	I don't know. Some people think More's damning history of Richard III is so OTT that it's a front and he was a Yorkist all along. Maybe Clement persuaded him his father – Warbeck – actually was Richard, Duke of York, and that Richard III was innocent. To cover his tracks and the boy's true identity, More wrote his sycophantic history. I admit, I don't really know. More never published his history in his own lifetime, so maybe he had second thoughts about it.
	Still more loose ends, but an intriguing theory, don't you think? Oh, and for what it's worth – and it's probably just a coincidence – Warbeck was hanged on 23 November, which is St Clement's Day.
Gates	And much to chew on.
Usher	The jury's back.
Gates	So, let's hear what they have to say. Your Leslau theory will have to wait.

Bibliography and Electronic Resources

Amin, N., *Henry VII and the Tudor Pretenders* (Amberley, 2020).

Amin, N., *The House of Beaufort* (Amberley, 2018)

André, B., *The Life of Henry VII*, trans. D. Hobbins (Ithica Press, 2011).

Bernard André, De Vita atque Gestis Henrici Septimi Historia, trans. D. Sutton. www.philological.bham.ac.uk/andreas/1e.html

Anglo, S., *Bulletin of the John Rylands Library*, Vol. 43 (September 1960), www.escholar.manchester.ac.uk/api/datastream?publicationPid=uk-ac-man-scw:1m2839&datastreamId=POST-PEER-REVIEW-PUBLISHERS-DOCUMENT.PDF

Annals of Ulster, B. MacCarthy (ed.) (HMSO, 1887), https://archive.org/details/annalauladhannal03magu/page/n5/mode/2up. For a more recent translation, CELT: Corpus of Electronic Texts: a project of University College Cork, https://celt.ucc.ie/published/T100001C/.

Anstey, H. (ed.), *Epistolae Academicae Oxon, Registrum F* (Clarendon Press, 1898), https://archive.org/details/epistolaeacademi02univiala/mode/2up?view=theater

Arthurson, I., *The Perkin Warbeck Conspiracy 1491–1499* (The History Press, 2009).

Ashdown-Hill, J., *Eleanor, The Secret Queen* (The History Press, 2010).

Ashdown-Hill, J., *Elizabeth Woodville: Lady Grey* (Pen & Sword History, 2019).

Ashdown-Hill, J., *The Dublin King* (The History Press, 2015).

Ashdown-Hill, J., *The Third Plantaganet* (The History Press, 2014).

Bacon, F., *The history of the reign of King Henry the Seventh*, B. Vickers (ed.) (CUP, 1998), https://archive.org/details/historyofreignof0000baco/page/n5/mode/2up.

Baldwin, D., *The Lost Prince* (The History Press, 2008).

Bennett, M., *Lambert Simnel and the Battle of Stoke* (Alan Sutton, 1993).

Bentley, S. (ed.), *Excerpta Historica, or Illustrations of English History* (S. Bentley, 1831), https://archive.org/details/excerptahistoric00bentuoft/page/n7/mode/2up.

Bibliographie Nationale (Brussels, 1938), vol. 27, www.academieroyale.be/ Academie/documents/FichierPDFBiographieNationaleTome2078.pdf.

Blockmans, W., 'The Devotion of a Lonely Duchess', in *Margaret of York, Simon Marmion, and the Visions of Tondal*, Thomas Kren (ed.) (1992), https://1library.net/document/zk88e81z-the-devotion-of-a-lonely-duchess. html.

Blunt, J.H., *Tewkesbury Abbey and Its Associations* (Simpkin, Marshall, Hamilton, Kent & Co, 1898), https://books.google.co.uk/books?id=Jw8 H A A A A Q A A J & p g = P A 7 7 & s o u r c e = g b s _ t o c _ r & c a d = 4 # v = onepage&q&f=false.

Bradley, S., *John Morton* (Amberley, 2019).

Brewer, J.S. & Bullen, W. (eds), 'Book of Howth' in *Calendar of the Carew Manuscripts*, Vol. 5 (Longman & Co, 1871), https://catalog.hathitrust.org/ Record/007689510.

Brown, J. & Brown, E., *The de la Poles, Earls and Dukes of Suffolk* (Wingfield, 2000).

Busch, W.H, *England Under the Tudors, King Henry VII* (Burt Franklin, 1895), https://archive.org/details/englandundertudo01buscuoft/page/n5/mode/2up.

Campbell, W. (ed.), *Materials for a History of the Reign of Henry VII* (1873–77), Vol. II, https://archive.org/details/materialsforhist02camp/mode/2up.

Carson, A., *The Maligned King* (The History Press, 2013).

Cavel, E. (ed.), *The Herald's Memoir, 1486–1490: Court Ceremony, Royal Progress and Rebellion* (Richard III Society and York History Trust, 2009).

CCR, Calendar of Close Rolls, 1476–1485 and 1485–1500, www.british-history.ac.uk/cal-close-rolls/edw4/1476-85, and https://catalog.hathitrust. org/Record/100884588, respectively.

Conway, A., *Henry VII's Relations with Scotland and Ireland 1485–1498 (CUP, 1932)*, https://archive.org/details/henryviisrelatio0000conw/page/242/mode/2up.

Coombs, B.J., *Scots Patronage of the Visual Arts in France, c. 1445–1545" (University of Edinburgh)*, https://era.ed.ac.uk/bitstream/handle/1842/11726/ Coombs2013vol1.pdf?sequence=2&isAllowed=y.

CPR, Calendar of Patent Rolls, (1399–1413), https://catalog.hathitrust.org/ Record/100574304; (1476–85), https://catalog.hathitrust.org/Record/100696925; (1485–1509), https://catalog.hathitrust.org/Record/100884609.

CPRR, Calendar of Papal Registers Relating To Great Britain and Ireland: Volume 14, 1484–1492, www.british-history.ac.uk/cal-papal-registers/brit-ie/vol14/pp305-309.

Crowland Chronicle, *Ingulph's Chronicle of the Abbey of Crowland with the Continuations by Peter of Blois and Anonymous*, https://archive.org/details/ ingulphschronicl00ingu/page/488/mode/2up.

CSPM, Calendar of State Papers and Manuscripts in the Archives and Collections of Milan 1385-1618, A.B. Hinds (ed.) (HMSO, 1912), www.british-history.ac.uk/cal-state-papers/milan/1385-1618.

CSPS, Calendar of letters, despatches, and state papers, relating to the negotiations between England and Spain, preserved in the archives at Simancas, Vienna, Brussels, and elsewhere, G.A. Bergenroth (ed.), Vol. 1, 1495–1509 (Public Records Office, 1862), https://catalog.hathitrust.org/Record/012410733.

CSPV, Calendar of State papers Relating to English Affairs in the Archives of Venice, www.british-history.ac.uk/cal-state-papers/venice/vol1, www.british-history.ac.uk/cal-state-papers/venice/vol4.

Curtis, *Calendar of Ormond Deeds*, Vol. III, www.irishmanuscripts.ie/product/calendar-of-ormond-deeds-vol-iii-1413-1509-6-vols-1932-43/.

David, S., *Last Champion of York; Francis Lovell, Richard III's Truest Friend* (The Crowood Press Ltd, 2019).

De But, *Chroniques relatives à l'histoire de Belgique sous la domination des Ducs de Bourgogne*, J.M.B.C. Kervyn de Lettenhove, (Commission Royale d'Histoire, Brussels, 1870), https://archive.org/details/chroniquesrelati01kervuoft/mode/2up (in Latin).

Dickson, T. (ed.), *Accounts of the Lord High Treasurer of Scotland* (H.M. General Register House, 1877), https://catalog.hathitrust.org/Record/011743009.

Ellis, H., *Original Letters, illustrative of English History*, 2nd ed. (Harding, Triphook & Lepard, 1825), https://catalog.hathitrust.org/Record/000310368.

Emden, A.B., *A Biographical Register of the University of Oxford to AD 1500* (Clarendon Press, 1957–59).

Excerpta Historica, or Illustrations of English History, S. Bentley (ed.) (S. Bentley, 1831), https://archive.org/details/excerptahistoric00bentuoft/page/114/mode/2up.

Fabyan, R., *The Great Chronicle of London*", A.H. Thomas & I.D. Thornley (eds) (Corporation of the City of London, 1938).

Gairdner, J., *History of the life and reign of Richard the Third, to which is added the story of Perkin Warbeck: from original documents* (CUP, 1898), https://archive.org/details/historyofliferei00gairuoft/mode/2up.

Gairdner, J. (ed.), *The Paston Letters, 1422–1509 AD* (A. Constable, 1895), https://catalog.hathitrust.org/Record/008957524.

Gairdner, R.B. (ed.), *Admission Register of St Paul's School* (G. Bell, 1884), https://archive.org/details/admissionregiste00stpa/page/n9/mode/2up.

Halliwell-Phillips, J.O., *Letters of the Kings of England: now first collected from the originals in royal archives, and from other authentic sources, private as well as public*, H. Colburn (ed.) (H. Colburn, 1846), https://catalog.hathitrust.org/Record/008644776.

Hall, E., *Hall's Chronicle : containing the history of England, during the reign of Henry the Fourth, and the succeeding monarchs, to the end of the reign of Henry the Eighth, in which are particularly described the manners and customs of those periods. Carefully collated with the editions of 1548 and 1550* (J. Johnson, 1809), https://archive.org/details/hallschronicleco00halluoft/page/n3/mode/2up.

Hammond, P., *The Children of Richard III* (Fonthill Media, 2017).

Harleian 433, http://ricardianresources.online.

Hayden, M.T., *Studies: An Irish Quarterly Review*, Vol. 4 (1925).

Hicks, M.A., *False, Fleeting, Perjur'd Clarence* (Alan Sutton, 1980).

Horne, *Fasti Ecclesiae Anglicanae 1300–1541*, www.british-history.ac.uk/fasti-ecclesiae/1300-1541/vol8/v.

HRSH, Historia Regis Henrici Septimi, a Bernardo Andrea Tholosate Conscripta, J. Gairdner (ed.) (Longman, Brown, Green, Longmans and Roberts, 1858), https://archive.org/details/historiaregishen00gair/mode/2up (partly in Latin).

Kleyn, D.M., *Richard of England* (The Kensal Press, Oxford, 1990).

LC, Chronicle of London (Vitellius A XVI), C.L. Kingsford (ed.) (Clarendon Press, 1905), https://archive.org/details/chroniclesoflond00kinguoft.

L&P, Letters and Papers Illustrative of the Reigns of Richard III and Henry VII, J. Gairdner (ed.), 2 volumes, https://archive.org/details/letterspapersill01gair.

L&P, Letters and Papers, Foreign and Domestic, Henry VIII, Vol. 1, 1509–1514, https://archive.org/details/letterspapersfor01greauoft/mode/2up; *Vol. 4, 1524–1530*, https://www.british-history.ac.uk/letters-papers-hen8/vol4.

Langley, P., *The Princes in the Tower : Solving History's Greatest Cold Case* (The History Press, 2023).

Leslau, www.holbeinartworks.org/#Bookmark40.

Lewis, M., *The Survival of the Princes in the Tower* (The History Press, 2017).

Leyland, J., in *Collectanea*, Vol. 4 (1774), https://catalog.hathitrust.org/Record/000273389

Madden, F., *Documents Relating to Perkin Warbeck, with Remarks on His History: Communicated to the Society of Antiquaries* (J.B. Nichols and Son, 1837), https://catalog.hathitrust.org/Record/000313271.

Mancini, D., *Domenico Mancini: de Occupatione Regni Anglie*, trans. by A. Carson (Imprimis Imprimatur, 2020).

Merriam, T., *Moreana*, XXV (1988), www.holbeinartworks.org/#Bookmark1.

Molinet, J., *Chroniques de Jean Molinet/publiées pour la première fois d'après les manuscrits de la Bibliothèque du roi; par J-A Buchon*, https://catalog.hathitrust.org/Record/000413249 (in French).

More, T., *Utopia*, trans. by D. Baker-Smith (Penguin Classics, 2012).

Nicholas, N.H., *Privy purse expenses of Elizabeth of York: Wardrobe Accounts of Edward the Fourth* (W. Pickering, 1830), https://catalog.hathitrust.org/Record/000313257.

Nichols, J. & Gough, R., *A Collection of All the Wills, Now Known to be Extant of the Kings and Queens of England, Princes and Princesses of Wales, and Every Branch of the Blood Royal* (J. Nichols, 1780), https://archive.org/details/acollectionallw00nichgoog/mode/2up.

North, J., *The Ambassadors' Secrets* (Phoenix, 2004).

Paul, J.B. (ed.), *Register of the Great Seal of Scotland, AD 1306–1668* (General Register House, 1882), https://archive.org/details/registrummagnisi02scot/mode/2up?view=theater.

Pollard, A.F., *The Reign of Henry VII from Contemporary Sources* (Longmans, Green and Co, 1913), https://archive.org/details/reignofhenryviif01polliala/page/n7/mode/2up.

Rymwwe, T. (ed.), *Rymer's Fœdera*, Vol. 12, www.british-history.ac.uk/rymer-foedera/vol12/pp672-682 (in Latin).

Regesta Imperii, Maximilliam I (1486/1493–1519), www.regesta-imperii.de/id/1497-11-17_1_0_14_2_0_1853_5512.

Rotuli Parliamentorum, *Parliament Rolls of Medieval England*, www.british-history.ac.uk/no-series/parliament-rolls-medieval (by date), https://books.google.co.uk/books?id=ZzFDAAAAcAAJ&printsec=frontcover&redir_esc=y#v=onepage&q&f=false (Volume 6, by page number).

Sanuto, M., *I Diarii de Marino Sanuto*, Vol. 1, cols 825–26 (in Italian) (F Visentini, 1879), https://archive.org/details/idiariidimarino00unkngoog/page/n405/mode/2up.

Schillings, A. (ed.), *Matricul de l'Université de Louvain* (1925).

Schofield, C.L., *The Life and Reign of Edward the Fourth, King of England and France and Lord of Ireland*, Vol. 1 (Longmans, Green and Company, 1923), https://archive.org/details/thelifeandreignofedwardthefo1/mode/2up?q=Monypenny.

Skidmore, C., *Bosworth* (Weidenfeld & Nicolson, 2013).

Smith, R.F.W. & Watson, G.L. (eds), *Writing the Lives of People and Things, AD 500–1700* (Ashgate Publishing, 2016), https://centaur.reading.ac.uk/57353/1/014_Chapter_5_Smith.f.1.pdf.

Spont, A., *La Marine Française Sous le Règne de Charles VIII, 1483–1493* (Bureaux de la Revue, 1894), https://catalog.hathitrust.org/Record/000455908.

Stapleton, T. (ed.), *Plumpton Correspondence: a series of letters, chiefly domestick, written in the reigns of Edward IV, Richard III, Henry VII and*

Henry VIII (Camden Society, J.B. Nichols and Son, 1839), https://archive. org/details/trent_0116401961713/mode/2up.

St Paul's School, https://archive.org/details/admissionregiste00stpa/page/n9/ mode/2up.

Stow, J., *The Annales or Generall Chronicle of England* (T. Adams, 1615), https://catalog.hathitrust.org/Record/100217153.

Sutton, A.F. & Hammond, P.W., *Coronation of Richard III: The Extant Documents* (Sutton Publishing Ltd, 1983).

The Ricardian, www.thericardian.online/the_ricardian.php#1997.

Tytler, P.F., *History of Scotland*, Vol. 4 (William Tait, 1831), www. electricscotland.com/history/scotland/history38s.pdf.

Vatican Regestra, *Calendar of Papal Registers Relating To Great Britain and Ireland: Volume 14, 1484–1492*, Vol. DCCLXIX, www.british-history.ac.uk/ cal-papal-registers/brit-ie/vol14/pp305-309#highlight-first.

Vergil, *The Anglia Historia of Polydore Vergil, A.D. 1485–1537*, D. Hay (ed.), Camden Series 3, Vol. 74, (Longmans, Green and Co, 1900–63), https:// catalog.hathitrust.org/Record/007560515.

Vergil, *The Anglia Historia of Polydore Vergil Anglia Historica (1555 Version); Henry VII*, D.F. Sutton, www.philological.bham.ac.uk/polverg/.

Wedgwood, J. (ed.), *History of Parliament: Biographies of The Members of the Commons House 1439–1509* (HMSO, 1936), https://archive.org/details/ in.ernet.dli.2015.210096/page/n959/mode/2up.

Weightman, C., *Margaret of York: The Diabolical Duchess* (Amberley, 2009).

Wilkins, D., *Concilia Magnae Britanniae et Hiberniae*, Vol. 3 (1737), https:// catalog.hathitrust.org/Record/001399780 (in Latin).

Williams, C.H., 'The Rebellion of Humphrey Stafford in 1486', *Eng. Hist. Rev.*, Vol. 43 (1928).

Williamson, A., *The Mystery of the Princes in the Tower* (Sutton Publishing, 2002).

Wroe, A., *The Perfect Prince* (Random House, 2003).

References

References below marked (*) are available electronically.

PART I

1. The current twenty-first-century format for numbering calendar years is adopted throughout this work, even though in the fifteenth century the year ran from 25 March (Lady Day) to the following 24 March. Thus, 1 February 1486 in the fifteenth century would be 1 February 1487 under our current system, where the new year begins on 1 January.

2. For legitimization by Richard II, S. Bentley, *Excerpta Historica* (London, 1831), pp.153–54(*). This act was reiterated by Henry IV (CPR, Henry IV, 1405–1408, p.284 (*)), but with the caveat that they be 'admitted to all honours, dignities, except to the royal dignity'. To complicate matters, while the original Act of Richard II was passed by Parliament, the reiteration, with its caveat, was not. Therefore, the caveat was legally contestable and the Beauforts still had something of a claim to the throne; Amin, N., *The House of Beaufort*, pp.82–83.

3. An Act of Parliament issued in 1484, better known as *Titulus Regius*, set out Richard III's right to the throne based on the invalidity of the marriage between Edward IV and Elizabeth Woodville, and thus the illegitimacy of their children; *Rot. Parl.*, 23 January – 20 February, 1494; Vol. 6, p.240 (*).

4. A full text of *Titulus Regius* can be found at www.richardiii.net/2_7_0_riii_documents.php.

5. Henry went into exile with his uncle Jasper Tudor after Edward IV regained the throne after the battles of Barnet and Tewkesbury in 1471; it was Duke Francis of Brittany who supported Tudor's aborted invasion of 1483. He subsequently fled to France in 1484 after being warned Richard III was negotiating with Piere Landois, Prime Minister of Brittany, to have him extradited; it was Charles VIII who supported the 1485 invasion.

6. Namely, Thomas Stanley, Earl of Derby, husband of Margaret Beaufort and stepfather to Henry Tudor, and his brother, William Stanley.

7. C.H. Williams, 'The Rebellion of Humphrey Stafford in 1486', *Eng. Hist. Rev.*, Vol. 43, No. 170 (1928), pp.181–89.

8. S. David, *Last Champion of York; Francis Lovell, Richard III's Truest Friend*, pp.14–23.

9. David, pp.158–61.

10. Usually referred to as Elizabeth of York, but not to be confused with the eldest daughter of Edward IV and Elizabeth Woodville, also known as Elizabeth of York and queen to Henry VII.

11. J. Brown & E. Brown, *The de la Poles, Earls and Dukes of Suffolk*.

12. J. Ashdown-Hill, *Eleanor, The Secret Queen*, pp.99–109.

13. Henry delayed the queen's coronation, however, to downplay any suspicion that his right to rule was *only* based on his marriage.

14. The report concerning these messengers appears in Bernard André's history before he reports on Lincoln leaving for Flanders, which was the beginning of February 1487.

15. The name of the Herald is left blank in André's account. Two possible names are John Wrythe, the Garter King of Arms, as suggested by Ashdown-Hill (*The Dublin King*, p.23), or Roger Machado, Richmond King of Arms and Henry VII's personal herald. Machado owned a house on Simnel Street in Southampton, which may be significant (*Writing the Lives of People and Things, AD 500–1700*, R.F.W. Smith & G.L. Watson (eds), Ashgate Publishing, 2016, Chapter 5 (*)); he was also involved in the search for Perkin Warbeck (see Part II). John Yonge, Falcon Pursuivant, who was sent to Ireland in the autumn of 1486 'on his [the king's] secret business', is a further possibility. R. Jones, *Ricardian Bulletin* (March 2012), p.49.

16. David, pp.206–13, for a discussion of a body found in Minster Lovell which *may* have been that of Francis Lovell.

17. J. Ashdown-Hill, *The Dublin King* (2015).

18. M. Bennett, *Lambert Simnel and the Battle of Stoke*.

19. N.A. Amin, *Henry VII and the Tudor Pretenders*.

20. *Chroniques relatives à l'histoire de Belgique sous la domination des Ducs de Bourgogne* (hereafter de But), J.M.B.C. Kervyn de Lettenhove, Commission Royale d'Histoire (Brussels, 1870), pp.210–717(*).

21. *Chroniques de Jean Molinet/publiées pour la première fois d'après les manuscrits de la Bibliothèque du roi; par J-A Buchon* (hereafter Molinet), Vol. 3 (*).

22. A. Carson, *The Maligned King*, p.336.

23. Bernard André, *The Life of Henry VII* (hereafter André/Hobbins), trans. D. Hobbins (Ithica Press, 2011). Bernard André, *De Vita atque Gestis Henrici Septimi Historia* (hereafter André/Sutton), trans. D.F. Sutton (*). The former translation appears closer to André's words, while the latter uses more contemporary language.

24. D.R. Carlson, 'André [Andreas], Bernard', *Oxford Dictionary of National Biographies* (hereafter ODNB) (2004).

25. *The Anglica Historica of Polydore Vergil, AD 1485–1537*, D. Hay (ed.), Camden Third Series, Vol. 74 (*) (hereafter Vergil/Hay); *The Anglia Historia of Polydore Vergil Anglia Historica (1555 Version); Henry VII*, D.F. Sutton (hereafter Vergil/Sutton) (*).

26. G. Smith, *The Ricardian*, Vol. 10 (1996), pp.502, 525 n. 29 (*).

27. W.J. Connell, *ODNB* (2004), *Vergil, Polydore*.

28. Most significantly, Elizabeth of York, the future queen.

29. Ashdown-Hill, *The Dublin King*, p.43; Bennett, p.121.

30. *York Civic Records*, A Raine (ed.), Vol. 2 (1941), pp.20–21.

31. E. Curtis, *Cal. Ormond Deeds*, Vol. III (1935), pp.vii, xxv, 261–63 (*); see also Ashdown-Hill, *The Dublin King*, pp.141–43. The year this letter was written is not stated and is open to debate. Langley, in defence of her assertion that the Dublin Pretender was Edward V, dates this letter as 1486, but this would only correspond to regnal year 1 of his reign if it dated from August 1485. P Langley, *The Princes in the Tower*, p.426; see also ref. 33, below.

32. https://virtualtreasury.ie/item?isadgReferenceCode=NLI%20 Ormond%2FD%2F1855.

33. For comparison, regnal year 1 Henry VI is 1422, the year he succeeded to the throne, despite the fact he was not crowned until he was 7 years old (1429; regnal year 8 Henry VI). He died in 1471, regnal year 49 Henry VI, the continuous numbering despite the intervening reign of Edward IV (1461–70).

34. Ashdown-Hill, *The Dublin King*, pp.136–41.

35. *Domenico Mancini: de Occupatione Regni Anglie*, trans. A. Carson, p.65. Mancini was an Italian, probably of the Augustinian order, working in England on behalf of Angelo Cato, Archbishop of Vienne, France, between late 1482 and summer 1483. He was essentially spying on behalf of the archbishop, possibly anticipating a war between England and France.

36. *Colchester Oath Book*, f 107r; *The Oath Book, or Red Parchment Book of Colchester*, W.G. Bentham (ed.) (1907), p.134. See also Ashdown-Hill, *The Dublin King*, pp.48–51, for a wider discussion.

37. Vergil/Hay, pp.22–23, '*Et quamuis ... corononatum*' (*). See also Smith, pp.510, 529 n. 81.
38. André/Hobbins, pp.44–45; André/Sutton, Section 54.
39. Vergil/Sutton, Henry VII, Entry 5 (*); Vergil/Hay, p.15 (*). Bennett, p.134.
40. F. Bacon, *The history of the reign of King Henry the Seventh*, pp.23–24 (*).
41. For more details, M.A. Hicks, *False, Fleeting, Perjur'd Clarence*, pp.128–69.
42. *Rot. Parl.*, January 1478, Appendix 1478 (*); Vol. 6, pp.193–95, esp. p.194 (*).
43. *Crowland Chronicle*, p.477 (*).
44. John Taylor had, confusingly, a son of the same name, who was a minor official in Edward IV's court. The two Taylors were both involved, to one degree or another, in the Simnel and Warbeck rebellions. Interestingly, the son was also pardoned by Henry VII (in 1488), at which time he seems to have been operating under a number of aliases (CPR Henry VII, 1485–1494, p.258) (*).
45. *Rot. Parl.*, October 1491, item 15 (*); Vol. 6, pp.454–55 (*). In a letter to a John Hayes, also formerly in the employ of George, Duke of Clarence, the pretender who had landed in Ireland was referred to as 'your Master's son'.
46. Molinet, Vol. 3, p.152 (*); Bennett, p.130.
47. De But, p.666 (*).
48. *Annuls of Ulster*, Vol. 3 (1895), p.299; *ibid.*, p.315.
49. Ankarette Twynyho was the daughter of William Burdon and his wife, Alana, whose first husband was Edward Haukestone (Calendar of Close Rolls (hereafter CCR), Edward IV, Edward V, Richard III 1476–1485, 16 February 1484, item 1186 (*)). Ankarette is cited as sister of Thomas Burdon, so her maiden name was not Hawkestone as previously suggested (J.E. Jackson, included in *Frome Society for Local Studies Yearbook*, Vol. 8 (2002), pp.90–93, originally published by Wiltshire Archaeological and Natural History Society, 1890), unless the CCR citation is erroneous and should read 'half-sister'. Alana herself was daughter to a Robert Kendalle of Sulton in Shropshire; Soulton Hall is *ca.* 2 miles from Hawkstone Park, using modern names.
50. John was the younger brother of William Twynyho, husband of Ankarette. Since William married Ankarette in 1441 when he was presumably aged about 20, it is likely John was born somewhat before his suggested birth year of *ca.* 1440.

51. Somerset Heritage Centre, DD\SAS\C/795/FR/54.

52. William was alive in 1470 (CCR, Edward IV, Vol. 2, p.124, Item 487, May 1470); his date of death is given as 1472.[51]

53. *History of Parliament : Biographies of The Members of the Commons House 1439–1509*, J. Wedgwood (ed.), p.887 (*).

54. She was executed at the age of 68 after spending over two years in the Tower of London. She was mother to Reginald (later Cardinal) Pole, who throughout his life was a thorn in the side of Henry VIII.

55. John Twynyho's will bequeaths to 'Dame Margery, my niece, nun of Shaftesbury' a silver and gilt goblet 'which had been presented to him by George, Duke of Clarence'. PROB 11/7/295, cited in Hicks, p.139.

56. *Rot. Parl.*, January 1478, item 17 (*); Vol. 6, pp.173–74 (*). A John Thursby was also accused of the poisoning of Clarence's son, Richard; Thursby was tried and executed on the same day as Ankarette Twynyho. A third accused was Roger Tocotes, a man loyal to Clarence, whose involvment in any conspiracy to poison the Duke's wife and son seems improbable. Tocotes avoided both capture and execution (Hicks, p.139).

57. J.H. Blunt, *"Tewkesbury Abbey and Its Associations*, pp.84–85 (*).

58. J. Ashdown-Hill, *Elizabeth Woodville: Lady Grey*, p.126, citing CPR, Edward IV, Henry VI, Edward V, Richard III, 1476–85, p.345.

59. CCR, Edward IV, 1469–70, items 541, 542 (*). Cited in Hicks, p.139.

60. De But, p.665 (*); see Ashdown-Hill, *The Dublin King*, p.111 for a translation.

61. Williams, p.183.

62. The rumour went on to say the earl had been brought to Lovell's care in York, which, though clearly inaccurate, does link Lovell and the Earl of Warwick at an early stage.

63. C. Weightman, *Margaret of York, The Diabolical Duchess*, pp.153, 233 n.30. Langley cites a further (undated) instance in the Dutch Archives of 'costs for a large group of men to help De Hertoghe van Clarens [The Duke of Clarence]', linking the Earl of Warwick (albeit erroneously naming him as his father) with Flanders (Langley, p.424, n.13). This entry then clarifies the entry the 'Duke of Clarence' as 'her brother's son (i.e. Clarence's son, Warwick) and by right succession and honour entitled to the crown of England'. Does this imply, at the time of this account entry, she was unaware of Edward V's survival?

64. The Channel Islands were often used as a staging post between England and Ireland and Calais/Flanders. For example, the flight of the Earls of Warwick and March after the route at Ludford Bridge in 1461 was to Calais via Jersey.

65. *Plumpton Correspondence: a series of letters, chiefly domestick, written in the reigns of Edward IV, Richard III, Henry VII and Henry VIII*, T. Stapleton (ed.), p.54 (*).

66. *Rot. Parl.*, November 1487, item 15 (*); Vol. 6, p.397 (*).

67. Smith, pp.517, 533 n.126 (*).

68. Ashdown-Hill, *The Dublin King*, p.158; Smith, p.525, n.36.

69. 'Book of Howth' in *Calendar of the Carew Manuscripts*, J.S. Brewer & W. Bullen (eds), Vol. V, p.188 (*).

70. M.T. Hayden, *Studies: An Irish Quarterly Review*, Vol. 4 (1925), p.629.

71. A.F. Pollard, *Dictionary of National Biography, 1885–1900*, Vol. 52, pp.261–63, 'Simnel, Lambert' (*), https://en.wikisource.org/wiki/Dictionary_of_National_Biography,_1885-1900/Simnel,_Lambert.

72. Cited in Hayden, pp.627, 629.

73. Vergil/Hay, p.17 (*); Vergil/Sutton, Item 6 (*).

74. D. Wilkins, *Concilia Magnae Britanniae et Hiberniaei*, Vol. 3 (1737), p.618 (*). A translation of this original Latin text can he found in Ashdown-Hill, *The Dublin King*, p.78, and Bennett, p.121.

75. *The Herald's Memoir, 1486–1490: Court Ceremony, Royal Progress and Rebellion*', E. Cavel (ed.), p.117.

76. 'And ther was taken the Lad that his Rebbells callede King Edwarde, whos Name was indede, Lambert, by a Vaylent'; J. Leland, in *Collectanea*, Vol. 4 (1774), p.214 (*). See also Bennett, pp.45, 46.

77. Ashdown-Hill, *The Dublin King*, p.79.

78. M.J. Bennett, 'Simnel, Lambert', *ODNB* (2004).

79. Ashdown-Hill, *The Dublin King*, p.80.

80. M Barnfield, *The Ricardian Bulletin*, September 2015, pp.51–53, available online to members of the Richard III Society (*).

81. Hayden, p.624.

82. Bennett, p.123. The original Latin text is given in *Letters and Papers Illustrative of the Reigns of Richard III and Henry VII* (hereafter *L&P*), J. Gairdner (ed.) (1861), Vol. 1, pp.94–96 (*).

83. *Calendar of Papal Registers Relating To Great Britain and Ireland: Volume 14, 1484–1492, Vatican Regesta*, Vol. DCCLXIX, 5 Janu,ary (*).

84. Bennett, p.132.

85. 'Roger Machado: a life in objects' *in Writing the Lives of People and Things AD 500–1700*, R.F.W. Smith & G.L. Watson (eds., pp.89–113 (*).

86. Vergil/Hay, p.25 (*); Vergil/Sutton, Item 9 (*).

87. *Book of Howth*, p.189 (*).

88. Vergil/Hay, p.13 (*); Vergil/Sutton, Entry 5 (*).

89. A.B. Emden, '*A Biographical Register of the University of Oxford to AD 1500, Oxford 1959*, Vol. 3, p.1841.

90. CPR 1476–1485; 1485–1494; 1494–1509 (*).

91. *Fasti Ecclesiae Anglicanae 1300–1541*, J.M. Horne (ed.) (1967) (*).

92. John Morton also had links to Oxford, so it was not exclusively a pro-York city; Smith, p.527, n.64; see also S Bradley, *John Morton* pp.11–12.

93. David, p.162.

94. David, p.173.

95. M. Heale, 'John Sante', *ODNB* (2015).

96. *Epistolae Academicae Oxon, Registrum F*, H. Anstey (ed.), Vol. II, pp.513–23 (*).

97. David, p.184.

98. M. Hicks, 'Robert Stillington', *ODNB* (2004).

99. André/Hobbins, p.45; André/Sutton, Entry 54 (*). Note that Edward's (Edward IV's) son could be either Edward or Richard, but André erroneously states elsewhere this is Edward's *second* son. The record 'when an organ-maker's son (Lambert Simnel), named one of king Edward's sons, came into Ireland', which appears in the reign of Henry VIII (*L&P*, Henry VIII, Vol. 4, pp.1066–1081, #2405 IRELAND (*)) cannot be taken in unambiguous support of Edward V and is most likely a simple reiteration of André, Henry VII's biographer.

100. S.G. Ellis, *ODNB* (2004), 'Fitzgerald, Gerald, Eighth Earl of Kildare'.

101. Hayden, p.635.

102. Vergil/Hay, p.27 (*) ; Vergil/Sutton, Entry 10 (*).

103. André/Hobbins, p.47; André/Sutton, Entry 56 (*).

104. Vergil/Sutton, Entry 9 (*). The entry in Vergil/Hay (p.25) merely states he was spared 'because he was a priest' (*).

105. Hayden, p.632.

106. Ashdown-Hill, *The Dublin King*, p.156.

107. R. Jones, *Ricardian Bulletin*, September 2022, pp.72–76.

108. *Book of Howth*, p.190 (*).

109. Hayden, pp. 626, 637; CPR, Henry VII, p.227 (*).

110. Hayden, p.630.

111. David, pp.20–23.

112. De la Pole Pedigree Roll, Ryland's Library, Latin MS 113, cited in Langley, pp.251, 453 n. 143. However, since this claim is made by the de la Pole family, its partiality has implications. A second source, de la Pole's seal matrix, provides additional indirect evidence (Langley, pp.251, 453 n. 144). See also Ashdown-Hill, *The Dublin King*, pp.64, 65.

113. Leyland, *Collectanea*, Vol. 4, T. Hearne (ed.), pp.208–09 (*); Bradley, p.61.

114. Vergil/Hay, p.17 (*) ; Vergil/Sutton, Entry 6 (*).

115. CPR, Henry VII, 1485–1494, p.179 (*).

116. *Materials for a history of the reign of Henry VII*, W. Campbell (ed.) (1873–77), Vol II, p.120 (*).

117. Wilkins, p.618 (*).

118. A letter from the Earl of Oxford to John Paston dated 24 January 1487 states that the king was aware on 17 January of news that Lovell had already fled the country, but some of the men Paston claimed had gone with him were still in the country; *The Paston Letters, 1422–1509 AD"*, J. Gairdner (ed.), p.329 (entry 892) (*).

119. *Rec. Convocation of Canterbury, Canterbury, 1444–1509*, Vol. VI, p.319; cited in Bradley, p.232, n. 26.

120. Leyland, p.209 (*).

121. Vergil/Hay, p.19 (*) ; Vergil/Sutton, entry 7 (*).

122. Leyland, p.249 (*).

123. Campbell, Vol. II, p.319 (*).

124. Harleian Manuscript 433, f308b (*).

125. J. Nichols and R. Gough, *A Collection of All the Wills, Now Known to be Extant of the Kings and Queens of England, Princes and Princesses of Wales, and Every Branch of the Blood Royal* (1780), p.350 (*).

126. For a full account of the post-burial rituals, see A.F. Sutton, L. Visser-Fuchs & R.A. Griffiths, *The Royal Funerals of the House of York at Windsor* (Richard III Society, 2005), pp.66–74.

127. It has been suggested that a hasty burial was consistent with Elizabeth Woodville having died of plague (E.C. Roger, *Social History of Medicine* (2019), pp.1–20). As a lay resident of Bermondsey Abbey, she would have been the least likely member of that community to come into contact with any plague-ridden traveller. So unless it can be established that other members of the abbey community died of plague in 1492, there is no reason to believe that this was the cause of Elizabeth's death. A more reasonable interpretation of the plague story is simply that Henry, as parents are ever wont to do, used this to soften the blow to the 6-year-old Arthur of his grandmother's (and godmother's) death and unceremonial burial – a story passed on to Henry VIII by his brother – rather than tell him (Arthur) what he (Henry VII) really thought about Elizabeth Woodville.

128. Campbell, p.148 (*).

129. Ashdown-Hill, *Elizabeth Woodville*, pp.184–93.

130. She was officially crowned on 25 November 1487.
131. Bradley, pp.66–67. Henry's distrust of Grey stems from his exile in Brittany when Grey, at his mother's bidding, tried to return to the Yorkist fold but was prevented from doing so by Henry Tudor. Grey was held back in Paris in 1485 and was not at Bosworth.
132. Hicks, p.163.
133. Thomas Langton, who, according to Richard III, 'knows the secrets of our heart', was sent to both the Pope and Charles VIII in 1484, plausibly to confide about the fate of Edward's son. Langton was in Mechelen in 1486, presumably to see Duchess Margaret, and this may have been the first indication she received that Edward's sons were alive (Langley, p.214).
134. P. Langley, *The Princes in the Tower*, particularly pp.173–81, 186–87.
135. *Register of the Great Seal of Scotland (Edinburgh, 1882)*, J.B. Paul (ed.), p.370, no. 1738 (*). There is no hard evidence that Lovell availed of this offer.
136. De But, pp.674–75 (*); Ashdown-Hill, *The Dublin King*, pp.151, 211 n.15.Edmund was not an earl at the time of the Battle of Stoke Field, but later became 3rd Duke of Suffolk; then, by decree of Henry VII, he was demoted to the position of earl in 1495.
137. *Matricul de l'Université de Louvain*, A. Schillings (ed.) (1925), III, p. 42, Entry 128; this is incorrectly dated as 1489 by Schilling and then reiterated unknowingly by Leslau. I am grateful to Carl Holdcroft for correcting this point in a private correspondence. The date of matriculation was recorded as February 1487 in the original documentation, which would be February 1488 under our current dating, as in the fifteenth century the new year began on March 25.
138. Schillings, p.423, Entry 86. There are two further entries for Clement: p.634, Entry 3 (1562), and p.738, Entry 55 (1568).
139. J. Leslau, Moreana, XXV, 98–99 (Dec 1988), pp.17–36 (*). See also https://mattlewisauthor.wordpress.com/tag/jack-leslau/.
140. In the original: *Prendre un engagement solennel sous la foi du serment revient évidemment à accomplir un acte juridique pour lequel if faut avoir la capacité requise.*
141. Leslau goes into great detail of the coded message on the identity of John Clement the Physician hidden in the Holbein portrait of the More family; see also J Leslau, *The Ricardian*, Vol. 4, no. 62 (1978), pp.2–14 (*).
142. J Dike, in Langley, Appendix 3, pp.311-326.
143. L Pidgeon, *Ricardian Bulletin*, March 2018, pp. 42-47
144. P.F. Tytler, *History of Scotland*, Vol. 4, Ch. III, p.371 (*).

145. Harliston was later with Warbeck at Deal: *Rot. Parl.*, October 1495, item 39 (*); Vol. 6, p.504 (*). Another veteran of Bosworth, Stoke and Deal was Rowland Robinson, who was in a jail in the town of Warwick in March 1488 along with Robert Bellingham, who captured Simnel at Stoke. What wouldn't we give to have been privy to their conversation? See CPR 1485–94, p.239 (*).

146. Tytler, p.372 (*).

147. *Rot. Parl.*, Henry VII, October 1491, Item 16 (*); Vol. 6, p.455 (*).

148. Wroe, p.85.

149. R. Fabyan, *The Great Chronicle of London*, A.H. Thomas & I.D. Thornley (eds), p.244.

150. *The King's Speech: Richard of England in his own words*, www.revealingrichardiii.com/two-pretenders.html.

151. *Rot. Parl.*, October 1495, entry 39 (*); Vol. 6, p.504 (*); Arthurson, p.317.

152. CCR Henry VII, Vol. 1, 1485–1500, Entry 372, p.104 (*).

153. CCR Henry VII, Vol. 1, 1485–1500, Entry 338, p.93; Entry 454, p.129 (*).

PART II

The main documents referred to are:

Setubal Testimony	Wroe, pp.525–28.
The Confession	Kleyn, Appendix VII, pp.205–07; Wroe, p.380; Arthurson, pp.13–14.
Tournai Archives	Kleyn, Appendix I, pp.188–90.
Letter to Mother	Kleyn, pp.136–37; Wroe, pp.412–13; Gairdner, *Richard III*, pp.329–30.
Letter to Isabella	Kleyn, Appendix II, pp.191–92; Madden, p.47.

1. A. Wroe, *The Perfect Prince*, p.489; D.M. Kleyn, *Richard of England*, p.155; *The Plumpton Correspondence*, T. Stapleton (ed.), p.141 (*).

2. Extended Project Qualification open to A-level (16–18 age group) students; it requires independent research and, usually, a lengthy dissertation.

3. www.youtube.com/watch?v=8D4CETT2tvs&ab_channel=HorribleHistories.

4. *Rot. Parl.*, October 1495, entry 27 (*); Vol. 6, p.489 (*).

5. A. Carson, *The Maligned King*, pp.75–90.

6. The various rumours are summarized in Wroe, pp.70–71 and notes on p.540.

7. *Domenico Mancini: de Occupatione Regni Anglie*, trans. by A. Carson (hereafter Mancini/Carson) (2021), p.65.

8. By this date, Henry VII had created his eldest son, Arthur, Duke of York.

9. The Earl of Warwick was a serious claimant to the English crown and as such was a threat to both Henry and his heirs. As a price for aiding Henry VI back to the throne in 1470/71, the Duke of Clarence was made second heir to the throne after the king's son, Edward, Prince of Wales. Both prince and king died at or immediately after the Battle of Tewkesbury in 1471, making Clarence (and subsequently his son) the prime Lancastrian heir to the throne. As the son of Richard, Duke of York's second surviving son, Warwick also had a better claim to the throne than Richard, Duke of Gloucester, after the death of Edward IV, although this was negated by Clarence's attainder for treason in 1477. There is speculation, but lacking proof, that Richard III may have considered revoking this attainder on the eve of Bosworth, thus making the Earl of Warwick also the prime Yorkist heir to the throne.

10. Dubeney was joint master of the Mint with Bartholomew Rede; K. Molloy, *Ricardian Bulletin* (January 2022), pp.56–60; T.F. Reddaway & L.E.M. Walker, *The Early History of the Goldsmiths Company 1327–1509* (Edward Arnold Ltd, 1975), p.177.

11. S.J. Gunn, 'Daubeney, Giles, First Baron Daubeney', in *Oxford Dictionary of National Biography* (hereafter *ODNB*) (2004).

12. https://en.wikipedia.org/wiki/Roger_Machado_(officer_of_arms).

13. C.L. Schofield, *The life and Reign of Edward the Fourth, King of England and France and Lord of Ireland*, Vol. 1, p.251 (*). For a history of both William and Alexander Monypen[n]y: B.J. Coombs, *Scots Patronage of the Visual Arts in France, c. 1445–1545*, PhD Thesis submitted to the University of Edinburgh (2013), pp.11–22 (*).

14. E.L. O'Brien, 'Harliston, Richard', in *ODNB* (2004); https://en.wikipedia.org/wiki/Richard_Harliston.

15. *Chroniques de Jean Molinet/publiées pour la première fois d'après les manuscrits de la Bibliothèque du roi; par J-A Buchon*, Vol. 2, p.402 (*).

16. *Letters and Papers Illustrative of the Reigns of Richard III and Henry VII*, J. Gairdner (ed.), 2 volumes (hereafter *L&P*), Vol. 1, p.xxv (*).

17. L. Visser-Fuchs, *The Ricardian*, Vol. 7, no. 95 (1986), p.316.(*).

18. A Goodman & A. Mackay, *Eng. Hist. Rev.*, Vol. 88 (2002), p.92 and note.

19. R. Fabyan, *The Great Chronicle of London* (hereafter *GC*), A.H. Thomas & D. Thornley (eds) (1938), pp.209, 212–13.
20. Wroe, pp.525–28.
21. Robert Ricart, *The Maire of Bristowe is Kalendar*, L. Toulmin Smith (ed.), The Camden Society, Vol. 230 (1872), p.46.
22. Crowland Chronicle (hereafter CC), p.491 (*).
23. *Calendar of Patent Rolls* (hereafter *CPR*) (1476–85), pp. 484, 514. While both entries appear in the autumn of 1484, the appointments are backdated to 7 July 1483 (*).
24. Mancini/Carson, p.67.
25. CC, p.490 (*).
26. Henry VII awarded his mother-in-law a pension of 400 marks p.a. after she was consigned to Bermondsey Abbey in 1487 – *Materials for a History of the Reign of Henry VII*, W. Campbell (ed.), Vol. II (1873–77), pp.319–20 (*) – compared to the 700 marks p.a. given to her by Richard III when she left sanctuary in Westminster. *Harl. 433*, Vol. 3, p.190 (*).
27. I. Arthurson, *The Perkin Warbeck Conspiracy 1491–1499*, p.205.
28. *Calendar of Close Rolls* (hereafter *CCR*), Henry VII 1485–1500, p.289 (*).
29. Wroe, p.139, note p.549.
30. Wroe, p.203. Somerset was the illegitimate son of Henry Beaufort, third Earl of Somerset, and thus a distant relative of the king.
31. Wroe, p.22; *CPR* Henry VII 1485–94, p.274 (*). For a summary of Brampton's life, B Williams, *The Ricardian*, Vol. 6, no. 84 (1984), pp.294–98 (*).
32. *CCR*, Edward IV, Edward V, Richard III, p.370, 21 August (*).
33. *CPR*, Edward IV, Edward V, Richard III, 1476–85, p.481 (*).
34. *Harl. 433*, Vol. 2, pp.187, 191 (*); see also Wroe, p.73 & note p.541.
35. *CPR*, Edward IV, Edward V, Richard III, 1476–85, pp.318, 413 (*).
36. Carson, *The Maligned King*, pp.153–54, 159–60; Langley, pp.67–68, and references therein.
37. J. Stow, *The Annales or Generall Chronicle of England*, p.460 (*).
38. R. Horrox, 'Tyrell, Sir James', *ODNB* (2008).
39. R. Horrox, 'Tyrell Family', *ODNB* (2008).
40. Worsley was himself arrested at this time.
41. *CPR*, Edward IV, Edward V, Richard III, 1476–85, p.241; W.E. Hampton, *The Ricardian*, Vol. 4, no. 63 (December 1978), p.19; Wroe, p.177 (*).
42. A. Williamson, *The Mystery of the Princes in the Tower*, p.115.
43. F. Madden, *Documents Relating to Perkin Warbeck, with Remarks on His History: Communicated to the Society of Antiquaries*, p.25 (*).

44. C.S.L. Davies, *The Ricardian*, Vol. 9, no. 199 (1992), p.336 (*).
45. *Rot. Parl.*, November 1487, entry 15 (*); Vol. 6, p.398 (*).
46. *Rot. Parl.*, October 1495, entry 39 (*); Vol. 6, p.504 (*).
47. *CPR*, Henry VII, 1485–94, p.139 (*).
48. Richard Harliston was attainted after Deal, returned to Burgundy and died there sometime after 1495; he never returned to England again.
49. Madden, p.4 (*); see also Kleyn, Appendix II, p.191.
50. Kleyn, Apendix VII, pp.205–07; Wroe, p.380; Arthurson, pp.13–14; LC, pp.219–22 (*). While copies of the confession were circulated throughout the country, the only surviving version now available is that translated into French, currently located in Courtrai, Belgium: *Courtrai Codex*, 111, f. 188r,v.
51. Wroe, p.383; these latter names only appear in the surviving French version of the confession.
52. For a summary of the relevant Archives of Tournai, see Kleyn, Appendix I, pp.188–90. Warbeck's sister, Jehanne, died in 1517 so would have been alive at the time of the trial.
53. *Courtrai Codex*, 111, ff. 188v-189r. Translations are given in Kleyn, pp.136–37; Wroe, pp.412–13; Gairdner, pp.329–30 (*) gives a French version by J. Weale, published by L Michel, *Bull. Hist. Soc. Tournai*, Vol. xx, p.127 (1880).
54. *Calendar of Letters, Despatches, and State Papers, Relating to the Negotiations Between England and Spain, Preserved in the Archives at Simancas, Vienna, Brussels, and Elsewhere*, G.A. Bergenroth (ed.), Vol. 1., 1495–1509 (hereafter *CSPS*), p.92 (*); Wroe, p.401; Kleyn, p.104.
55. *CSPS*, pp.92, 111 (*); Wroe, p.410. It seems various monarchs were vying to help Henry, however implausible their offers: see Gairdner, pp.313–14 (*).
56. This refers to a letter from Henry VII to Sir Gilbert Talbot. J.O. Halliwell-Phillipps, *Letters of the Kings of England: Now First Collected from the Originals in Royal Archives and from other authentic sources, private as well as public*, H. Colburn (ed.), Vol. 1, p.172 (*).
57. I. Arthurson, *Nott. Med. Studies*, XXXV (1991), pp.134–54.
58. 'Journals of Roger Machado' in *Historia Regis Henrici Septimi, a Bernardo Andrea Tholosate Conscripta* (hereafter *HRHS*), J. Gairdner (ed.), pp.157–94 (*).
59. Wroe, p.43; Rui de Pina, *Crónica de el-Rei D Joao II*, pp.70–71.
60. *Calendar of State Papers and Manuscripts in the Archives and Collections of Milan 1385–1618* (hereafter *CSPM*), A.B. Hinds (ed.) (HMSO, 1912), p.331, 21 October 1496 (*).

61. Wroe, pp.404–05 notes p.579.
62. Kleyn, p.134.
63. The letter containing news of the death of a 'John Perkin' arrived on 20 September 1497,[61] and Warbeck's letter to his mother is dated 13 October of that year.[53] No exact date of death for Jehan (John) de Werbecque is recorded, though the Tournai Archives state that his wife, Nicaise, didn't sell the family home until December 1498 (Wroe, p.513, citing ref. 222). It is this that has led to the belief that Warbeck's father didn't die until December 1498 (Kleyn, p.138).
64. D. Desmons, *Un Tournaisien Prétendant au Trône d'Angleterre, Rev. Tournaisienne*, Vol. 6, Nos 4–5 (1910), p.45.
65. Warbeck's letter to his mother links the death of Jehanne with the birth of another daughter, so it is possible that two Jehannes did exist and one was still living into the sixteenth Century. The letter also refers to a brother, Thiroyan, who, if he existed, must also have died young as neither he nor the putative first Jehanne appear in the Tournai Archives. However, the translation of the letter from its original French has been disputed, and it is argued that it actually refers to Warbeck's grandfather, not another brother.[52, 63] Gairdner's transcription (cited by Wroe) of the French is '*mon frere*' (p.330) which indisputably means 'my brother'. Conversely, Desmons[64] (cited by Kleyn, p.138) transcribes the relevant wording as '*mon aïeul*', my grandfather, i.e. Dieric/Thiery Warbecque.[52] It is unclear which author is correct on this. though Desmons (perhaps unsurprisingly) claims Gairdner's version is a reproduction of an earlier mistranslation; Desmons does not give a name to the brother/grandfather, unlike Gairdner. Both versions of the letter link the death of Jehanne and that of the brother/grandfather, which, if the letter refers to the grandfather, means these two deaths must have taken place before May 1474, when Dieric/Thiery Warbecque died.[52] This would imply that a Jehanne was possibly born before Perkin and that their parents married a year or more earlier than generally suggested, which is usually based on Perkin being the oldest child.
66. Arthurson, p.59.
67. Wroe, p.382 & note p.576.
68. Wroe, pp.415–16.
69. *CPR*, 1485–1509, p.274 (*).
70. Wroe, pp.393–95. There may be more to this aspect than has previously been appreciated. In a document attributed to Richard, Duke of York, he claims to be able to play the clavichord (Langley, pp.195, 205–06).

71. *Bibliographie Nationale* (Brussels, 1938), Vol. 27, cols 152–59 (*).

72. Gaspar hailed from Oudenaarde, some 30km from Tournai. Warbeck's grandfather hailed from Beveren, which is 70km from Oudenaarde; in the French version of the confession, Warbeck's cousin, Jehan Steinbeck, continues to live there (Wroe, p.388), though in the English version, Steinbeck lives in Antwerp, where Beveren is a suburb.[50]

73. Wroe, p.96.

74. Wroe, pp.31, 32. It seems da Cunha, and presumably Warbeck, left Portugal for Africa in 1489, broadly the time Richmond Herald was in Lisbon. Warbeck cannot have played a part in arranging this voyage, but it may have been a serendipitous convenience if he felt Henry's men were on his trail.

75. Wroe, p.198.

76. A. Spont, *La Marine Française Sous le Règne de Charles VIII*, 1483–93, p.34, note 6 (*).

77. Wroe, p.48.

78. F. Bacon, *History of the Reign of King Henry VII*, p.109 (*).

79. *CPR*, 1494–1509, p.44 (*); Carrickfergus, then named Knockfergus/Knokvergece, is in the north-east of Ulster, barely 30 miles from Galloway, Scotland.

80. J. Ashdown-Hill, *The Dublin Pretender*; see also Part I for further discussion on this point.

81. It has been claimed[80] that there were two Earls of Warwick in simultaneous existence. In this scenario, in 1477 the Duke of Clarence substituted his son for a doppelganger, sending his true son to either Ireland or Flanders for safety. It was this Earl of Warwick who was crowned king, probably (but by no means certainly) Edward VI, in Dublin in 1487. His fate after the Battle of Stoke Field in 1487 in unknown. After Clarence's arrest and execution in 1477/78, the surrogate Earl of Warwick passed to the care of Thomas Grey, Marquis of Dorset, then Richard III, before falling into the hands of Henry VII in 1485, who imprisoned him in the Tower of London until his execution in 1499. While there is a forceful argument to support this narrative, it is by no means widely accepted. This is more fully discussed in Part I.

82. C. Weightman, *Margaret of York, The Diabolical Duchess*, pp.129–44.

83. Kleyn, Appendix III, p.193.

84. Spont, p.35 (*).

85. Wroe, pp.93, 94.

86. *Rot. Parl.,* Henry VII, October 1491, item 15 (*); Vol. 6, p.454 (*).

87. Interestingly, the same John Taylor was involved in the plan to replace Clarence's son with an imposter, taking the real earl to safety in either

Ireland or Flanders;[80, 81] *Rot. Parl.*, Vol. 6, p.194 (*). This is discussed in Part I.

88. C.S.L. Davis & M. Ballard, *Hist. Res.*, Vol. 62 (1989), pp.245–59.

89. Wroe, p.119; *Rymer's Fœdera*, T. Rymer (ed.), Vol. 12, 14 December (*).

90. Wroe, p.129; Langley, pp.327–29.

91. Wroe, p.131.

92. N.H. Nicholas, *Privy Purse Expenses of Elizabeth of York: Wardrobe Accounts of Edward the Fourth*, pp.126, 141–45 (*).

93. Wroe, pp.176–78; Kleyn, p.84.

94. *The Anglia Historia of Polydore Vergil, A.D. 1485–1537*, D. Hay (ed.), Camden Series, Vol. 74, p.69 (hereafter Vergil/Hay) (*); *The Anglia Historia of Polydore Vergil Anglia Historica (1555 Version); Henry VII*, D.F. Sutton (hereafter Vergil/Sutton), Entry 25 (*). *L&P*, Vol. 1, p.235 (*).

95. Wroe, pp.148–51.

96. Molinet, Vol. 4, pp.393–96 (*).

97. Wroe, p.245.

98. *CSPV*, vol. 4, pp.482–83, 22 September (1495) (*).

99. Wroe, p.132.

100. Gairdner, *History of the life and reign of Richard the Third, to which is added the story of Perkin Warbeck: from original documents*, p.282 (*). In a letter of 1493, Maximilian states the three distinguishing signs as his mouth, one of his eyes and a mark on his thigh (Langley, p.437, n.84). In the Setubal Testimonies,[20] Tanjar also commented on distinguishing features named by Perkin's father, including thin legs and him being a bit of a fool, but these latter attributes can hardly be counted as 'distinguishing'.

101. Kleyn, Appendix 3, p.194.

102. Isabella of Portugal (d. 1471) was the great granddaughter of Edward III through John of Gaunt and his daughter, Phillipa of Lancaster.

103. Wroe, p.164.

104. Wroe, p.200.

105. Weightman, p.132.

106. Wroe, p.232, note p.560. Albrecht in fact leant 30,000 gold florins, while Engelbert II of Nassau leant 10,000 gold ecus, both considerable sums (Langley, p.196).

107. Wroe, p.230.

108. Weightman, pp.152–53.

109. Maximilian may have been more involved, albeit less directly, than this answer suggests (Langley, p.176).

110. W.A.J. Archbold, 'Sir William Stanley and Perkin Warbeck', *Eng. Hist. Rev.*, Vol. 14 (1899), pp.529–34. A translation of the Latin is in the Richard III Society Barton Library, Non-Fiction Papers.

111. *CPR*, Henry VII, 1494–1509, p.13 (*).

112. Wroe, p.226.

113. Vergil/Hay, p.75 (*). Vergil/Sutton, Entry 27 (*).

114. Gairdner, in the notes to Archbold,[110] is of the opinion Stanley was hedging his bets in offering support for Warbeck.

115. E. Hall, *Hall's Chronicle : containing the history of England, during the reign of Henry the Fourth, and the succeeding monarchs, to the end of the reign of Henry the Eighth, in which are particularly described the manners and customs of those periods. Carefully collated with the editions of 1548 and 1550*, p.469 (*).

116. *CPR*, Henry VII, 1484–94, p.85 (*).

117. Wroe, p.192.

118. *Excerpta Historica, or Illustrations of English History*, S. Bentley (ed.) (1831), p.100 (*). Richard/Warbeck claimed in a proclamation delivered from Scotland in the summer of 1496 that Henry had bought Clifford off: 'He has offered large sums of money to the rulers of several countries to apprehend us, and has tried to persuade some of our personal servants to murder us, and to persuade others, such as Sir Robert Clifford, to leave our service and our cause.' See Ref. 147, Part 1.

119. An extensive account of all those implicated in the plots of 1493–95 is given in Wroe, pp.176–91.

120. Madden, pp.19, 20, 24–26 (*).

121. Humphrey Savage is later cited in the Attainder against William Stanley: *Rot. Parl.*, October 1495, Item 39 (*); Vol. 6, p.504 (*).

122. N. Amin, *Henry VII and the Tudor Pretenders*, p.180.

123. Arthurson, p.123; *ibid.*, Appendix B, p.317. Hall's Chronicle (p.472) claims 160 men were captured, of which five were captains (*). The London Chronicle (pp.205–06) suggests the Deal invasion force comprised *ca.* 800 men in fourteen ships, of which *ca.* 160 were taken prisoner after the failed landing (*).

124. Wroe, p.308.

125. G. Mattingly, *Eng. Hist. Rev.*, Vol. LV, Issue CCLXVII (1940), pp.30–34.

126. Wroe, p.309.

127. W. Busch, *England Under the Tudors, King Henry VII*, pp.113–14 (*).

128. In reality, the code wasn't cracked until 1862, by a Prussian, G.A. Bergenroth.[129] Perhaps the most famous example of Tudor code-breaking

concerns the secret letters of Mary, Queen of Scots, which ultimately led to grounds for her execution.

129. G.A. Bergenroth, *CSPS*, Vol. 1 (1485/1509), p.lxxxiv (*); Kleyn, p.148.
130. C. Skidmore, *Bosworth*, p.145.
131. Wroe, p.264; Ellis, Vol. 1, p.29 (*); *CSPV*, Vol. 1, 21 May (*).
132. P.F. Tytler, *History of Scotland*, Vol. 4, p.371 (1828) (*).
133. Tytler, p.372 (*).
134. *Accounts of the Lord High Treasurer of Scotland*, T. Dickson (ed.), Vol. 1, p.130 (*).
135. Tytler, p.373 (*).
136. Tytler, p.375 (*).
137. Dickson, pp.263–64, 267 (*).
138. Arthurson, p.186.
139. Tytler, pp.378–79 (*).
140. H. Ellis, *Original Letters, Illustrative of English History*, 2nd Ed., Vol. 1, p.22 (*).
141. Dickson, p.296 (*).
142. Kleyn, p.109.
143. Wroe, p.286; Ellis, pp.23–24 (*).
144. Tytler, p.381 (*).
145. Tytler, p.376 (*).
146. Wroe, p.297.
147. Tytler, p.377 (*).
148. Ellis, p.27 (*).
149. Ellis, p.26 (*).
150. Wroe, pp.312–14; *Treasurer's Accounts*, pp.301–03 (*).
151. Dickson, pp.342–43 (*).
152. *Annals of Ulster*, B. MacCarthy (ed.), Vol. 3, pp.419, 423 (*).
153. *CSPM*, 16 September 1497 (*).
154. Wroe, p.332.
155. Dickson, pp.360, 371 (*).
156. In fact, Daubeney became isolated during the confrontation (the Battle of Deptford Bridge) and was captured by the rebels; remarkably, he was freed unharmed.
157. Wroe, p.329; a less numerous force, 'a thousand-strong', is quoted in D.M. Yorath's *The Devon Historian*, Vol. 84 (2015), p.56, while rumours cited by A F Pollard – *The Reign of Henry VII from Contemporary Sources*, Vol. 1, p.165 (*) – speak of about 5,000 men. In Venice, the news was of 6,000–8,000 men; Pollard, p.166; *CSPV*, Vol. 1, 11 October 1497, item 755 (*).

158. *CSPM*, 16 September 1497 (*); Pollard, p.163 (*).
159. *CSPV*, Vol. 1, pp.223–24, 19 September 1495 (*).
160. Rymer, Vol. 12, pp.578–82, 24 February 1496 (*).
161. Wroe, pp.333–36. Perhaps significantly, William Courtenay switched to supporting the Yorkist claimant, Edmund de la Pole, after 1499, while his son, Henry, was later beheaded for supporting another Yorkist claimant, Reginald Pole.
162. Wroe, p.339.
163. Sanuto, *Diarii de Marino Sanuto*, Vol. 1, cols 825–26 (in Italian) (*).
164. Wroe, p.356.
165. *CSPM*, p.329, 21 October (*).
166. *Regesta Imperii* RI XIV, 2 n. 5512 (*). Note: Ehg = Erzherzog, which refers to the Archduke Philip; Hg = Herzog or Duke, which refers to the Duke of York. Suggestions that there were additional children or at least a second pregnancy can be found in reference 238.
167. Bentley, pp.115–18, 121 (*).
168. Wroe, p.442.
169. S. Anglo, *Bull. John Rylands Lib.*, Vol. 43 (1960–61), p.27 (*).
170. *Chronicle of London (Vitellius A XVI)* (hereafter *LC*), C.L. Kingsford (ed.), p.223 (*); *GC*, p.287.
171. Wroe, p.435.
172. Wroe, p.447.
173. *CSPS*, p.152.
174. A long list of people who would have known Richard of York and could have made a judgement on his authenticity or not is given in Wroe, p.438.
175. B. Williams, *The Ricardian*, Vol. 5, no. 73 (1981), pp.341–45 (*).
176. In fact, de Sousa had died in 1498, and although there is no precise date for his birth he must have been in late life when he made his testimony at Setubal in 1486.One genealogical website gives '*ca.* 1423' for the date of his birth but without quoting a source: www.geni.com/people/Rui-de-Sousa-1°-senhor-de-Beringel-e-Sagres/6000000003253102911.
177. *CSPS*, p.92.
178. Wroe, pp.370–71.
179. Wroe, p.455.
180. Wroe, p.456 and notes p.583.
181. Sanuto Diaries, col. 1023 (*).
182. Kleyn, p.146.
183. Wroe, pp.475–86.
184. Kleyn, p.154.

185. This is based on a comment in Hall's Chronicle – p.490 (*) – that after fourteen years in the Tower, Warwick 'could not descerne a Goose from a Capon'. This probably means he was somewhat lacking in knowledge of the outside world rather than in any way mentally impaired.

186. Wroe, p.490.

187. Thomas Stangeways was spared and pardoned in July 1500; *CPR*, Henry VII, 1494–1509, p.205 (*).

188. The treaty formed the basis for the Treaty of Perpetual Peace, signed in 1502.

189. Wroe, p.428.

190. Rymer, Vol. 12, p.675, 10 February 1498 (*).

191. Wroe, p.429; A. Conway, *Henry VII's Relations with Scotland and Ireland 1485–1498*, Appx. I, pp.242–43 (*).

192. Wroe, pp.431–32.

193. Wroe, pp.467–68.

194. *Excerpta Historica*, p.115 (*).

195. *CSPS*, pp.185–86 (*).

196. *CSPS*, p.196 (*).

197. W.E.A. Moorhen, *The Ricardian*, Vol. 11, no. 139 (1997), pp.191–213 (*).

198. Wroe, pp.375–77.

199. *HRHS*, pp.73–75 (*).

200. Margaret (b. 1489) and Mary (b. 1496); another daughter, Elizabeth (b. 1492), had died (1495) before Katherine Gordon was brought to London.

201. The marriage was never annulled, even after Warbeck's execution. Katherine Gordon did not remarry until 1509, by which time Henry VII was dead.

202. Wroe, p.461.

203. If the pre-contract between Edward IV and Eleanor Butler was true, then the sons of Edward IV and Elizabeth Woodville were bastards and not royalty, so from this perspective the title 'princes' is inappropriate.

204. This is based on reports that the royal physician was visiting the elder boy, Edward, regularly in the Tower of London, suggesting an ongoing illness. See Mancini[7] and the associated note 144, p.108.

205. A.F. Sutton & P.W. Hammond, *Coronation of Richard III: The Extant Documents*.

206. Wroe, pp.516–18.

207. Wroe, *Ricardian Bulletin*, pp.25–30 (December 2003).

208. J. Ashdown-Hill, *The Third Plantaganet*, p.154.

209. Wroe, pp.77, 78.

210. Weightman, p.153.

211. While a link between Clarence's son and Jehan le Sage is highly unlikely, a case has been made that Clarence succeeded in a scheme to send his son to safety in Ireland and/or Flanders.[80] Rumours that the Earl of Warwick had escaped from the Tower of London and was on Guernsey cannot be true, but would be consistent with the son of Clarence, also the Earl of Warwick, pausing at Guernsey on his way from Ireland to Flanders.; C.H. Williams, *English Historical Review* (1928), vol. 43, p.183. Furthermore, it is known that Francis Lovell took a boy named Edward from Flanders to Dublin, where he was crowned king, but it is far from clear whether this was as Edward V (i.e. Edward IV's eldest son) or Edward VI, the title the Earl of Warwick would have assumed. The identity of the pretender crowned in Dublin is as big a mystery as the identity of Perkin Warbeck. This is discussed more fully in Part I of this book.

212. *CSPM*, p.292, 11 February 1495 (*).

213. Weightman, p.185.

214. W. Blockmans, 'The Devotion of a Lonely Duchess', in *Margaret of York, S Marmion, and the Visions of Tondal*, Thomas Kren (ed.) (1992), pp.29–46 (*).

215. Wroe, p.208.

216. Weightman, p.192.

217. Weightman, p.186.

218. Henri of Berghes was a bastard son of John II of Glymes.

219. Z. Maula, *Ricardian Bulletin* (December 2020), pp.54–58; L. Visser-Fuchs, *ibid.* (June 2021), pp.24–25.

220. Wroe, p.515. It is likely that this Anthony was also a bastard brother of John III, though a legitimate son of John III of the same name also existed.

221. Arthurson, p.55.

222. P.A. du Chastel de la Howarderie, *Bull. Hist. Lit. Soc. Tournai*, Vol. XXV, pp.410–14 (1892–94); translation available from the Barton Library, Richard III Society.

223. *The Missing Princes Project* (November 2023; Langley, pp.189–227) has now revealed that, after fleeing London, Richard of York initially resided in Paris and remained there for 'a long time', albeit that this is unquantified. He later spent time in Flanders, plausibly Tournai, though how long he remained there is, as yet, unknown. This may be the genesis of Henry's Simnel-like cover story to cloud the identity of the second pretender.

224. Wroe, pp.492–93. There are mixed accounts of whether Warbeck stated his confession (Hall, p.491) or simply had his written confession

displayed (*LC*, pp.227–28; *GC*, p.291; Langley, p.434, n.50). Given Warbeck's physical condition at the gallows, it is quite possible that he was unable to speak his last words, or that it was inaudible to the extent his final words had to be read for him from his Taunton confession.

225. Molinet, Vol. 5, p.121 (*).
226. The bishop visited at the end of July 1498 and Warbeck was executed in late November 1499.
227. André/Hobbins, p.67. This is not stated in the André/Sutton translation, entry 78 (*).
228. Wroe, p.454; W.E.A. Moorhen, *The Ricardian*, Vol. 12, no. 156, p.417 (*).
229. Wroe, p.520.
230. P. Hammond, *The Children of Richard III*, pp.52–59.
231. D. Baldwin, *The Lost Prince*, pp.19–38. There is no credibility to the part of the rumour that Richard was taken to Richard III's tent on the eve of Bosworth. *TMPP* has provided evidence that Richard, Duke of York, was taken from the Tower to Paris (initially) in the summer of 1483 (Langley, pp.193–99).
232. Hammond, pp.45–51.
233. *Letters and Papers, Foreign and Domestic, Henry VIII*, Vol. 1, 1509–14, p.322 (*).
234. Wroe, p.147.
235. J. Leslau, *The Ricardian*, Vol. 4, No. 62, pp.1–14 (*). See also M. Lewis, *Leslau, Holbein, More and Clement*, https://mattlewisauthor.wordpress. com/2014/07/26/leslau-holbein-more-and-clement/.
236. J. North, *The Ambassadors' Secrets*.
237. There is a good case to be made for a third 'royal', John Clement, to exist. In 1510, Henry VIII organized a tournament, a feat of arms, to celebrate his accession to the throne. On 1 June, of the ten combatants in addition to the king, nine were of royal blood or closely associated with the king's household, including Arthur Plantaganet, illegitimate son of Edward IV and later to become Lord Lisle. The tenth was a John Clement. *L&P*, Henry VIII, Vol. 1, 1509–14, pp.1533–77, Appendix, 3 June 1510; www. british-history.ac.uk/letters-papers-hen8/vol1/pp1533-1557. See also, Lewis, *Survival of the Princes in the Tower*, pp.213–14. Who was he and how did he fit into the assortment of men close to the king? He could not be John Clement the physician (only aged about 10 in 1510), and is unlikely to be John Clement the Louvain student (acceptable age but not of a military disposition). However, a John Clement exists who was a spearman of Calais, a member of the Calais garrison, thus probably a career soldier. Is it possible that this John Clement was John of Gloucester

(sometimes known as John of Pontefract), illegitimate son of Richard III? John of Gloucester would have been about 37 in 1510 and was made Captain of Calais (a purely titular role at this point in his life) by his father in 1485 (*Harl. 433*, Vol. 1, p.271; Hammond, p. 6). There is thus a Calais connection, and as a Calais spearman he would be of the correct background to fight in a feat of arms. There is a suggestion that John of Gloucester was executed at the same time as Perkin Warbeck and the Earl of Warwick (Hammond, p.47, and references therein), but there is no hard evidence to substantiate this claim, nor is it mentioned in any of the contemporary London chronicles in their descriptions of the 1499 executions.

238. There is a suggestion that there may have been a second child (HRSH, p.70: '*cum suis liberis*'; Gairdner, pp.319, 324; *CSPV*, Vol. 1, p.264, 11 October: 'leaving his wife and children at … Penryn' (*)), or at least that Katherine was pregnant when they landed in Cornwall (Wroe, p.374).

239. Wroe, p.374.

240. Wroe, p.301 and note p.568. While this could possibly relate to Richard of York, he had by this time left Flanders to attempt to regain the throne (1495). Moreover, it's more likely that an infant, rather than a pretender to the throne, would have a bedroom named in his honour.

241. Blockmans, p.35 (*).

242. Colet's buildings were completed by 1510, so that is logically the earliest date Clement could have enrolled at the school, though the earliest pupil records, including Clement, are for the period 1512–22. *Admission Register of St Paul's School*, R.B. Gardiner (ed.), pp.7, 19 (*).

243. Clement is mentioned in More's first letter to Peter Giles, which is in the accompanying documents associated with *Utopia*. Despite describing Clement as 'his servant', Clement was clearly well-educated, as More goes on to describe him as follows: 'this young plant who is just putting out green shoots in Latin and Greek will give us a splendid harvest'.[244]

244. T. More, *Utopia*, trans. D. Baker-Smith, p.12; see also T. Merriam, *Moreana*, XXV (1988), pp.145–52 (*).

245. Baker-Smith, p.xiv.

246. Weightman, p.142.

247. https://fr.wikipedia.org/wiki/François_de_Busleyden (*).

Index